WILLS AND TRUSTS

IN A NUTSHELL

By

ROBERT L. MENNELL
Former Professor of Law

WEST GROUP

1994

Nutshell Series, In a Nutshell, the Nutshell Logo and the WP symbol are registered trademarks of West Publishing Co. Registered in the U.S. Patent and Trademark Office.

COPYRIGHT © 1979 WEST PUBLISHING CO.

COPYRIGHT © 1994 By WEST PUBLISHING CO.
                          610 Opperman Drive
                          P.O. Box 64526
                          St. Paul, MN 55164–0526
                          1–800–328–9352

Printed in the United States of America

Library of Congress Cataloging-in-Publication Data

Mennell, Robert L., 1934–
    Wills and trusts in a nutshell / by Robert L. Mennell. — 2nd ed.
        p.   cm. — (Nutshell series)
    Includes index.
    ISBN 0–314–04025–0
    1. Wills—United States. 2. Trusts and trustees—United States.
I. Title. II. Series.
KF755.Z9M38 1994
346.7305 ' 4—dc20
[347.30654]   94–12517
                                                                CIP

ISBN 0–314–04025–0

 *TEXT IS PRINTED ON 10% POST CONSUMER RECYCLED PAPER*

DEDICATION
of Second Edition

To my fellow lawyers,

Ann I. Mennell, J.D., University of Michigan, of Foley & Lardner, Milwaukee, Wisconsin,

and

James A. Mennell, J.D. cum laude, Duke University, of Popham, Haik, Schnobrich & Kaufman, Ltd., Minneapolis, Minnesota,

neither of whom really needed this book at all.

*

DEDICATION
of First Edition

Those who gave inspiration for this book are divisible into three groups:

THE HOME BASE: Toni, Ann, John, Jim and Betsy, to whom this book represents time not shared.

THE COLLEAGUES: My colleagues in this field who provide inspiration, especially M. Arnold Lyons, Thomas L. Shaffer, Jesse Dukeminier, Edward C. Halbach, Jr., Richard V. Wellman and Neill H. Alford, Jr.

THE STUDENTS: Fifty classes in Wills, Trusts or both gave me more pleasant moments than I can list. I remember with especial fondness the following students, among others: George D. Bane, Richard G. Berg, Mary L. Cox, Mary E. Delaplane, Patricia B. Fry, Paula C. Gentile, Lawrence Gingold, Paulette W. Lee, George Nazarian, Leonard Pape, Verna L. Porter, Julius Rabinowitz, Anne-Marie Saunders, Emanuel Sedacca, Earl R. Siddell, Dennis J. Tonsing, Robert Whitmore, Zbignieu M. Wojciechowski and Norman Zafman.

With that much inspiration, one would have expected a better product.

*

DEDICATION
of First Edition

PREFACE

This book is designed to help law students in their efforts to master the course in Wills and Trusts and to pass examination questions in that subject. As such, it does not attempt to teach how to draft wills, trusts or other related documents, nor does it give a comprehensive presentation of the subjects. This book, alone, will not present an integrated coverage of the subject. It is designed to supplement traditional coverage by pointing out particular areas of difficulty and suggesting approaches. A few subjects (such as the nuncupative will) are totally ignored; others (such as exoneration of devises) are given very short treatment. Other subjects (such as anti-lapse and pretermission) are given extensive coverage because of the difficulties they present when they interact with other doctrines.

A few references are made to cases which are found in many of the common casebooks, but references[1] are generally omitted. The book is designed to be read easily so that the student can tie together classroom and casebook presentations.

ROBERT L. MENNELL

Roseville, Minnesota
February, 1994

---

1. One footnote is considered sufficient for this book.

*

OUTLINE

PART I. WILLS

PART II. DECEDENT'S ESTATE ADMINISTRATION

OUTLINE

*

TABLE OF CASES

References are to Pages

WILLS AND TRUSTS

IN A NUTSHELL

*

PART I

WILLS

CHAPTER 1

INTESTACY

Intestacy is the blackboard upon which the law of wills is written. Property not effectively disposed of prior to death or by will passes in accordance with the appropriate law of intestacy in effect at and in regard to those persons living at the decedent's death.

A. THE MEANING OF "HEIR"

"Heir" has a precise meaning when used in its technical sense. The heir is the intestate taker of property which a decedent did not otherwise dispose of.

Among the connotations of "Heir" are the following:

• There are times when the word "heir" is used as a "convention" like "not guilty" in criminal law or "Four No–Trump" (the Blackwood Convention) in bridge. At those times, the word "heir" is said

1

to be used as "words of limitation and not as words
of inheritance (or purchase)." Thus, a conveyance
to "A and his heirs" is a conveyance in fee simple to
A, not a conveyance to A (for life?) and then to A's
heirs.

● Originally, the "heir" was the intestate taker of
realty while the "next of kin" shared the personalty. This limitation of "heir" has practically disap-
peared, but the word "heir" does have some flavor
of its original "realty" dimension while "next of
kin" retains the personalty connotation (but is far
less frequently used).

● Heirs are persons designated by statute: Each
jurisdiction has its own statute(s) of "descent" (connoting realty) and "distribution" (connoting personalty). Generally, the distinctions between realty
and personalty have been eliminated, but traces
may remain. These statutes prescribe a specific
pattern by which persons have priority to the property based upon relationship to the decedent. The
statutory pattern makes no distinction based upon
the length of time of the relation (for example, a
newlywed spouse is treated the same as one who
was married to the decedent 50 years) nor of the
degree of friendliness or animosity between the
decedent and the statutory "heir."

● The heir does not necessarily receive any property. In many cases, the decedent may leave no
property to be disposed of at his death. Even a
person of great wealth may "leave" nothing because

of will-substitute provisions, commonly joint tenancies, life insurance, gifts and trusts.

● Even if a decedent died leaving property not disposed of during life, the heir may not receive because there is a valid and effective will disposing of the property. The Statute of Wills was enacted to allow testators to dispose of property at death in a manner contrary to the applicable intestacy scheme.

● Although the heir may not receive the property (either because there was none or because it was disposed of by will), the heir is still "heir." To be disinherited is to receive nothing, not to be dethroned from the "heir" position. Heirship is a position like the shortstop in baseball. One remains a shortstop when he or she does not have the ball, indeed even when his or her team is at bat rather than in the field.

● Heirs apparent and presumptive are not yet heirs. They have no interest in the property of their living predecessor. Their rights are inchoate and "mere expectancies" like a chance on the Irish Sweepstakes. In this regard, they are similar to the usual situation of a life insurance policy beneficiary during the life of the insured. Among the implications of the inchoate status of the relationship is the fact that the "expectancy" cannot be sold or assigned except that a court of equity will enforce, in appropriate cases, an assignment which was made for consideration, but then only after the contingency is resolved, i.e., it is no longer an expectancy.

• Heirship is determined as of one point in time—
the death of the intestate. No one is an "heir"
before that time. The terms "heir apparent" and
"heir presumptive" describe those persons who
would be the heir if the predecessor in interest died
at this moment. An "heir apparent" is one who
will be the "heir" upon the death of the predecessor
if two existing conditions are maintained: The
"heir apparent" survives the intestate and remains
in the relationship (spouse, child etc.) which qualified him or her for the inheritance. The "heir
presumptive" is one who must satisfy the conditions of an "heir apparent" and also not be dis-
placed by someone having a preferred heirship position. For example, a widowed mother of the intestate will be an heir only if he does not marry and
leave issue surviving him. Under most intestate
statutes, surviving issue and a surviving spouse
would be the only heirs. Only when there are no
surviving issue (and sometimes when there is also
no surviving spouse) does a parent take a share by
intestacy.

• Since there is only one time at which an "heir"
would achieve that status, there is no statutory
substitute for the person living at the time of the
intestate's death who disclaims his or her intestate
share of the estate. There is no "Vice–Heir" to
claim title to the property unless the fiction is
indulged in that the "heir" was dead at the time of
the intestate's death.

• Different intestacy statutes may apply to the
estate of the same decedent. Under conflict of laws

rules, the *situs* of realty determines the applicable law. Therefore, if an intestate possessed realty in all 50 states at the time of his or her death, the law of each state would apply to the parcel of realty located within it. Although most jurisdictions would state that the personalty would be distributed according to the law of the domicile of the intestate, the jurisdictions might not agree in their independent determinations of what jurisdiction is the domicile. In addition, a few courts might assert jurisdiction over large items of tangible personalty which were habitually kept in the jurisdiction even though it was not the intestate's domicile.

● Within any particular jurisdiction, there may be a further division of types of heirs based upon some characteristic of the property. Remnants of the realty-personalty distinction remain. In community property states, different intestate schemes are provided in many cases for community (or former community) property and separate property. When distribution is to be made among remote relatives, the historical source of the property may be relevant, e.g., in "ancestral property" or "half-and-half" statutes.

B. TYPICAL INTESTACY SCHEMES

Blackstone's 2 *Commentaries* * 200 to * 236 set forth the English common law Canons of Descent. The Canons of Descent, in common with all intestacy statutes, call for an order of taking to be followed until there is a taker. Unlike modern intestacy statutes, the Canons of Descent sought a single taker (except that females, when allowed to take, could take equally).

Uniform Probate Code §§ 2–102 and 2–103 are typical of modern provisions for intestate succession. They provide roughly as follows:

1. The intestate share comes only after certain benefits are paid to the surviving spouse and (usually minor or dependent) children. These rights supersede intestacy.

2. A surviving spouse always has an intestate share, which is in addition to the superseding rights mentioned above. The surviving spouse usually shares the estate with the children who are stepchildren to the surviving spouse or the decedent's parents if there are no children. The 1990 version of the Uniform Probate Code gives the surviving spouse the first $100,000 to $200,000 in sharing situations. The Uniform Probate Code is unusual in both the dollar sum and in giving the entire estate to the surviving spouse if "all of the decedent's surviving descendants are also descendants of the surviving spouse".

3. Generally, descendants take the balance of the estate after the spouse's share. Surviving children usually take equal shares; other issue take "by right of representation".

4. If there are no surviving issue, the surviving spouse may take the entire estate or share it with the surviving parent(s).

5.   If there is neither issue nor spouse surviving, the estate is distributed to the intestate's parents (or their issue) as follows:

a.   Equally if both parents are alive;

b.   Entirely to the survivor if one is alive;

c.   To their issue (or the issue of either of them) by right of representation.

6.   If there is no person who is within the foregoing categories, the search for the heir(s) proceeds to the grandparents and their descendants under most systems.

7.   If there is no person who is within the foregoing categories, the Uniform Probate Code and five states would have the estate escheat. Other systems would trace the family tree further and cause an escheat only for failure of proof or claiming by the "heirs."

8.   Escheat makes the state the ultimate heir, but is usually treated separately from intestacy.

An intestacy provision found only in the UPC is the requirement that an "heir" survive by 120 hours. This useful provision solves many simultaneous death problems. Generally an heir is only required to survive for an instant.

Few problems arise with the intestacy rules, but a solid knowledge of the rules is essential to mastery of Wills. Among the problems which do occur are the problems of division among co-takers and possibility of escheat when there are otherwise eligible "heirs" who cannot take for some reason such as disclaimer, slaying the predecessor in interest etc.

C. DIVISION AMONG CO–TAKERS

A single heir takes the entire estate. Multiple heirs share the estate in one of three ways: Equally, by right of representation and by other methods.

(1) Equally gives each taker the same size share as any other.

(2) By right of representation is a method of distributing property among the descendants (issue) of some specified person.

(3) The "other" category indicates that any other distribution scheme can be adopted. The only "other" situations which regularly appear are those which divide the estate between the surviving spouse and a child. For example, a statute may provide that the spouse will receive one-half if there is one child (i.e., equally) but two-thirds if there are "children" (which is equally when there are two children, but can only be described as an "other" distribution when there are three or more surviving children.)

D. BY RIGHT OF REPRESENTATION

Issue (or the more difficult to spell synonym "descendants") are the potentially unending stream of progeny of some specified person. In order to determine the identity of the takers when such a description is used, it is necessary to know two things: the identity of the ancestor (i.e., *whose* issue) and the time when the particular issue are to be determined, (i.e., as of *when*?) The composition of the stream "issue" is like the water composition of a river. Unless we freeze (literally, or by taking a still photograph) the river, we cannot say *which* particles of water form the river. When it is frozen, however, we can determine the members who form the whole. If the stream dries up, there are no particles to form the river. Similarly, if there are no descendants living, there are no members of the group. If there is only one descendant, he or she takes the entire portion and there is no problem of division.

The first generation of issue are the children of the named ancestor. There is no difficulty in distributing among the issue of an intestate ancestor who has no deceased children or has no deceased child who left more than one descendant surviving the intestate. The problems arise when there are deceased children who are "represented" by other issue who survive the intestate ancestor.

"By right of representation" and its Latin form, *per stirpes,* is a method of distributing among multiple issue, usually in different generations. The concept of right of representation allows a deceased member of one generation who leaves descendants who survive until the time for distribution (usually the death of the intestate ancestor) to be "represented" by the living descendants. The gift is substitutional; the share of a deceased ancestor is divided among his issue. A living ancestor prevents his issue from taking a share even though such issue are in existence at the time for distribution. The issue stand in the shoes of their ancestor, but only if the shoes are empty.

An illustration shows both the similarities and the differences in various aspects of "by right of representation":

ILLUSTRATION
BY RIGHT OF REPRESENTATION

Assuming that A & B, the children of the common ancestor, predecease him, as did a grandchild F and that each is survived as follows:

A is represented by two issue, his children C and D, who are the grandchildren of the intestate common ancestor.

B is represented by two children, E and G and two grandchildren, H and I, the children of a deceased child, F. E and G, grandchildren of the intestate common ancestor represent, along with H and I who are great-grandchildren of the intestate common ancestor, their ancestor, B, in taking a share of the estate.

When all the children of the intestate common ancestor are dead, jurisdictions vary in approach and results. Classic per stirpes distributions start the process of representation at the highest possible level, i.e., at the A and B level of "children" even though all children are dead. This results in one-half of the estate being divided among the issue of A, i.e., one quarter each to C and D. (Note that X, having the linking ancestor still alive, cannot step into his or her shoes.) This system was used in Maud v. Catherwood (1945). Under this system, E and G would each have one third of the one-half of B (i.e., one sixth each) and H and I would share one-half each of the one-third that F would have taken of the half that B would have taken, i.e., one-twelfth each.

The Uniform Probate Code has had two "representation" schemes. The original approach of Uniform Probate Code § 2–106, probably the majority approach in the United States, is to divide the stock at the highest generation *at which there are living members*. Thus, in the Illustration, the division would be at the grandchildren level since there are no children surviving. Thus, C, D, E and G each receive one-fifth and H and I share (one-tenth each) the fifth which F would have taken had F survived.

In 1990 the Uniform Probate Code substituted a concept called "per capita at each generation". In the illustration on page 11, the Uniform Probate Code results are the same: The grandchildren C, D, E and G take equal one-fifth shares while H and I receive one-tenth each. However, under the new "per capita at each generation" distribution scheme, the shares of H and I would change if D is dead, leaving X alive. Now the three great-grandchildren, X, H and I, would each receive two fifteenths (i.e., one third of the two-fifths pooled shares of the two deceased grandchildren, D and F).

E. VARIATIONS ON "CHILDREN": ADOPTED AND ILLEGITIMATE

1. ADOPTIONS

The process of adoption results in the complete grafting of the branch from one family tree onto another tree. Statutes may, however, be incomplete in specifying that the adopted child shall be treated as if born into the new family for all aspects of inheritance: By, from and through the new family and not by, from or through the old family. The aspects are the following four issues as to each of the original and the adopting families:

1. Does the adopted child inherit from the adopting parent?

2. Does the adopted child inherit through the adopting parent from the adopting parent's family?

3. Does the adopting family inherit from the adopted child?

4. Does the adopting family inherit through the adopted child, e.g., will the adopting father inherit from his grandchild traced through the adopted, but now deceased, intervening generation?

If the statute is incomplete, it is usually in the failure to specify the inheritance *through* the relationship (i.e., where the intestate or the potential heir was not directly involved in the adoption) or in the failure of the statute to specify that the rights of the old family are terminated.

2. INHERITANCE–MOTIVATED ADOPTIONS

The technique of adopting a person to qualify as "issue" of the adopter, usually for the purpose of an already established irrevocable trust, meets with varied judicial reaction. In a strict sense, the adopted person qualifies; as a practical matter, the adoption is often a sham which has little substance of the traditional adoption.

3. ILLEGITIMATES

At common law the illegitimate child was "the child of no one" and did not inherit from his father. Three relatively modern trends have expanded the ability of an illegitimate child to inherit: a narrower definition of illegitimacy, some statutory trend toward allowing illegitimates to inherit (especially from their mothers), and increasing constitutional protection.

1. **Expanding the Definition of Legitimacy.** In a strict sense, only the parentage is illegitimate, but the stigma has traditionally been case upon the child conceived out of wedlock. Increasingly, statutes declare children legitimate when the parents marry prior to (and in some cases after) birth of the child. In most jurisdictions a child can be legitimated by acknowledgment (or other act short of marrying the mother) by the father.

2. **Statutory Permission to Inherit by Children of Illegitimate Parents.** Especially in the case of inheritance from (and in some cases through) the maternal line, statutes tend to permit "illegitimate children" to inherit. This statutory trend has been accelerated by the constitutional approach next described:

3. **Constitutional Rights of Bastards to Inherit.** Starting with wrongful death actions in 1968 and probably not yet concluded, is a trend toward federal constitutional protection of the right of illegitimates to inherit, but a majority of the

United States Supreme Court upheld the constitu-
tionality of the restrictive Louisiana inheritance
statute in Labine v. Vincent (1971). North Dakota
found its statute restricting the inheritance rights
of illegitimates to be unconstitutional on both state
and federal grounds.

CHAPTER 2

SUPERSEDING RIGHTS OF THE SPOUSE AND ISSUE

A. SUMMARY OF SPOUSAL RIGHTS

Certain rights have been granted to the surviving spouse (and sometimes minor or other dependent children) in the strongest possible terms: Those rights supersede both intestacy and any will that could be written. Thus, the probate estate available for distribution by will or intestacy is that which is left after the rights of quarantine, homestead, exempt property, family allowance, small estate procedures, dower, curtesy, statutory substitutes or community property.

1. QUARANTINE

At common law, the widow (who was not an heir of realty, but was "next of kin" for personalty) was allowed to remain as occupant of the principal house of the deceased husband for forty days after his death. This right was in addition to the "dower" right and is related to the "probate homestead" concept.

2. HOMESTEAD AND EXEMPT PROPERTY

Most states have adopted from Texas the concept of exempting from execution and other judicial process the principal dwelling house and certain amounts of personal property, usually clothing, furniture and equipment used to earn a living. This protection from execution is often extended beyond the death of the head of the family. Often special statutory provisions permit a "probate homestead" to be set aside to the surviving spouse (and sometimes to minor or other children).

The term "homestead" is given varying meanings among various jurisdictions and often within the same jurisdiction. The probate homestead may be the same as, in lieu of or in addition to the homestead which is exempt from execution and there may be still a third type of exemption for tax, especially local realty tax, purposes.

3. FAMILY MAINTENANCE ALLOWANCE

In addition to the other rights of the spouse and dependent children, most jurisdictions authorize relatively liberal periodic payments of cash to the surviving spouse, dependent children or both. These payments, often characterized as extensions of the duty of support of the decedent, are often given priority over almost all other debts and expenses of the decedent and his or her estate. The family maintenance allowance is very important in

practice, but seldom is the subject of questions on
examinations. Among the issues which prompt litigation (or need to be covered by a statutory provision) are the following: Is the amount flexible according to a "station in life" test or fixed? Must
the estate be (and remain) solvent? Can the allowance be granted retroactively? Ex parte? Does the
court consider the other assets and sources of income of the person applying for the family allowance? Are children and other issue entitled? If so,
must they have been minors or dependent upon the
decedent for support?

The family allowance is designed as protective
legislation, but is often used offensively against
other claimants from the estate. The shield of the
wicked stepmother becomes a battering ram.

4. SMALL ESTATE LEGISLATION

Statutory provisions permitting persons to obtain
possession of assets or take small estates without
full probate proceedings are additional procedures
available to the surviving spouse (and, often, the
children and other close relatives). These techniques are extremely practical, but almost never the
subject of examinations.

5. DOWER, CURTESY, STATUTORY EQUIVALENTS OR COMMUNITY PROPERTY

Almost every jurisdiction has some provision permitting the surviving spouse to claim a portion of

the estate of a decedent despite a valid will attempting to dispose of it to others. The same right does not exist for children or other relatives except for the Louisiana *legitime* for legitimate children.

Dower is the common law right of the widow to a life estate in one third of the realty of which the husband was seised at any time during their marriage. Curtesy was the corresponding right of the husband, but had the additional requirement that children be born of the marriage.

Dower and curtesy, being rights in the probate estate, were both inchoate until one spouse died. Nine states have the community property system which is very similar in effect at death, but which is characterized by equal rights of both spouses in the "community" during their joint lives. Generally, community property of a married couple is that which is acquired onerously (i.e., not gratuitously) during marriage and domicile in a community property state.

Most states have varied the dower provisions. The fraction of the estate has often been increased from one-third to one-half. The property affected has been expanded from realty only to both realty and personalty. The time of ownership has tended to be changed from "seised during marriage" to "owned at death" with extensions to certain lifetime dispositions which are considered to be will substitutes, e.g., joint tenancy, life insurance, gifts, revocable trusts etc. The type of interest given to the surviving spouse has been expanded from a life estate to a fee in most cases. The statutes often make identical provisions for widows and widowers.

A summary of the aspects of dower, statutory substitutes and community property is as follows:

Aspect	Dower/Curtesy	Statutory Substitute	Community Property
Who:	Widow/Widower	Either Spouse	Either Spouse
How Long:	Life Estate	Fee Simple	Fee Simple
Fraction:	⅓	⅓ to ½	½
Nature:	Realty	Realty or Personalty	Realty or Personalty
Time Owned:	During Marriage	At Death and Some Will Substitutes	Acquired Onerously During Marriage and Domicile in Community Property State

Newman v. Dore (1937), is a leading case for the concept of an "illusory transfer": A surviving spouse was granted her forced share not only from the probate estate, but also from a revocable trust. Other jurisdictions, using either or both a "fraud" theory and emphasis upon the intent to defeat the share of the surviving spouse, have similarly allowed the surviving spouse a share of property otherwise disposed of by certain will substitutes. Not all jurisdictions accept the concept of an illusory transfer. Where established by decision or statute, the coverage is seldom as complete as the provisions of Uniform Probate Code § 2–201 which establishes the concept of the "augmented estate" subject to the forced share right of the surviving spouse.

B. WHO IS A WIDOW OR WIDOWER?

Traditionally, a widow or widower was a person who had entered into a valid marriage which had not been terminated by divorce prior to the death of the decedent. This concept has undergone some stretching and may see further changes concerning unconventional "marriages."

Until a divorce is "final" under the applicable domiciliary law, a couple remains married for the purposes of probate law. Although affinity traditionally initiates the marital status, it is not required to continue it. In jurisdictions which employ the concept of the interlocutory divorce, the divorce is not final until a final decree is entered and it may be impossible to enter the decree after the death of one of the parties. In jurisdictions with the decree nisi, the divorce is final upon entry, even though it could be set aside because of a reconciliation.

Normally certain marriages are voidable while others (usually incestuous and bigamous) are void for most, if not all, purposes. The "putative" spouse is one who innocently enters a marriage which is void because of a prior unterminated marriage of the other spouse. Courts sometimes create for a putative spouse equitable analogs to the rights of the spouse.

The unmarried couple who lives together, whether of the same sex or not, generally does not have a sufficient marriage upon which surviving spousal rights can be granted. There is little case law concerning the rights of members of a homosexual marriage or common law marriage where permitted by law, but it appears that they should have the same rights as other widows and widowers.

C. THE POST–WILL SPOUSE

While some states permit *any* spouse to assert the right to a marital share (statutory substitute for dower and curtesy), most do not give the right to take a full intestate share.

In one situation, however, most jurisdictions permit the surviving spouse to take his or her intestate share as if there were no will: When a person writes a will, marries, does not change the will and does not make other provision for (or express the intention to exclude) the spouse and then dies without changing the pre-marital will, the post-will spouse is usually permitted to take his or her intestate share of the decedent's estate. This is usually phrased in terms of being a revocation of the will to the extent necessary to satisfy the share of the post-will spouse.

Two amplifications of this doctrine:

1. Although the term "pretermission" is sometimes used with the spouse, certain purists insist that pretermission applies only to issue and the post-will spouse is a distinct category.

2. Since the post-will spouse (and in some cases any spouse with a statutory forced share) is allowed to take despite the will's language (unless the will

specifically provides for him or her as spouse or shows an intention to exclude the post-will spouse), secondary questions often arise as to how much of the will's dispositive scheme can be salvaged and in what order other bequests should abate to satisfy the spouse's share.

D. PRETERMISSION

We have seen that the "forced share" or dower share or community property share of a spouse cannot be disposed of by will without the spouse's consent, or at least acquiescence. Similar rights for children do not exist except in Louisiana where the *legitime* right of children will prevail over any will provision. Other rights of the spouse (and sometimes the children) of the decedent will also prevail over the specific language of the will; these include the quarantine, family allowance, homestead and exempt property and small estate set-aside provisions. These provisions are available in both testate and intestate estates.

The rights of the post-will spouse and the rights of pretermitted issue are in an intermediate class. They generally operate only against a will (giving what is usually the intestate share) if the will does not provide to the contrary. This leads to "boiler-plate" provisions which declare a blanket non-application of both doctrines. On rare occasions, as in In re Estate of Torregano (1960), the court will stretch to avoid that will's blanket fiat that the pretermission (or post-will spouse) provision will not apply. Torregano is a riptide with the main thrust of the statute's provisions going in the opposite direction.

Pretermission occurs when a will fails to provide for or show intention to exclude a protected descendant. Usually the protected descendants are only the first generation, i.e., children, and most of the pretermission statutes limit themselves to children born after the execution of the will. These statutes operate on the assumption that the testator would have wanted to provide for the child, but inadvertently neglected to do so.

The Uniform Probate Code has a specific provision giving a share of the estate to a child living at the time that the will was executed, but whom the testator believed to be dead. (Wishful thinking on the part of testators is apparently impermissible.)

A common situation, solved by the Uniform Probate Code and a few other code provisions, involves the after-born child of a testator who disposed of his or her entire estate to his or her spouse despite the existence of other children. In this case, the common testamentary reliance upon the surviving parent to take care of all the children is disturbed by the pretermission claim of the youngest children. A guardianship is usually required to manage a fraction of each item in the estate. The Uniform Probate Code broke ground in examining the entire testamentary plan of the testator. It also avoids the problem in small estates by giving the first

$100,000 to $200,000 to the surviving spouse as part of the intestate share.

The statutes also vary as to what evidence of intention to exclude the descendant will be admitted. While settlements or advancements or ademptions by satisfaction are generally allowed as evidence of intention to exclude the descendant, extrinsic evidence (including direct statements of the testator as to his or her intention) is occasionally excluded. In approaching a pretermission problem, it is necessary to have a specific statute in mind and be aware of the range of the statutes.

One of the most detailed statutory approaches is the following:

UNIFORM PROBATE CODE § 2–302

(a) Except as provided in subsection (b), if a testator fails to provide in his [or her] will for any of his [or her] children born or adopted after the execution of the will, the omitted after-born or after-adopted child receives a share in the estate as follows:

(1) If the testator had no child living when he [or she] executed the will, an omitted after-born or after-adopted child receives a share in the estate equal in value to that which the child would have received had the testator died intestate, unless the will devised all or substantially all of the estate to the other parent of the omitted child and that other parent survives the testator and is entitled to take under the will.

(2) If the testator had one or more children living when he [or she] executed the will, and the will devised property or an interest in property to one or more of the then-living children, an omitted after-born or after-adopted child is entitled to share in the testator's estate as follows:

(i) The portion of the testator's estate in which the omitted after-born or after-adopted child is entitled to share is limited to devises made to the testator's then-living children under the will.

(ii) The omitted after-born or after-adopted child is entitled to receive the share of the testator's estate, as limited in subparagraph (i), that the child would have received had the testator included all omitted after-born and after-adopted children with the children to whom devises were made under the will and had given an equal share of the estate to each child.

(iii) To the extent feasible, the interest granted an omitted after-born or after-adopted child under this section must be of the same character, whether equitable or legal, present or future, as that devised to the testator's then-living children under the will.

(iv) In satisfying a share provided by this paragraph, devises to the testator's children who were living when the will was executed abate ratably. In abating the devises of the then-living children, the court shall preserve to the maximum extent possible the character of the testamentary plan adopted by the testator.

(b) Neither subsection (a)(1), subsection (a)(2), nor subsection (c) applies if:

(1) it appears from the will that the omission was intentional; or

(2) the testator provided for the omitted after-born or after-adopted child by transfer outside the will and the intent that the transfer be in lieu of a testamentary provision is shown by the testator's statements or is reasonably inferred from the amount of the transfer or other evidence.

(c) Except as provided in subsection (b), if at the time of execution of the will the testator fails to provide in his [or her] will for a living child solely because he [or she] believes the child to be dead, the child is entitled to share in the estate as if the child were an omitted after-born or after-adopted child.

(d) In satisfying a share provided by subsection (a)(1), devises made by the will abate under Section 3–902.

Pretermission is a doctrine which applies to wills and probate estates. Although pretermission may be affected by a transfer made during the testator's life (e.g., an advancement or settlement will prevent pretermission), the doctrine of pretermission is not applied to will substitutes such as trusts, gifts, life insurance or joint tenancies.

Adopted children pose the additional dual problems of whether they are covered by the pretermission statutes and whether the effective date in relation to the will is the date of birth of the child or the date of adoption. Is a child born before, but adopted after, the date of the will covered by the statute?

QUIZ ON PRETERMISSION

Assume in each situation below that the decedent had no issue other than those mentioned and that the decedent dies leaving a valid will which made no provision for the issue surviving him except as stated. Is any issue pretermitted under the Uniform Probate Code or other statutory provisions?

1 through 3: T died survived by one child, C, and one grandchild, G. C is the parent of G. The will provides:

1. $1 to C. Is C pretermitted?

2. $1 to C. Is G pretermitted?

3. "I intentionally omit C." Is C pretermitted?

4. Testatrix had six children. All of her prior wills indicated an intention to benefit only two daughters while making token gifts to the other four. Her last will gave the entire estate to the two daughters and showed no intention to exclude the other four and a seventh child born after the making of the will.

5. A prior will gave $5,000 to a son, the balance of the estate to the spouse. A new will gave the

entire estate to the spouse, but did not mention the son or a daughter born after the making of the new will.

6. T's will provided, "I bequeath my entire estate to my daughter, D, if she survives me by 30 days; and, if not, to my friend, X." D survives T by 10 days and dies leaving a grandson, G. Is G pretermitted?

7. T created an irrevocable trust by which her children became income beneficiaries upon T's death, but T's will was written before the birth of her children.

8 through 10: T died survived by a post-will son who was neither mentioned nor disinherited by T's will. The son was the beneficiary of a substantial life insurance policy on the life of T. Concerning T's intention that the life insurance policy be in lieu of a testamentary provision there is evidence:

8. that T intended it;

9. that T did not intend it;

10. that is inconclusive concerning T's intent.

11 and 12: T died survived by C, his post-will son. C was raised by "foster parents"; is C pretermitted if the foster parents did or did not adopt him?

11. Is C pretermitted if adopted "out"?

12. Is C pretermitted if not adopted by others?

13. T died survived by five children one of whom was born after the making of the will. Her will did

not mention, provide for, nor disinherit them. In a separate typewritten document not admissible to probate, T explained to her executrix that she intentionally made no provision for her five children. Are they pretermitted?

14. T dies survived by one son, S, born after the making of the will, who is not mentioned or otherwise provided for in the will, but S is an employee of T and T left a bequest of $50 to each of his approximately 50 employees. Is S pretermitted?

15. T's will provided: "I give my estate to my son and my brother or the survivor of them." Brother survived T, but son predeceased T, leaving a daughter (T's granddaughter). Is the granddaughter pretermitted?

16. Although T's will did not mention a deceased child nor the child's living issue, it contained a clause giving "$1 to anyone who claims to be an heir of" T. Are the issue pretermitted?

17. T, survived by a widow, four living children and issue of a deceased child, left a will providing "all property is to be divided among the four children mentioned, if living at that time and if any of them should die, then to be divided between the rest living and not their heirs or any other relatives or friends of mine."

18. T's will leaves $1,000 to his predeceased son, but does not mention the son's surviving issue.

19 and 20: T's will leaves $1 to his son and the residue to T's friend, X, but does not mention the

son's daughter, G. The son renounces as permitted by law:

19. Is the son pretermitted?

20. Is the granddaughter pretermitted?

21. The only provision or mention of the post-will son is a devise of Cragthorn, a parcel of realty which T owned in joint tenancy.

22. While waiting for his wife to deliver their first and only child, testator executed his will, giving his entire estate to his wife, but making no mention of the child. His wife and child survived him. Is the child pretermitted?

23. T dies a widower with one son, and a valid will which makes no dispositive provision other than a statement, "I give no part of my estate to my son." Does the son take any part of the estate?

ANSWERS TO QUIZ ON PRETERMISSION

1. No. The token gift to C in the will indicates both that the omission was intentional (Uniform Probate Code and all others) and that C is not after-born (Uniform Probate Code and most states).

2. No. Disregarding the issue whether G is after-born, the Uniform Probate Code covers only children. Five states have pretermission statutes that protect other issue. In those states, it is a matter of terminology whether G is pretermitted or not. G's intestate share is zero. His parent, C, is

the heir. It is possible to say that G is not pretermitted or that G is pretermitted, but his intestate
share is zero.

3. No. The will shows sufficient intent to disinherit C in all jurisdictions. A token gift is unnecessary except to show the intention to exclude.

4. The four children living at the time the will
was written do not take under the Uniform Probate
Code, but would take under statutes (like that in
Washington state) not limited to after-born children
unless the prior wills are accepted as evidence to
exclude. The prior wills might be acceptable alone
as evidence; otherwise, they could be combined
with the will by the doctrine of dependent relevant
revocation. If so combined, the issue arises whether the after-born child is also limited to a token
bequest. The after-born seventh child is entitled to
take under the Uniform Probate Code; the more
difficult issue is the share it receives. The Uniform
Probate Code is unclear in the situation in which
various children receive varying bequests. The
share is apparently one-third under Uniform Probate Code § 2–302(a)(2) rather than the one-sev-
enth of intestacy.

5. Uniform Probate Code § 2–302(a)(1) prevents
the after-born daughter from taking a share because all or substantially all of the estate was devised to the other parent of the child. The son
living at the time the will was executed is not
pretermitted under the Uniform Probate Code. A
few jurisdictions could permit both to take as pre-

termitted issue if their statutes are not limited to after-born children and they do not include the Uniform Probate Code § 2–302(a)(1) limitation described above.

6. No. G is not pretermitted because the Uniform Probate Code applies only to children. In the five jurisdictions which extend pretermission to all issue who are heirs, G is also not pretermitted because G was not an heir. Additionally, the alternate bequest to X may show that the testator had an intention to the contrary.

7. Possibly the provision in the trust instrument would prevent pretermission. Uniform Probate Code § 2–302(b)(2) requires that "the intent that the transfer be in lieu of a testamentary provision is shown by the testator's statements or is reasonably inferred from the amount of the transfer or other evidence."

8 through 10. T's intention as to his after-born child will control where it is available. Where there is no evidence, the child will be pretermitted under the general rule of Uniform Probate Code § 2–302(a) because no exception has been proved. The burden of proof is on those asserting the exception to defend the will.

11 and 12. It is probable that a child adopted away from the testator would not be entitled to an intestate share, but some jurisdictions may not have severed the intestacy link between the parents who gave birth and the child who was adopted by others. It is possible to put a strained interpretation upon

the initial clause of Uniform Probate Code § 2–302(a): "... if a testator fails to provide in his will for any of his children born or adopted after the execution of his will ...". That section does not have the words "by him" after "adopted". A child could be (1) born and (2) adopted out. The statute only appears to require (1) or (2). Nevertheless, a definition of the parent and child relationship in Uniform Probate Code § 2–114(b) and the definition of "child" in Uniform Probate Code § 1–201(5) indicate that an adopted person is no longer a "child" of the natural parents.

13. The post-will fifth child, born after the date of the will, is pretermitted under Uniform Probate Code § 2–302(a). Evidence of intention to disinherit (except because of advancement) must appear "from the will". Extrinsic evidence is excluded. Other rules of evidence which exclude statements of a decedent may also apply. The other children are not pretermitted under the Uniform Probate Code because they were not born after the execution of the will. A few state statutes would treat them as pretermitted even though alive when the will was executed.

14. S is pretermitted if T has failed "to provide". Did T? On one side of this close question is the fact that there is some economic benefit flowing to the post-will child. On the other hand is the fact that it is a token amount and not given in his capacity *as child*. Some post-will spouse cases, by analogy, require that the bequest in a premarital

will be to the spouse as spouse, not as other relative or friend.

15.   No.   Uniform Probate Code § 2–302 covers only children.   In the few states in which the right of pretermission extends to all issue who are heirs, G would be pretermitted.

16 to 19.   No.   Uniform Probate Code § 2–302 covers only children.   In the few states in which the right of pretermission extends to all issue who are heirs, the following additional issues are reached:

16 and 17.   Does it appear from the face of the will that the omission was intentional?   Yes, in 16. In 17, the "four children mentioned" does not include the issue of a fifth deceased child, but the broader language "any other relatives . . . of mine" does cover those issue.

18.   Does the anti-lapse statute pass the $1,000 bequest to the issue of the predeceased son, thereby "providing for" them?   Probably.

19.   The son is not pretermitted because the intention to exclude is shown on the face of the will. Occasionally a case or statute will use the language that a disclaimed bequest will be treated "as if it were not made."   Extension of this fiction would permit the son to disclaim under the will and take a (larger) intestate share by pretermission, but this does not seem to be a proper application.   Perhaps a broad reading of Uniform Probate Code § 2–302(b)(1) would say that "it appears from the will

that the omission [from a larger share] was intentional".

20. The granddaughter, of course, would not be covered by the Uniform Probate Code. Can the son's disclaimer make the granddaughter a pretermitted heir in the few jurisdictions which extend the pretermission statute to issue other than children? Disclaimer provisions often state that the property passes "as if the disclaimant predeceased the testator". This fiction probably should not be extended to the pretermission and heirship provisions to make the granddaughter, otherwise not an heir, an heir for the purpose of pretermission. One purpose of the statute of wills is to allow a testator to avoid having his heirs participate in his estate if he so desires. To apply pretermission in disclaimer situations would give the heirs too strong a weapon against wills.

21. No. Probably an ineffective bequest would be sufficient to prevent pretermission. The testator omitted to make sufficient provision for the child, but did "provide". This result is more likely even though it exalts form over substance.

22. No. The child is not pretermitted under Uniform Probate Code § 2–302(a)(1), last clause, because the will devised all of the estate to the other parent of the child. Many states do not have a provision similar to the clause which controls in this situation. In those states, the child would be pretermitted because born "after the execution of the will".

23. Yes. The son takes, not by pretermission, but by intestacy since the testator failed to make an effective disposition. The only alternative would be an escheat on the theory of carrying out the testator's intention to disinherit and no person being named to take.

CHAPTER 3

THE STATUTE OF WILLS
A. INTRODUCTION

Each jurisdiction has enacted its own version of
the Statute of Wills. Naturally there are conflicts
in the terms and constructions of the various statutes. A preliminary issue therefore is *which* Statute of Wills applies to the estate of a particular
decedent.

The traditional, and probably majority, thinking
among states of the United States is that the validity of a will and the administration of a decedent's
estate are governed by the law of the location of
"immovables" and by the law of the decedent's
domicile as to "movables". Naturally, the jurisdictions are far from uniform in determining what is a
"movable" and what is not.

There is a trend, spearheaded by the Restatement, Second, Conflict of Laws § 269 to stress
other variables, but the fact remains that the nature (real or personal) of the decedent's property is
the main test for jurisdiction. Thus, a decedent
possessing realty in 50 states of the United States
could require 50 separate probate proceedings, of
which one would be the "domiciliary" administration and 49 would be "ancillary" administrations.

Finally, even if the involved jurisdictions can agree on what is a movable and what law, such as the law of the decedent's domicile, should apply, there may be an unresolvable conflict about which state is the decedent's domicile. The states agree that a person may have only one domicile at a time and that the domicile at the time of death generally determines the validity of the disposition of the personalty (or at least those parts of the personalty classified as "movables"), but different states may reach differing conclusions as to where the decedent was domiciled at the time of his death.

Once the jurisdiction has been selected, usually by itself, as being the appropriate jurisdiction, the Statute of Wills of that jurisdiction must be examined. The state will generally permit one, two or three types of wills (excluding Louisiana variations): Nuncupative (oral), Formal (witnessed) and Holographic (handwritten). The nuncupative will appears to have been designed to waste the time of law students. The terms and conditions under which it is permitted vary greatly from state to state. Only a low value amount of personalty can be involved in any state. This leaves for serious discussion the formal will (which every state permits) and the holographic will (which is permitted in 22 states, but may be validated in others because of Conflict of Laws rules concerning execution of wills, see e.g., Uniform Probate Code § 2–506).

B. FORMAL WILLS

Statutes specifying the requirements for a formal will range from the relatively simple Uniform Probate Code § 2–502 through New York Estates, Powers & Trusts Law § 3–2.1. The two statutes are set forth below with notations of points for comparison in brackets:

NEW YORK ESTATES, POWERS & TRUSTS LAW § 3–2.1

(a) Except for nuncupative and holographic wills [2] ... every will must be in writing [1], and executed and attested in the following manner:

(1) It shall be signed at the end thereof [3] by the testator

* * * [4]

(2) The signature of the testator shall be affixed to the will in the presence of each of the attesting witnesses [5], or shall be acknowledged by the testator to each of them to have been affixed by him or by his direction [6]. The testator may either sign in the presence of, or acknowledge his signature to each attesting witness separately.

(3) The testator shall, at some time during the ceremony or ceremonies [7] of execution and attestation, declare to each of the attesting witnesses that the instrument to which his signature has been affixed is his will.

(4) There shall be at least two [8] attesting witnesses, each of whom shall, at the request of the testator, [9] sign his name [10] and affix his residence address at the end [3] of the will. The failure of a witness to affix his address shall not affect the validity of the will. [11]

* * *

UNIFORM PROBATE CODE § 2–502

(a) Except as provided in subsection (b) and in Sections 2–503, 2–506, and 2–513, [2] a will must be:

(1) in writing; [1]

(2) signed [3] by the testator or in the testator's name by some other individual in the testator's conscious presence [5] and by the testator's direction [4]; and

(3) signed by at least two [8] individuals, each of whom signed within a reasonable time [7] after he [or she] witnessed either the signing of the will as described in paragraph (2) or the testator's acknowledgment [6] of that signature or acknowledgment of the will.

(b) A will that does not comply with subsection (a) is valid as a holographic will, whether or not witnessed, if the signature and material portions of the document are in the testator's handwriting.

(c) Intent that the document constitute the testator's will can be established by extrinsic evidence,

including, for holographic wills, portions of the document that are not in the testator's handwriting.

————

The numbered entries represent a pock-marked
battlefield upon which will contests have been
fought for centuries. The Uniform Probate Code
sought to smooth the surface of the battlefield. It
is improbable that the denial of a handhold to
contestants will diminish the number of will contests, but the number of wills defeated by the
statutory requirements should be reduced as the
number of statutory formalities are reduced.

The 1990 revision to the Uniform Probate Code
introduced to the United States the saving doctrine
of "harmless error" in Uniform Probate Code § 2–
503: A document otherwise insufficient as a will
can be admitted to probate if the proponent establishes by clear and convincing evidence that the
testator intended a testamentary act, i.e., creation,
revocation, amendment or revival of a will. This
revolutionary doctrine has not been adopted in very
many states.

Despite the fact that contests concerning improper execution are seldom motivated by an impartial
desire to improve the symmetry of the law, courts
have been notoriously quick to penalize the decedent by denying admission to a will executed without the full statutory pomp. They protect the decedent into intestacy.

The major areas and differences in the Statute of Wills are, as indicated by the bracketed numbers in New York Estates, Powers & Trusts Law § 3–2.1 and Uniform Probate Code § 2–502, as follows:

1. WILLS MUST BE IN WRITING

This is the basic rule, stemming from the 1677 Statute of Frauds (not the original Statute of Wills in 1540). The requirement excludes non-written wills but does not answer the questions of what is a writing and in what language it must be written.

The writing apparently can be in any language, so long as there is someone who can translate it. The most extreme example in this area was a private code used by the decedent and explained only by his sons, the beneficiaries of the will, in an 1856 English case. In that case, there was intent to make a gift shown in English, so the amount, written in a jeweler's code, was more a matter of ambiguity than translation.

Writing materials are as varied as the imaginations and needs of testators. Atkinson, *Wills* § 63 suggests that only a test of permanence is appropriate; he would therefore deny probate to a will written in the dust or the vapor on a panel of glass.

2. EXCEPTIONS TO THE "WRITTEN" REQUIREMENT

If a jurisdiction will permit both holographic or nuncupative wills, as New York does, or one of

them, as the Uniform Probate Code does, or even
the unusual Uniform Probate Code provision permitting a separate writing to dispose of tangible
articles of personalty, permission normally appears
at this point. The absence of the "Except ..."
clause (and any other provision giving specific permission) is treated as authority for the proposition
that holographic wills are not permitted.

The Uniform Probate Code recognizes the "foreign" will (i.e., one not executed with the formalities required in this jurisdiction, but permissible
under the law of some other jurisdiction having a
defined nexus with the will, the decedent or his
property) as an exception to the requirements of
Uniform Probate Code § 2–502. The International
Wills Act, added as Uniform Probate Code §§ 2–
1002 through 2–1010, permits another technique
which (as is the common case for other "foreign"
wills in many jurisdictions) exists as an unmen-
tioned exception to Uniform Probate Code § 2–502.

3. "SUBSCRIBED," "SIGNED AT THE END"

"Subscribed," "signed at the end" or the redun-
dant "subscribed at the end" as a requirement
imposed upon the testator, the witnesses or both,
has impaled many wills and therefore is excluded
from the Uniform Probate Code. "Signature"
which can be almost any act intended as a signature
(i.e., act, combined with intent) is still required of
the testator. "Subscription" adds the requirement

that the signature be "at the end" of the will. Without the "subscribed" requirement, the court must decide whether the name is signed wherever it is written, for example, "Will of Anna England" or "I, Lovina Bauman" at the beginning of the will or "Bonds belonging to Helene I. Bloch" in the body of the document.

What is "the end" of the will? A literal interpretation would require the signature to be the final entry (which is often true of the witnesses' signatures, but not the testator's). The "spatial end" test mechanically searches for the signature at such a spot. The "logical end" test, on the other hand, reads the text of the will and finds the end to be at the conclusion of the testamentary provisions. (Testamentary provisions include not only the dispositive provisions, but also the revocation of prior wills and the nomination of executors.) This approach saves many wills in which the decedents exercised frugality of paper by signing in margins, on reverse sides of the page, at the bottom of a cover page to which attachments were made etc.

Generally, a purported will which fails the statutory test of "subscribed" is not a valid will. In some cases, the courts (or occasionally a statutory provision such as the following) use amputation instead of capital punishment:

NEW YORK ESTATES, POWERS & TRUSTS LAW § 3–2.1(a)(1)

(A) The presence of any matter following the testator's signature, appearing on the will at the time of its execution, shall not invalidate such matter preceding the signature as appeared on the will at the time of its execution, except that such matter preceding the signature shall not be given effect, in the discretion of the surrogate, if it is so incomplete as not to be readily comprehensible without the aid of matter which follows the signature, or if to give effect to such matter preceding the signature would subvert the testator's general plan for the disposition and administration of his estate.

(B) No effect shall be given to any matter, other than the attestation clause, which follows the signature of the testator, or to any matter preceding such signature which was added subsequently to the execution of the will.

———

The amputation approach is strengthened by those courts which are willing to indulge in a presumption that material after the testator's signature was added after the signature and witnessing of the will.

4. SIGNATURE BY ANOTHER
FOR THE TESTATOR

In view of the infirmities of those who are close to death, an alternative for signature by the testator is provided by most jurisdictions including the Uniform Probate Code and New York. The procedure for signature by another is often in addition to provisions for signature by "X" (which is a "signature" by the testator); both procedures have detailed requirements which tend to be strictly enforced. The portion of New York Estates, Powers & Trusts Law § 3–2.1(a)(1) states:

(1) It shall be signed at the end thereof by the testator or, in the name of the testator, by another person in his presence and by his direction, subject to the following:

* * *

(C) Any person who signs the testator's name to the will, as provided in subparagraph (1) shall sign his own name and affix his residence address to the will but shall not be counted as one of the necessary attesting witnesses to the will. A will lacking the signature of the person signing the testator's name shall not be given effect; provided, however, the failure of the person signing the testator's name to affix his address shall not affect the validity of the will.

These additional requirements of "presence" and "request of the testator" and the signing of his own name by a person who is not also a necessary witness to the will make this provision particularly difficult to comply with. An easier provision for signature by another exists in the International Wills Act provision found in Uniform Probate Code § 2–1003(d).

5. "PRESENCE" OF THE TESTATOR

Signing or acknowledging in the *presence* of the testator, when required, as it is in New York and many states, has led to prolonged debate about whether the "presence" is a strict "line of sight" test in which each person must be in view of the others or a liberal "conscious presence" test in which persons in the next room qualify as being in the "presence" if they are able to "hear" the testator (or the other witness, if required by statute) sign. More difficult problems arise when the parties are connected by telephone or videophone or remote two-way television. The Uniform Probate Code eliminates this troublesome requirement except for the person who is signing the testator's name for him in lieu of an "X" or more complete signature.

6. SIGNING OR ACKNOWLEDGING

The testator normally would *sign* in the presence of both witnesses; a totally alternative provision is to permit the testator to *acknowledge* that a signature already made is his or her signature on the will. Some jurisdictions require that both witnesses follow the same alternative; i.e., either both see

the testator sign or both hear him or her acknowledge that it is his or her will.   The requirement
that both witnesses observe either the signature or
the acknowledgment (but not one doing each) is
often found in statutory language that the witnesses observe the signing or acknowledgment "at the
same time."   New York and the Uniform Probate
Code both permit a liberal mixing of the two techniques to permit the additional possibility of one
witness seeing the testator sign and the other hearing the testator acknowledge that it is his or her
will.   Which must be acknowledged by the testator:
That it is the testator's *signature* or that it is the
testator's *will*?   New York says "signature"; the
Uniform Code permits either.   Whether New York
would permit acknowledgment that it is the testator's "will" to be an acknowledgment that it is his
or her signature upon the will is left for court
interpretation.

7. AT THE SAME TIME

New York is unusual in admitting that the various signings and other acts required of a formal will
are "ceremonies" rather than "a ceremony"; further, New York allows a very extended time (up to
30 days) to complete all the ceremonies; this is
extremely unusual.   Normally, the formalities of
execution are considered as one ceremony to be
completed "at the same time"; courts have extended the time to some extent under the concept that
the signings are a "continuous transaction."

8. NUMBER OF WITNESSES

Most jurisdictions require two witnesses for a formal will. Louisiana has unique provisions and requires three witnesses. Other requirements for witnesses are discussed below.

9. REQUEST BY THE TESTATOR

The requirement that the testator "request" the witnesses to witness his signature to his will has been carried to such dryly logical extremes, as in In re Hales' Will (1956) [client in lawyer's office for the signature of the will failed to ask legal secretaries to witness his signature to attorney-prepared and secretary-presented will]. The abuses of the requirement explain its absence from the Uniform Probate Code.

10. SIGN "HIS" NAME

The extent to which the unexpected can defeat a will is shown by one case in which a will was held invalid because the statute required that the witness "sign his name" (as New York presently does) and the witness signed the *testator's* last name instead of his own! The Uniform Probate Code's appropriate response to that type of interpretation was to delete the requirement as to whose name the witness should sign, although a court could still so interpret the requirement of a signature.

11. ADDRESSES FOR WITNESSES

The non-essentiality of the witnesses' addresses is a sharp contrast to the mandatory language of the balance of the statute; it serves as support for the position that the remaining provisions are essential to the validity of the will.

C. WITNESSES TO A FORMAL WILL

Witnesses are required for formal wills. In jurisdictions which do not recognize holographic or noncupative wills (and in all jurisdictions as to wills which do not satisfy those requirements), the only possibility of a will with fewer than two witnesses being valid is if it qualifies as an international will or other foreign will which was valid under the laws of a jurisdiction which has sufficient connection with the will (e.g., domicile of testator, location of realty or place of execution).

The requirements to be a witness (other than being "disinterested") are not different from the requirements of a witness generally. The witness should be able to observe, understand, remember and relate the events which happened at the signing of the will. There is no minimum age for being a witness to a will, although it is common to require the testator to be an adult in order to create a valid will.

As of when is the witness role most important? In testing the "competence" or "credibility" of a witness, there are at least two possible times: The time that the will was signed and after the testator's death at the time the will is to be proved. Generally, the focus is upon the time that the will was signed. Thus, a will is generally not invalid even though both of the witnesses are deceased or unable to testify as to the events of the execution. Some jurisdictions have a "self-proving" provision as in Uniform Probate Code § 2–504 and the International Will, Uniform Probate Code § 2–1005. In those jurisdictions, the time of the execution should properly be the only appropriate time for consideration. The timing may be a material factor in the case of a witness who is "interested" at one time, but not at another, e.g., a bequest to a class such as "my employees" which class includes the witness at the time of execution, but not at the time for proving the will.

D. THE "INTERESTED" WITNESS

There are three basic postures for dealing with the problem of a will in which a necessary witness is an interested party:

1. Older common law (and statutory posture) by which the entire will would be held invalid if a bequest was made to a person who served as a witness to it. An extreme case is Crowell v. Tuttle (1914) in which the court invalidated a will witnessed by a guarantor of a promissory note by a church. The note itself, but not interest due on it, was barred by the statute of limitations. The will purported to bequeath $300 to be "applied to the

reduction of the present mortgage" on the church. There were five other guarantors in addition to the witness to the will and the security for the (barred) note was adequate. Note that this posture of the law caused the entire will to fail, i.e., it was a question of the "external" validity of the will as a will rather than a question of the "internal" validity of the bequest within the will.

2. A second posture is found in statutes such as in Illinois which specifically state (or imply) that the will is externally valid, but find the bequest to the interested witness to be invalid:

ILL.—SMITH–HURD ANN.
755 ILCS 5/4–6

(a) If any beneficial legacy or interest is given in a will to a person attesting its execution or to his spouse, the legacy or interest is void as to that beneficiary and all persons claiming under him, unless the will is otherwise duly attested by a sufficient number of witnesses ... exclusive of that person; ... but the beneficiary is entitled to receive so much of the legacy or interest given to him by the will as does not exceed the value of the share of the testator's estate to which he would be entitled were the will not established....

———

Typically a statute of this type makes the bequest to the "necessary" interested witness void unless one of three exceptions applies:

a. The "interested" witness is not "necessary," i.e., he or she is a "supernumerary." The typical instance of this is a will witnessed by three persons, one of whom is "interested", in a jurisdiction which requires only two witnesses. In that case, the "interested" witness is not "necessary" and is permitted to take his or her bequest (usually without regard to the order of signing of the will). A more difficult question arises when two or more of the witnesses are interested.

EXAMPLE: T, whose heir is H, writes an otherwise valid will in which his estate is given to A, B and C, who are the only witnesses to the will. Although each of A, B and C could maintain that there are two "disinterested" witnesses as to the bequest to him or her, it is probably the better view that there are no disinterested witnesses because of the possibility of collusive action.

b. A parallel to the instance where the witness is unnecessary occurs when the bequest is unnecessary in the sense that the bequest to the interested witness does not exceed what the witness would otherwise have received. The better phrasing of the alternative is "as if the will were not established" although it is occasionally (and inexactly phrased) "as if there were no will." The differences between the two phrasings is seen if the interested witness has participated in the execution of a second or subsequent will or is an heir (intestate taker).

This provision is the key to many intricate examination possibilities. A series of wills could be executed with varying problems of execution. If there is a necessary witness who is beneficially interested in the latest will, it is necessary to determine the validity of each previous will (even though otherwise revoked by the last will) to determine what share the beneficially interested necessary witness would otherwise take.

EXAMPLE: If H is the heir-presumptive of T and T writes the following testamentary documents, valid as formal wills only, what share does each beneficially interested witness take?

Will #	Disposition of Estate	Witnesses
1	One-half each to H and A	H and A
2	One-third each to H, A and B	H, A and B
3	One-third to H, two-thirds to A	H and A
4	One-third to H, residue to A	H and A
5	Revocation of one-third to H	H and A

The foregoing example serves as a vehicle for understanding a logical approach to a Wills problem expressed in the aphorism, "First Deed, Last Will." The "First Deed" aspect indicates the general rule that a chronological approach to irrevocable transactions made during life is logical. Since a deed is irrevocable, the first valid and effective deed disposes of the property involved. If, however, the transfer is revocable or by a will (which is typically revocable), the *last* transaction, chronologically, is the first to examine logically. The most efficient approach to a Wills question therefore looks first to irrevocable inter vivos dispositions, then to the revocable inter vivos dispositions which are effective unless revoked, expressly or by implication, by a subsequent transaction. In some cases, the will itself may revoke an inter vivos revocable disposition. Finally, property not effectively disposed of during lifetime and owned by the decedent at death is disposed of by the last valid and effective will. The external validity of the wills is examined in reverse chronological order. Once the validity of the will as a will (external validity) is established, the provisions should be examined for effectiveness (internal validity).

Applying this approach to the Example, we would start with the fifth testamentary transaction and work backwards. Will # 5 was a written revocation of part of Will # 4 and would probably be called a codicil to it. Note that the Illinois statute does not specifically cover a written revocation, as opposed to an execution of a new will. Ordinarily the court would extend the section's language to include a written revocation. Although the common law older posture would declare the entire act to be void because the revocation would increase the share of A who is a necessary witness, the Illinois statute (if applicable) implies that the will is valid by voiding the bequest to the necessary witness to the extent "as does not exceed the value of the share of the testator's estate to which he would be entitled were the will not established." The share given by the will is compared to a hypothetical share of an estate. The need to establish this hypothetical share of the estate opens the door for multiple additional will questions. The details of execution could be given for each will (instead of specifying that they are otherwise valid) to include variables such as failure to "subscribe at the end." In the example posed, however, the only defect is the interest of the witnesses in the will. A preliminary question involves interpretation of the statutory language "given in a will" when Will # 5 takes away rather than gives. It makes no difference in the problem posed, but if the witnesses to Will # 4 were C and D, two disinterested parties, would A's role as a witness to Will # 5 cause the effect of Will # 5 to be changed?

Consider the application of the Illinois statute to the Example if testamentary documents ## 4 and 5 were the only such papers: The share of A is increased actually, but not theoretically, by the revocation of H's share. In actuality, A will receive another third of the estate; in theory, A will continue to receive "the residue." The Illinois statute is helpful in stating that A, the interested witness in Will # 5 receives so much of the "interest given to him by the will as does not exceed the *value* of the share of the testator's estate to which he would be entitled were the will not established". [Emphasis added.] Thus, A would not be entitled to the final third of the residue because it exceeds the value of the share which he would otherwise take. Note that H was also a witness to a will, but his interest was cut down by Will # 5; therefore, he suffers no additional penalty and the will is valid as to him.

But the problems with the Example are not finished at this point. H and A were also witnesses to Wills ## 3, 2 and 1. These documents need to be examined in the search for the share to which A "would be entitled were the will not established". Taking the documents in reverse chronological order, we see the following: Comparing the provisions of Wills # 3 and # 4, they seem to be identical; thus A's share was not increased in Will # 4. (Note, however, that Will # 4's designation of A as the residual taker made A potentially able to receive more, e.g., failed gifts or the revoked gift in Will # 5.)

Comparing the provisions of Wills ## 3 and 4 with Will # 2, the share of H remains the same, but A's share is increased from one-third to two-thirds. Therefore, A would be entitled to only one-third of the estate if Wills ## 2, 3, 4 and 5 were the only documents. But A was a witness to Will # 2, also. In Vermont, a three-witness jurisdiction, A would clearly be necessary. In a two-witness jurisdiction if the other two witnesses, H and B, were "disinterested," A would be a "supernumerary" or unnecessary witness and allowed to take his share. Despite the appeal of the claim that there are two disinterested witnesses to the bequest of A's one-third of the estate, the problem of collusive action dictates that A's share under Will # 2 be reduced to the lower of the bequest in Will # 2 or the amount which A would have received had Will # 2 not been established. This calls for a comparison (and determination of the validity) of Will # 1. Under Will

1, A (disregarding A's role as a necessary witness) would receive one-half of the estate. Thus, A's bequest in Will # 1 does not limit the bequest in Will # 2. Unfortunately, however, the ubiquitous witness, A, also "did his thing" with Will # 1. Since the amount which A would have received without Will # 1 was zero (A was not the heir), the share which A would have received under all of the wills is therefore zero.

A similar determination can be made as to B's bequest in Will # 2, if it is material; it is not material under the Example's facts, except to determine the share of H.

The share of H is complicated by the fact that H is the heir. Thus, the bequests in wills which H witnessed in the Example did not increase the share which H would receive: In all the wills, the bequests to A and to B were invalid because the bequests exceeded amounts otherwise given to those necessary witnesses. Any intermediate valid and effective bequests to a person other than H would reduce the share which H would otherwise receive.

The Illinois statute's use of the term "value of the share" and the fact that the "heir" status is determined at the time of death both introduce problems of changes which occur between the time that the will is written and the time of the testator's death. As of when is the value determined? Does an heir apparent or heir presumptive at the time of execution have a share "to which he would be entitled were the will not established"? It seems that facts at the time of execution, rather than the decedent's death, should be determinative, but courts may vary in their interpretations of the statute.

Who is a "Beneficially Interested Witness"?

The Illinois statute resolves the question whether the spouse of a beneficiary has a "beneficial interest." We have seen the extreme treatment of a co-guarantor of a church's note being held "beneficially interested" (supra, p. 52) when the will provided for a $300 payment against that debt. On the other hand, some jurisdictions will not attribute the interest to any other person, even a spouse. In the middle ground are bequests to persons (e.g., children) or organizations (e.g., churches) to which the witnesses are related. The parent-child relationship is more obvious than the minister-church relationship. There is also a question of what is an "interest" "given" in the will: usually a person named as executor can serve as a witness and still be entitled to administer the estate and collect fees for so doing. The bank officer who witnesses a will in which his bank is named as executor is generally not penalized by making his bank unable to serve.

Sometimes the "interest" of a necessary witness is the result of an interaction with other provisions of the law. For example, if the will contained a bequest to a son and the son's daughter (testator's granddaughter) witnessed the will and then received her father's bequest under anti-lapse provisions, should she be prevented from receiving that bequest?

In some cases, statutory provisions may clarify that certain persons are *not* beneficially interested: for example, a specification that a general charge in the will for the payment of debts will not make the creditors "incompetent" as witnesses to the will or prevent the payment of their debts.

The third exception to the statutory rule arises in jurisdictions (unlike Illinois) which permit holographic wills. If the will is otherwise valid as a holograph, the witnesses' signatures may be ignored as "surplusage." This is really a variation upon the "necessary" witness theme.

3. Uniform Probate Code Posture:

The Uniform Probate Code has no specific provision which invalidates either the will or the bequest. Rather, the Uniform Probate Code considers the interest of a necessary witness to the will to be a factor to be considered in determining whether undue influence (or fraud) has been exerted upon the testator. Thus, the most modern approach leaves the field in uncertainty in order to avoid mechanical injustice.

E. HOLOGRAPHIC WILLS

Approximately half the states permit as an alternative to the formal, witnessed will a holographic will. Louisiana, having kicked the "H" out of the name, refers to it as "olographic." The key requirement is that the will be in the "handwriting" of the decedent. The most lenient phrasing of the requirements is that contained in Uniform Probate Code § 2–502:

UNIFORM PROBATE CODE § 2–502(b)

A will which does not comply with subsection (a) [dealing with formal wills] is valid as a holographic will, whether or not witnessed, if the signature and the material provisions are in the handwriting of the testator.

———

The key requirements are that the will be in the handwriting of and signed by the decedent. Other statutes impose greater restrictions by stating that the will be "entirely" in the handwriting of the decedent and a few states require that the will be dated.

1. HANDWRITING

Script handwriting in reasonably durable form poses few problems. Block printing, especially if that is the style of writing commonly used by the decedent, is generally acceptable. Although most types of writing require the use of some instrument other than the "hand" itself (e.g., pen or pencil) courts have generally declined to admit documents as holographic wills when they were typed, even if that was the customary method of writing used by the decedent.

2. "ENTIRELY"

In jurisdictions which use the term "entirely in the handwriting of the decedent" the court is often faced with the question of whether portions not in the handwriting (e.g., printed letterheads or the signature of one or more witnesses or printed text or caption of a stationer's form "Will") can be ignored. A mechanical approach would allow the trimming of upper or lower edges in order to validate an otherwise valid holographic will. It is more difficult to ignore non-handwritten material in the body of the will, such as machine-printed clauses on a form. The most extreme case is In re Estate of Thorn (1920) in which a single word, not necessary to the meaning of the will, was stamped by rubber stamp into the body of the will; the will was denied probate because it was not "entirely" in the decedent's handwriting.

3. "SIGNED"

Almost any act performed with the intention that it be a "signature" will suffice as a signature. Thus, the signature need not be legible, nor be the full or formal name of the decedent. Problems of what is intended as a signature arise when the decedent has written his or her name in a spot where it may not have been intended as a "signature," e.g., at the top in a space starting "Will of

_____" or in the beginning as "I, _____, hereby make my will." This problem of deciding when the writing of one's name is intended as a "signature" gave rise to the requirement that the testator "sign at the end" or "subscribe" in the formal will requirements. As we have seen, that requirement raised additional problems of defining what is the "end." Many otherwise-valid wills were denied probate because of the misplacement of the signature.

4. "DATED"

Few requirements produced such unwanted results as the "dated" requirement. California and Louisiana, especially, invalidated countless attempted wills by strict adherence to the requirement that holographic wills be "dated." The requirement was exalted above substance to the point where it was immaterial both that it was possible to determine when the will was written and that there was no legal difference regardless of the will's date. The date must be complete—month, day and year; apparently the decade is necessary; but the century may not be necessary. The date can be expressed in numbers. Louisiana until 1975 did not permit extrinsic evidence to establish the exact date when a numbered date contained a day numbered "12" or less and therefore was capable of being confused with the number for the month. The date does not have to be correct, but is usually rebuttably presumed to be correct.

Note that the Uniform Probate Code tends to eliminate the major "trouble" spots of statutory wills requirements: For the formal will, the "subscribed" and "both present at the same time" requirements and for the holographic will the "entirely" and "dated" requirements. In jurisdictions which do not have as permissive a statute, an astonishing number of otherwise-valid wills which everyone concedes were intended as wills by persons not suffering from any undue influence, fraud, duress, mistake nor lack of capacity are denied probate for failure to comply with the exact requirements of the statute. Although courts will occasionally twist to fit within a term (e.g., ignoring as surplusage the signature of a single witness to a holographic will or accepting initials as a signature), failure to satisfy the precise statutory requirements causes the purported will to be denied probate; it is a nullity.

F. STRICT v. LIBERAL INTERPRETATION

It is easy to divide court attitudes toward wills into two camps—strict and liberal. It is not so easy to determine in advance which attitude will control a particular situation. The ambivalent attitude of the courts toward the preparation and validity of wills has existed as long as wills themselves. The purposes of the Statute of Wills—to eliminate fraud and undue influence and to allow people to provide in a clear, inexpensive, easy and certain manner for the post-death ownership of their property—are themselves divisible into "strict" and "liberal" purposes. Strictness or liberality are not matters of "majority" or "minority" jurisdictions, although the trend is clearly in favor of liberalization of the formalities for will execution. Differing attitudes are often found within the same jurisdiction, although the flexibility within a particular jurisdiction is often limited by the terms of the applicable statute of wills itself and the judicial doctrine of stare decisis.

G. TESTAMENTARY INTENT

Every legal act is a combination of some type of act and some type of intent. For example, a "signature" is a combination of some writing or marking of one's name, nickname or initials or other symbol (the act) combined with a peculiar type of intent called the intention to sign (*animus signandi*). The intention to sign is a mental intention that the act be a "signature," i.e., that the formality and finality which accompany a signature be present.

In a similar manner, every will is the product of a certain act (the testamentary formalities required by the applicable statute of wills) and the intention to make a will (*animus testandi*). While the formalities are almost always set out in a statute, the description of *animus testandi* is left for common law development. The essence of testamentary intent is that the transaction be effective at (and not before) death with no interest vested before that time.

Testamentary intent is involved in two different equations: First, those dispositions during life intended to take effect at death in which the formalities of the statute of wills are not satisfied. Second, those written documents which satisfy the requirements of the statute of wills but which may not have been intended to be a will. In summary, since both act and intent are required, the problems usually arise when there is intent without the act or act without the intent.

Dispositions during the lifetime of a person may have some relation to his or her death. Whether these dispositions are valid will substitutes or not turns on whether they fit into certain narrow categories. The will substitutes which are commonly accepted include gifts and trusts, legal and equitable life estates which expire upon death, life insurance and other contractual designations of successors upon the death of the insured or other party to the contract and joint tenancy with its right of survivorship. These will substitutes are commonly accepted without any requirement of testamentary intent and distinguished from wills because they presently vest an interest in the successor (although the life insurance beneficiary is often said to have a "mere expectancy" like an heir presumptive).

Certain arrangements tend to fail as will substitutes and as wills. These include undelivered deeds, incomplete gifts and agencies which lack the formality (or court construction) to be trusts. Thus, an instruction to one's agent to deliver upon one's death is a "self-destruct" device: It fails as a gift (will substitute) because there is no delivery. (Contrast the situation if the agent is the agent of the donee or is a neutral third person "escrow holder".) It fails as a will if the formalities of the statute of wills are not complied with. It cannot succeed as an agency because agencies terminate upon the death of either principal or agent. (The Uniform Probate Code has given impetus to the concept of the durable power of attorney.)

The preceding portion of this chapter dealt with situations in which the testamentary formalities did not exist; in those cases, it was irrelevant whether testamentary intent was present since there was no valid will. Now we examine situations in which the formalities exist, but intent is questionable: Letter wills, conditional wills, mock wills and sham wills.

Letter Wills. Particularly in jurisdictions which permit holographic wills, the issue arises whether certain writings were intended as wills. Two of the most common categories are suicide notes and letters of instructions to attorneys. In both cases the "this very paper" test is traditionally applied to admit documents which are deemed to have been dispositive or appointive in this very paper rather than contemplating that a further document will be written. Thus a letter to an attorney stating "Please draft a will which states . . ." is not itself a will. On the other hand, a letter which states "This is my desire; it'll do until I put it in more formal style" does demonstrate testamentary intent.

Conditional Wills. It is generally conceded that a testator may make either a bequest or the entire will conditional upon the happening of some event. (Of course, all wills are conditional upon the death of the testator.) This ability to limit by condition is often in sharp contrast to the ability to create a will which is "revoked" under certain conditions. Thus, the phrasing of the determinative event as a condition which must exist for the will to arise will generally be given effect while the same event may not be acceptable as a condition upon which the will is automatically "revoked." The issue of whether a will is truly conditional often arises in the context of a self-drawn will in which the testator makes psychologically-explainable rationalizations as to why he or she is writing the will: "In case I fail to return from the trip to Idaho which I am making, this is my will." The testator completes the journey successfully, retains the will and then dies. Was the preamble a true condition or simply an explanation of why the will was being written? If the former, the condition has not been fulfilled and there is no will because of a lack of intention that the document be his or her will. If the latter, the dispositive provisions will be carried out. Courts have tended to be reasonable in determining that most supposed "conditions" are not such when the will has been retained and it appears to do more justice to admit rather than deny probate to the will.

Mock Wills and Sham Wills. There are some occasions when a will, satisfactory in form and

apparent intent, is not truly intended as a will:
Law professors demonstrating a sample will, initi-
ation rites or efforts to impress or induce action by
another person.   Atkinson, *Wills* § 46 indicates
that "Upon clear proof that an instrument in the
form of a will was intended as a joke or a sham, the
instrument will be denied probate and all testamentary effect."   Courts, however, require clear proof,
not supposition.

The lack of testamentary intent is also the cor-
nerstone for will contests which are based upon the
broad equitable concept that one must intend to do
a legal act as a matter of capable decision without
compulsion or fraud.

H. WILL CONTESTS: INCAPACITY, FRAUD, UNDUE INFLUENCE

There are many phrasings for the factors which
prevent the testator from being able to form the
intention to make a will.   Incapacity, Fraud and
Undue Influence are almost always included in any
such list.   Other terms such as Duress or Menace
may also be used.   You will note that these factors
are "equitable overrides" in the sense that the
courts of equity would negate an otherwise valid
transaction (be it a purported will, contract, trust or
other arrangement) if one of these overriding inten-
tion-eliminators is present.

Among the implications which flow from the nature of these grounds of will contest are the following:

- Each case must be determined on a case-by-case approach, dependent upon its particular facts.

- The grounds are predominantly decisional, rather than statutory. Although a statute may state the name of the ground (e.g., "lack of capacity"), the development of what is capacity and incapacity has been left to the courts.

- Being a decisional field, there is no authoritative statement of the exact terms (cf. a statute). Therefore, the definition of a particular ground will vary within a jurisdiction as it is stated and restated by the courts.

- While there is great variation within a single jurisdiction, the decisional nature of this area of the law tends to create a greater uniformity among various jurisdictions as the decisions from one are used in the others. For example, almost identical definitions of incapacity may exist although statutes use such differing terms as "Sound Mind," "Sound and Disposing Mind and Memory" or "Capacity."

- Results are more unpredictable because of the case-by-case approach. Certainty of result is sacrificed for "fair" results.

- Common sense, tempered by the application of certain legal realities (such as the fact that persons who make wills are often ill or close to death) will generally lead to acceptable results.

- The grounds of contest dealt with here are involved only in the attorney function of will contest and not in the attorney function of will preparation. There is no language which can, or should, be inserted into a will to avoid challenges for incapacity, fraud or undue influence.

● Examinations in this area are particularly unrealistic because the number of factual details given is finite and not capable of being enlarged. In practice an attorney would continue to investigate and might discover additional facts or variations on the facts as they originally appeared.

● Discussion in an examination answer would be lengthier because of the need to examine each relevant fact with no particular fact being immediately determinative.

1. INCAPACITY

Mental derangement sufficient to invalidate a will is generally said to consist of one of two forms: First, insanity of such broad character as to establish mental incompetency generally, or, second, some specific and narrower form of insanity under which the testator is the victim of some hallucination or delusion.

In the delusion situation, the evidence must establish that the will itself was the creature or product of such delusion, that the delusion bore directly upon and influenced the creation and terms of the will and that the testator devised his property in a way which, except for the existence of such delusion, he would not have done. Thus, the delusion that one is Napoleon is more obviously linked to a purported devise of Louisiana to the Empress Josephine than to a devise of one's house in New York to his wife, Mabel.

One has testamentary capacity if he is able to understand and carry in mind the nature and extent of his property and his relationships to his relatives and those around him, with clear remembrance as to those in whom and those things in which he has been mostly interested, capable of understanding the act he is doing and the relation in which he stands to the objects of his bounty. This is often divided into the following sub-abilities.

a. Ability to know the nature and extent of his own property, although a perfect knowledge is not required.

b. Ability to know the persons who "have claims upon his bounty."

c. Ability to dispose of his property to his beneficiaries in a rational manner, although authorities differ as to the extent to which the testamentary plan itself should serve as the basis from which capacity may be deduced.

d. Ability to relate the previous three abilities to each other, i.e., to form a rational plan for the disposition of one's property to the objects of one's bounty.

The tests for general mental capacity are relatively easy to satisfy. More rigid tests would invalidate many wills because of the common tendency to postpone making a will until one is weaker and in contemplation of impending death through old age, sickness or injury. Isolated instances of unusual behavior, especially when not related to the testamentary process of disposing of property to people, probably will not invalidate a will.

A weakened state of mind may be relevant for other grounds of will contest. For example, if the issue is undue influence, the fact that the testator is of weakened mental condition tends to show the relative ease of overpowering that mental condition and imposing another person's desires in place of the testator's.

2. FRAUD

Fraud consists of willfully false material statements of fact made by the heir or will beneficiary with the intention of deceiving the decedent, which do deceive the decedent and which cause the decedent to write or change (or refrain from writing or changing) a will in reliance upon such statements.

Although "Fraud" is essentially an equitable ground (which suggests that it should be broadly interpreted) in Wills the fraud ground is given a much narrower interpretation. The foregoing description is held to be required in all of its parts so that if a person making a false statement believes the statement to be true, or makes it for a purpose other than to deceive the decedent or if the decedent is not thereby "caused" to write his will, the will is not denied probate.

The most common phrasing of the causation test asks whether the bequest would have been made "but for" this fraud. A second phrasing asks if the fraud was the "sole motive" for the gift. Thus in In re Estate of Carson (1920) [in which the residual bequest to the decedent's "husband" was challenged on the ground that the marriage was void because it was bigamous] the appellate court remanded the matter to the trial court for evidence concerning the inducement effect of the marriage upon the bequest and whether "the bequest would not have been made except for that belief."

The Carson case also stands for the proposition that part of a will may be invalid due to fraud with the untainted portion being valid. Partial invalidity is also possible due to undue influence and possibly because of a delusion, but generally the entire will fails for improper execution, lack of intent or a generalized mental (or age) incapacity.

Fraud is a ground to prevent the probate of a will which has been duly executed. Another application of fraud, but not involving a "will contest," is the equitable action to impose a constructive trust to avoid unjust enrichment. Thus, where beneficiaries of a purported will which was to be executed alleged that the beneficiary of a prior will murdered the testatrix in order to prevent the execution of a new will, a constructive trust for the purported new will beneficiaries was the proper remedy, not the denial of probate of the earlier will, Latham v. Father Divine (1949).

Purportedly fraudulent wills are sometimes divided into two types: Fraud in the factum (or execution) cases involve a spurious will which is signed by the testator after he is told that it is another type of document. These are generally easy cases because there is no intention to write a will. The other type of fraud, fraud in the inducement, is more difficult. In fraud in the inducement cases, there is a generalized intention to create a valid will; the rigid "but for" causation test will be applied. It is possible that the erroneous belief of the testator was the product of mistake, rather than fraud.

Courts give short shrift to claims that the testator made a mistake in executing his will. For example, in Gifford v. Dyer (1852) [testatrix believed her son to be dead and expressed to the will draftsman her intention to exclude him even if living], the court stated in dictum that the mistake must appear on the face of the will and what would have been the will of the testatrix but for the mistake must also appear. This position sharply contrasts with claims that the testator made a mistake *in revoking* his will, a situation which calls for the application of the doctrine of dependent relative revocation. Without strong proof, the court is reluctant to nullify the formally stated words of the decedent in order to give credit to claims by the living of what they believed the testator wanted. Similarly, mistakes in the execution of a will, e.g., the signing of a will prepared for one's spouse, are seldom rectified by the court.

Between the two points—the unremediable mistake and the fraud which voids the will—is the innocent beneficiary of another's fraud. Is his or her gift more in the nature of a mistake which will be left uncorrected or is it so tainted by the fraud that it must be set aside? Courts differ. In a nonprobate action for fraud, it may depend upon whether the relief sought is equitable (constructive trust) or legal (a tort action for deceit).

3. UNDUE INFLUENCE

Undue Influence is the kind of influence that destroys the testator's free agency and substitutes another person's will for his own. Mere general influence, however strong or controlling, not brought to bear on the testamentary act is not enough. It must be influence used directly to procure the will and must amount to coercion destroying free agency on the part of the testator.

The evidence of undue influence is usually a combination of factors. For example, where one who unduly profits from a will sustains a confidential relationship to the testator and is active in procuring the execution of the will, the burden is usually shifted to the proponent to show that the will was not induced by undue influence. Similarly, there are indicia of undue influence when the following factors are present:

(a) The relationship between the proponent and the decedent afforded the proponent an opportunity to control the testamentary act. (Confidential Relationship);

(b) The decedent's condition was such as to permit a subversion of his free will (Weak Condition). It is in the weakened condition of the testator that there is an overlap between undue influence and incapacity;

(c) The proponent was active in procuring the instrument to be executed (Participation); and

(d) The proponent "unduly profited" as beneficiary under the challenged will (Undue Profit). The relative nature of "undue" is elaborated on a case-by-case basis. Equally vague is the concept of "natural objects of bounty," but the exclusion of such an "object" is often balanced by "undue profit" to another person.

These factors permit several inferences to be drawn from the same facts. For example, a statement that "We were like sisters" both indicates a confidential relationship and tends to indicate that the profit was not undue; i.e., the evidence could be used by either side in the will contest.

Returning to the problem of the beneficially interested necessary witness to a formal will and the Uniform Probate Code position of making no specific provision, it can be seen that such a person has participated and profited. In some cases, the courts have deduced a confidential relationship from the act of requesting the person to assist in the preparation of the will, but this seems to be an unwarranted blending of the elements.

A more difficult area is the attribution of the action of a participant to another who is the beneficiary, e.g., a father influences testatrix to devise her estate to his son or a wife induces the bequest by her mother-in-law to her son. Generally, the courts have been reluctant to attribute to a beneficiary the exertion of undue influence by a non-beneficiary. A possible exception is action by members (including clergymen) of a church to induce devises to the church. A few states still have so-called Mortmain statutes restricting bequests to charities to a certain percent of the estate or if the will is made at a time close to death. The great majority of states follow the Uniform Probate Code practice of having no specific provision and leaving the area for coverage as an instance of undue influence.

CHAPTER 4

REVOKING AND CHANGING WILLS

A. REVOCABILITY AS A WILL'S SINE QUA NON

The essential characteristics of a will are that a will is secret (in the sense of no person needing to know the contents other than the testator), ambulatory (in the sense that the will's provisions apply to property acquired after it is executed) and revocable. Although a testator is free to disclose the terms of the will and may specify that property subsequently acquired shall not be governed by the will, attempts to destroy the essential characteristic of revocability are often unsuccessful. For example, a provision in the will itself that the will shall be revoked upon the occurring of some event may be treated as a nullity because it is an attempt to revoke the will in a manner not specified in the applicable statute. (Another approach would be to treat the will as a conditional will in which the condition for effectiveness has failed to occur.) Similarly, even though the testator contractually promises not to revoke his or her will, he or she still has the power to revoke the will (but may be liable for a breach of the contract or a constructive trust might be imposed upon the takers of the estate).

B. REVOCATION BY OPERATION OF LAW

The provisions for the post-will spouse and for pretermission of children unintentionally omitted from the will are on the definition borderline as to whether they are revocations by operation of law. Both Uniform Probate Code § 2–508 and § 2–804(f) provide that no change of circumstances other than divorce or homicide revokes a will or part of it. Nevertheless, the Uniform Probate Code has provisions for the omitted post-will spouse (§ 2–301), pretermitted children (§ 2–302) and detailed provisions for a forced share to the spouse which have the effect of overruling portions of the will.

Uniform Probate Code § 2–804 provides that nonprobate provisions and dispositive and appointive provisions of a will in favor of a spouse or a relative of the ex-spouse are revoked by divorce or annulment (and revived if the couple remarries). Many jurisdictions do not have statutes comparable to the Uniform Probate Code provision and therefore have the unbalanced position that marriage revokes a will (or part of it) while divorce does not.

It must be borne in mind that the *effect* of a will could be eliminated by a constructive trust, but the will itself would not be "revoked."   Similarly, changes in a will by a codicil or the inability of a beneficiary to take or enjoy the share which the will purportedly gives him or her are not, technically, "revocations" although they have the same effect as far as the beneficiary is concerned.

C. INTENTIONAL REVOCATIONS

Revocations are either by operation of law or intentional. Intentional revocations of wills are similar to the creation of wills in that they consist of a generally undefined "intention" to revoke (animus revocandi) combined with an act (either a new testamentary writing or an act done to the old writing on the paper). All intentional revocations require that there be animus revocandi. In order to form this intention, there must be the same capacity and freedom from undue influence and fraud as is necessary to execute a will.

The acts which comprise a valid revocation are typically set out in a statute such as the following:

UNIFORM PROBATE CODE § 2–507

(a) A will or any part thereof is revoked:

(1) by executing a subsequent will that revokes the previous will or part expressly or by inconsistency; or

(2) by performing a revocatory act on the will, if the testator performed the act with the intent and for the purpose of revoking the will or part or if another individual performed the act in the testator's conscious presence and by the testator's direction. For purposes of this paragraph, "revocatory act on the will" includes burning, tearing, canceling, obliterating, or destroying the will or any part of it. A burning, tearing, or canceling is a "revocatory act on the will," whether or not the

burn, tear, or cancellation touched any of the words on the will.

(b) If a subsequent will does not expressly revoke a previous will, the execution of the subsequent will wholly revokes the previous will by inconsistency if the testator intended the subsequent will to replace rather than supplement the previous will.

(c) The testator is presumed to have intended a subsequent will to replace rather than supplement a previous will if the subsequent will makes a complete disposition of the testator's estate. If this presumption arises and is not rebutted by clear and convincing evidence, the previous will is revoked; only the subsequent will is operative on the testator's death.

(d) The testator is presumed to have intended a subsequent will to supplement rather than replace a previous will if the subsequent will does not make a complete disposition of the testator's estate. If this presumption arises and is not rebutted by clear and convincing evidence, the subsequent will revokes the previous will only to the extent the subsequent will is inconsistent with the previous will; each will is fully operative on the testator's death to the extent they are not inconsistent.

––––––

The code section therefore provides two alternate categories of revocation: writing and revocatory act. Within each category there are sub-categories:

Written revocations can be express or implied. Revocatory acts include burning, tearing, canceling, obliterating or destroying.

D. REVOCATION BY WRITING: EXPRESS AND IMPLIED

The statute concerning revocation may require interpretation as to what type of "writing" is sufficient as a revocation. If the statute permitted *any* type of writing, the testamentary formalities need not be complied with. If a "will" is required the question arises whether a codicil is included or whether a writing which satisfies the testamentary formalities but does not dispose of property or appoint personal representatives is a will, e.g., a document, duly executed which states "I hereby revoke my will." The Uniform Probate Code answers the problem by defining "will" (the term used in the foregoing § 2–507) in Uniform Probate Code § 1–201(56): " 'Will' includes codicil and any testamentary instrument which merely appoints an executor, revokes or revises another will. . . ." Most statutes require a testamentary writing to revoke a will.

Express revocations seldom present difficulties unless they are ambiguous or encounter the doctrine of dependent relative revocation. The revocation could be hopelessly ambiguous, e.g., "I revoke some, but not all, of my prior will." The revocation may be ambiguous to the point where it resolves nothing, e.g., "To the extent this disposition is inconsistent with my earlier disposition, the earlier disposition is revoked."

Implied revocations are involved only when there is no express written revocation, but an implied revocation is often less ambiguous than an act of revocation. As a practical matter, wills drafted by attorneys traditionally include an express revocation of prior wills, but such a clause only states what would occur in any case because of the inconsistency in the dispositions. A subsequent testamentary document without an express revocation clause does not wholly revoke a prior will (and is therefore a codicil to the prior will) unless it is wholly inconsistent with it (in which case it would be the single new will), but the subsequent testamentary document does change any terms which are inconsistent with it. Thus, the "Last" will is the first to be examined. Similarly, the statement that a document is the "Last" will (and how does one really know that it will be at the time that it is written?) is a slim straw upon which to base the claim that the document revokes all prior dispositions by implication.

When is a subsequent disposition "inconsistent"? Some cases are easy, such as disposition of the same, unique chattel or realty to different persons or different dispositions of the residue of the estate.

EXAMPLE: A's first will makes a bequest of $5,000 to B. Subsequently, another testamentary document (obviously containing no express revocation clause) makes a bequest of $10,000 to B without mentioning the prior bequest. Is the second bequest "inconsistent" with the first? Does B receive $10,000 or $15,000? Is the second bequest "substitutional" or "supplementary"? Obviously, the intent of the testator is controlling, so no absolute answer is possible, but what presumption should prevail in the absence of evidence to the contrary? Jurisdictions differ.

More as a matter of semantics than practical value is the distinction between an equitable inconsistency (Blackacre to A in document # 1 and Blackacre to B in document # 2) and a formal inconsistency (entire estate to A in document # 1, entire estate to A in document # 2). In the formal inconsistency case, the second document is probably a "will" totally replacing the prior document even though it is the same disposition. This type of distinction affects the terminology used ("will" v. "codicil") and procedures (Which document(s) should be admitted to probate?), but often not the recipients of the estate.

EXAMPLE: A's first will makes a bequest of $5,000 to B, Blackacre to C and the residue to D. Subsequently, another testamentary document, without an express revocation clause, devises Blackacre to E and the residue of the estate to D. Does B receive the $5,000 bequest? The testator's intent is controlling, but what did A intend? The devise of Blackacre to D is equitably inconsistent with the devise of the same property to C; therefore, C's devise is clearly revoked. The bequest of the residue to D in both documents is inconsistent in a formal sense, but makes no practical difference, unless we regard the second instrument as intended to be a complete disposition of the estate in which case the second bequest of the residue to D impliedly revokes the $5,000 bequest to B.

E. REVOCATION BY ACT

The requirements for a revocation by act (like creation of wills) involve rigid interpretations of the statute and precise adherence to its language to produce many results which offend common sense.

EXAMPLE # 1: T crumples her will and throws it into the wastebasket where it is subsequently dumped into the trash and taken to a land-fill operation. The will is not revoked because the act done did not fall within the precise language of the statute; it was not burned, torn, canceled, obliterated or destroyed "by the testator."

EXAMPLE # 2: T telephones his lawyer and says "Rip up that will of mine; I want to revoke it." If the lawyer hangs up the telephone and complies, the will is not revoked because the act for a testator by another person must be "in his presence."   Query whether maintaining the telephone connection would consist of being "in his presence."

EXAMPLE # 3: T tells nephew, the will beneficiary, "Burn that will." Nephew removes the will from inside the envelope and burns the envelope in the next room. The revocation was not prevented by the nephew's fraud because it would not have been effective since not in the testator's presence.

EXAMPLE # 4: T writes in the margin of his will "I hereby cancel this will." Is it canceled? No, according to the prevailing view (and contrary to the UPC position) because a "cancellation" is a crossing of the writing; here the writing of the will was not "crossed". What effect does the writing have? None, legally. It showed intention, but the act was missing. Can it be a revocation by writing? No, because not signed by the testator (and not witnessed in jurisdictions which do not permit holographic wills).

As the foregoing examples demonstrate, a precise knowledge of and adherence to the statutory requirements for revocation is demanded.

Despite the strictness of the foregoing, there is a situation in which the courts operate by "presumption". We have seen that an act and the intention is required for a revocation of a will. In the situation where the will is in the "secure possession" of the decedent (which is open for investigation, especially since that person is dead and unable to explain the circumstances or protect the will) and the will is either not found or found in an altered condition, these two facts (secure possession and not found unchanged) raise the presumption that the testator did the act of changing or destruction and that the testator intended it to be a change or revocation of the will. In summary, the court presumes all that the statute requires in such a situation.

F. PARTIAL REVOCATION BY ACT

The Uniform Probate Code specifically permits partial revocation of a will by act. Approximately half of the states do not permit partial revocation by act, usually as a matter of interpretation of the applicable statute with a consideration to the difficulty of determining how much of the will is intended to be revoked. If the signature to the will is cancelled, it can be inferred that a total revocation was intended, but partial burnings or other cancellations may not be so clear. When a partial revocation is combined with an attempted, but invalid, addition to the will (e.g., the names of the beneficiaries of two specific bequests are crossed off and transposed without testamentary formalities), the doctrine of dependent relative revocation may be invoked.

A jurisdiction which does not permit partial revocation by act does not avoid questions; it merely raises different ones: If the will cannot be partially revoked, is it totally revoked or is the provision which the testator did not desire to retain preserved despite that intention?

G. LOST WILLS

It is possible to have a valid will which has not been revoked, but which cannot be proved because

of the absence of the required degree of proof.
Some states have statutory provisions for the proof
of "lost" wills, but the vast majority of states leave
the proof of the terms of the document, in the
absence of the document itself, to the general law of
evidence, requiring, however, "clear" proof of the
terms of the will.

The statutes concerning the proof of lost wills
generally impose greater standards for proof of the
lost will and restrict the number of reasons for the
loss which are accepted. Thus, the only wills which
may be admitted as lost wills under a typical statute
might be those which are shown to be "in existence" at the death of the testator, fraudulently
destroyed before his death without his knowledge or
destroyed by public calamity. Each of the grounds
requires interpretation and raises new questions.
For example, is a will "in existence" if it is in
physical existence (the paper document exists) or
legal existence (the will, as a concept, has not been
revoked)? Is the "fraudulent" destruction capable
of being expanded by a "constructive" fraud, e.g.,
where the attorney entrusted with the original will
accidentally destroys it? How public must a public
calamity be?

Statutes may require two witnesses to prove the
terms of the will.

The "missing" or "lost" will is the meeting point
of a number of wills doctrines: The will may never
have been created. If created, it may have been
intentionally revoked by the testator and proof of

either the intention and destruction or the secure possession (which raises the presumption of destruction with intention to revoke) may be available. In those cases, there is no valid will. It is possible that some person fraudulently destroyed the will document, leaving the will as a concept to be proved if there is evidence of the will's terms. If there is proof of a will, but no proof of destruction which falls into either of the two categories presented (by testator or fraudulently by another), the will is not revoked, but can be proved only by clear evidence of its contents (or two witnesses if such are required by a statute).

> EXAMPLE: T leaves his valid will in his automobile which is compacted. There was no intention to revoke the will at that time, but T decides, eventually, that he does not want to recreate the document and that he prefers to die intestate. Is the will revoked? T has not done an act of revocation with the intention to revoke; the usual course is to say that the will is not revoked. If the terms of the will could not be proved, T has a valid, unrevoked but not proved will. If the terms of the will could be proved, it would be admitted to probate unless a "lost will" statute imposes a greater set of conditions (e.g., that the destruction be without his knowledge or fraudulent or that the will be proved by two witnesses).

H. REVIVAL

How should one treat a document which is designed to take effect at death when there has been an intervening revocation and an elimination of the revocation? Is the first document a balloon from which the air has been let out gradually but that is capable of being reinflated or has the balloon burst?

Naturally, the testator is capable, while living, of re-executing the first document, i.e., going through the steps of creating a new will as if it were a matter of first instance. It is when he or she does not do so that the problem of revival of a revoked will arises.

Jurisdictions vary from flat approaches that a will is always or never revived in such a situation to a preference for one or the other position which controls in the absence of the testator's intention to the contrary. Thus, within any particular jurisdiction, a particular approach has been adopted and the only issue is whether the testator has clearly indicated a desire contrary to the statutory approach.

We have seen that the Uniform Probate Code will revive a will's provisions concerning a former spouse, otherwise revoked by divorce or annulment, when the parties remarry. Uniform Probate Code § 2–509 deals with revocations of revocations. Different presumptions arise when the original revocation was partial or complete. In the case of a complete revocation there is no revival unless "it is evident from the circumstances of the revocation of the subsequent will or from testator's contemporary or subsequent declarations that the testator intended the previous will to take effect as executed." This approach is probably the most common form;

it states that a prior will is not revived by revocation of the revoking instrument unless the testator's intention to the contrary is established. Note that revival usually involves the elimination of written revocations and usually does not involve revocations by act. UPC § 2–509(a) would permit revival based upon circumstances of the revocation or the testator's declarations.

Revival can be distinguished from dependent relative revocation in a manner similar to distinguishing a divorce from an annulment. In revival, there was a revocation for a period of time; in divorce, there was a marriage for a period of time. In dependent relative revocation situations, the application of the doctrine results in a finding that there never was a revocation, just as an annulment finds that there never was a marriage.

I. DEPENDENT RELATIVE REVOCATION

1. THEORIES AND APPROACHES

Described in terms of its result, dependent relative revocation eliminates a revocation of a testamentary document or part of it. The stage is set for this decisional doctrine when there is a valid will, an otherwise valid revocation of part or all of the will and some reason why that revocation will not carry out the intention of the testator. Probably the better view is that dependent relative revocation is essentially an equitable doctrine which is applied only in appropriate cases. Therefore, it is not capable of being reduced to a simple formula, is less predictable and appears more threatening to the student attempting to learn the subject. The terminology used, including the name of the doctrine, tends to cloud rather than clarify the issue. The revocation of the valid will is said to be dependent upon the validity of some other disposition (usually a subsequent, but imperfectly executed, purported will).

EXAMPLE # 1: T, having previously created valid Will (# 1), unsuccessfully attempts to create a new Will (# 2). Believing the second document to be a valid will, T destroys Will # 1. Did T die testate? The second document is not a will; the first one has been revoked. T died intestate unless the court determines from facts not given (e.g., a comparison of the provisions of the two wills and intestacy and the reasons for the attempted change) that dependent relative revocation should apply to eliminate the revocation of Will # 1.

Another approach to dependent relative revocation is more mechanical. It looks to the connection between (rather than a comparison of) the revocation and the ineffective disposition:

EXAMPLE # 2: T crosses off the signature on his valid will, intending to write a new will, but dies before writing the new will. Is the old will revoked? In most cases, the mere intention to make a new will should not be enough, but if the revocation and new will were found to be part of "one scheme," dependent relative revocation might apply. Some courts apply the concept of a unified action (revocation of one and creation of the second) to achieve mechanical results. The better approach appears to be to examine the circumstances to determine the intention of the testator and carry it out as closely as possible.

The better approach seems to be that dependent relative revocation should not be applied mechanically. In many, if not most, cases it should not be applied at all. It is a riptide flowing contrary to the main current of revocation. The reasons for applying the doctrine should be apparent.

Terminology of "mistake" is often used in this field. It is possible to say in the examples given above that the revocation of the first instrument was a mistake. In Example # 1, it is possible to say that there was no intention to revoke by the act of revocation because T was under the mistaken impression that the revocation clause in the second instrument had been effective to revoke the will. (It would not be so effective in a jurisdiction which required the testamentary formalities for a revocation; if all that was required was "a writing" for a revocation, then the doctrine of dependent relative revocation would arise without the subsequent act of destruction of Will # 1.) Perhaps "mistake" is too broad a term for this usage because there are situations on both sides of the dependent relative revocation situation which could use the same terminology. On one side is a mistaken destruction of the will without intention to revoke, e.g., an accidental burning. Here, there is no intention to revoke. On the other side is the claim by the disgruntled former beneficiary that T did "not understand" him and made a "mistake" in revoking the bequest to him.

Some jurisdictions decline to apply dependent relative revocation to eliminate a written revocation, although accepting it to declare an act of revocation is ineffective. The justification for the distinction is that the act is inherently ambiguous. The court is seen as having the power to construe the ambiguous act to determine what the testator did, but not to disregard an express statement to carry out the court's conception of what the testator should have done. The inherently ambiguous nature of the acts of revocation is also cited as the reason for the admission of extrinsic evidence to prove the circumstances of the revocation.

Dependent relative revocation goes against many of the trends in the law of wills: The strict interpretation of and demand for rigid adherence to the specific language of the statutes concerning the making and revocation of wills and the philosophy of the parol evidence rule are given little weight in the case by case determinations of whether dependent relative revocation should apply. The court in making the decision should consider the testamentary pattern of the decedent (the terms of the prior wills and the direction they were taking in regard to intestacy), the respective shares and identities of the beneficiaries under the old and purportedly new will, the nature of the defect which prevents the

purported new will from taking effect, the trustwor-
thiness of the evidence of the reasons for the testator's desire to make the changes and the proximity
of the desired objective to the prior testamentary
plans and as contrasted to intestacy.   Note the
anomaly involved: While proclaiming that it will
not "write a new will for the testator," the court
examines the very document which it rejects as a
will in order to determine whether it should restore
a prior will.   The court will not make a new will,
but it will scrape away revocations to breathe new
life into an old will that achieves the same objective.

2.   INTERACTION WITH OTHER
WILLS DOCTRINES

Dependent relative revocation presents difficulties in addition to doctrinal differences and the
uncertainties inherent in an equitable doctrine
which is applied on a case by case basis: Often
dependent relative revocation is an alternate theory
applied after some preliminary theory (revival,
mortmain, beneficially-interested witness, partial
revocation by act, interlineation) has been applied.
Additionally, dependent relative revocation could
apply internally or externally to a will, i.e., to part
or all of it.

EXAMPLE # 3: T having previously executed
valid Will # 1 and valid Will # 2, revokes valid
Will # 2 in the belief and desire that Will # 1 be
effective. If the jurisdiction permits "revival,"
the first document is revived. If the jurisdiction

does not permit revival, should the second will be retained by the application of dependent relative revocation to its revocation?

The type of revocation may be very material in this area. Some courts apply revival only to written revocations, probably on the basis that acts of revocation are instantly effective. Some courts resist applying dependent relative revocation to written revocations because they are less ambiguous than acts.

EXAMPLE # 4: T's valid Will # 1 contains a valid bequest to a charity which does not violate the applicable "mortmain" statute (which limits the amount, or voids, bequests to charities made by wills executed too close to death). Valid Will # 2 repeats the bequest and changes the executor. T dies within the statutory period. Is the bequest in Will # 1 preserved by dependent relative revocation?

In In re Estate of Kaufman (1945) the California Supreme Court applied dependent relative revocation to make Will # 2 a codicil to Will # 1 despite express language to the contrary in the document and testimony that the testator, after having the effect of the mortmain statute and the difference between wills and codicils explained to him stated, "I want a new will. I don't want a codicil."

The Mississippi Supreme Court reached the opposite result, stressing the written nature of the revocation, in Crosby v. Alton Ochsner Medical Foundation (1973).

EXAMPLE # 5: T's valid Will # 1 makes a bequest to A. Will # 2 repeats that bequest and changes another part of the dispositive plan. A is a necessary witness to Will # 2. What result? Review pages 52 to 61.

Unless the provision for necessary witnesses is given, all possibilities should be covered. Will # 2 may be invalid as a will (Posture # 1 of the common law when there was an interested witness). The revocation contained in it would also fail—unless the jurisdiction was one of these permitting a written revocation to be less formal than a will. In that case, dependent relative revocation should be considered. But there are very few jurisdictions which retain either of those doctrines—voiding the will if there is an interested witness or permitting a revocation with less formality than a will.

Posture # 2, in which the bequest to the beneficiary is declared to be invalid, is more likely. The Illinois statute apparently would not invalidate the bequest because it "does not exceed the value of the share of the testator's estate to which he would be entitled were the will not established." ILL.— SMITH–HURD ANN. 755 ILCS 5/4–6. But, in In re Estate of Lubbe (1962), similar statutory language was interpreted to mean the *intestate* share and a non-heir who was beneficially interested in the will he witnessed was denied his bequest under both the interested witness statute and the refusal to apply dependent relative revocation to revive the bequest in Will # 1.

Posture # 3, typified by the Uniform Probate Code, has no provision concerning either the interested witness or dependent relative revocation; the only issue involved is possible undue influence.

EXAMPLE # 6: T's valid Will # 1 contains a bequest of "$1,000 to A." T crosses off the numerals "$1,000" and writes in "$500," initialing and dating the change. How much does A receive, if anything, from T's estate?

In order to reach the dependent relative revocation issue, we must examine the law concerning codicils, testamentary effectiveness of holographs and partial revocations by act:

• If both instruments were holographic (or if the jurisdiction permits holographic codicils which may "incorporate" non-holographic material in a witnessed will) and if the jurisdiction both permits holographic wills and accepts initials as a "signature," then the attempted changes are valid.

• If the changes are not an acceptable holograph (e.g., no internal integration as a complete will, not valid as a holographic codicil because not "entirely in handwriting," not "signed" or simply because holographic instruments are not accepted), we note that the crossing off of "$1,000" is an acceptable act of revocation. If the jurisdiction does not permit partial revocation by act, is the will entirely revoked or still intact? The latter choice produces the same result as dependent relative revocation, but on the same mechanical method as the theory of the unified act (revocation linked to new disposition).

• If the changes are not an acceptable holograph and a part, or all, of the bequest would fail because of the act of revocation, should dependent relative revocation apply to restore the bequest? Note that here we have the most difficult case: The bequest has been cut down. What would the testator prefer if he knew that the $500 bequest was ineffective: $1,000 or nothing at all? If the issue is evenly balanced, then the advocates of dependent relative revocation have probably failed to prove their case. In the attempt to determine the intention of the testator, the general rule (revocation) should apply in those instances in which the intention to the contrary has not been proved.

J. CODICILS

A codicil is a subsequent will which does not wholly revoke a prior will. In determining that a particular document is a codicil, a court arrives at three conclusions:

1. The subsequent document satisfies the requirements of the applicable statute of wills;

2. There is in existence a prior document which also satisfies the requirements for testamentary formality; and

3. The later document does not expressly or by necessary inference revoke the entire prior document.

A testamentary document could be written at different times. If two or more of the parts are capable of standing alone as far as the requirements for testamentary formalities, then the earliest is the "will" and all supplements (at least until the point at which the original will is entirely superseded) are codicils. If the testamentary formalities are satisfied by only one of the documents, it is the will. Changes to a formal will after it is executed generally require a complete re-performance of all the testamentary formalities in order to be valid. On the other hand, some jurisdictions permit a holographic will to be written from time to time, even having a number of dates, so long as all the provisions are in the handwriting of the testator.

> EXAMPLE: T purportedly executes a valid will, but it is invalid for reasons unknown to him, e.g., only two witnesses in a three-witness jurisdiction. T subsequently validly executes a document called a "codicil" which makes a slight change in the purported original will. What documents, if any, should be admitted to probate, on what theory and what should they be called?

Technically, the second document is not a codicil because there are not two or more properly executed documents. It would not be unusual, however, for the court to refer to the two papers as two separate documents—the will and its codicil. This could be supported under the theory of "re-execution" by the second document of that which was never executed properly in the first place, i.e., it is a "bootstrap codicil" since the "codicil" provides the validity for both itself and the underlying will.

A second approach would be to treat the two pages as one document, i.e., a will executed at the time of the codicil. Any internal discrepancies could be resolved by constructional rules about later portions (even in the same document) prevailing over the former. When carrying out the intention of the testator is used as a guiding principle, this type of validation and construction appears to be appropriate.

In cases in which the requirements for incorporation by reference are satisfied, the second document could be the only one admitted to probate, but it would incorporate the earlier one by reference.

K. INTEGRATION

"Integration" of a will is the act of deciding what parts constitute the will. Integration problems are more frequently encountered in jurisdictions which permit holographic wills. The term "integration" is used in both the external and internal integration sense:

1. EXTERNAL INTEGRATION

External integration is the process of determining what *pages* constitute the will. The pages which constitute the will are exactly those pages which the testator intended to be his or her will—but how is the intention determined? Where the several writings are connected by sequence of thought, folded together or physically forming one document, they are integrated if it may reasonably be inferred that the testator meant all the papers together to constitute his will.

Formal (witnessed) wills may pose another problem: If the applicable statute of wills requires that the will be subscribed "at the end," the addition of a page to the document below the signature page may appear to cause the entire will to fail. Usually, the court will focus upon what pages were present at the time that the testator signed or acknowledged the document to the witnesses as "my will." If there is no evidence, the court may indulge in the presumption that pages below the signature were added after execution, thereby admitting to probate the pages before the signature while giving no effect to the subsequently-added pages.

2.   INTERNAL INTEGRATION

When there are different writings by the testator, often on the same page, internal integration is the process of determining what *writings* (as opposed to what pages) constitute the will or will and codicil(s). Again the touchstone for formal (witnessed) wills is to admit the writings which were present when the document was executed. In the case of holographic wills, however, courts have tended to admit all writings which are in the handwriting of the testator. A construction preference may exist which would exclude items not in the testator's handwriting and not obviously intended by him or her to be incorporated into the will, e.g., a printed letterhead when the jurisdiction required that the will be "entirely" in the handwriting of the testator.

EXAMPLE: T wrote entirely in her own handwriting 21 pages of dispositive provisions. The materials used (type of paper, ink, etc.) and provisions (references to persons born and dying between the relevant dates) indicate that the will was written in three stages. Each of the pages has T's name written on it; there are three different dates on the document. What, if anything should be admitted to probate? Is it a will or a will and codicils? Probably the most common, but not the only position, would be to treat the document as one 21–page will and admit it to probate. Also possible is to proclaim it a will with two codicils. An unfortunate possibility is to hold that the document has no certain date (since it has three possible "certain" dates). Utilizing such an approach, it is possible that Louisiana might invalidate the document as an olographic will.

L. REPUBLICATION

A codicil republishes a will. Re-execution of the will in accordance with the testamentary formalities also republishes a will. So what? The republication gives a new point in time to the testamentary scheme. There are situations in which the time of the will makes a significant difference. Some of these are, or are becoming, obsolete. In each of the following instances, consider a will executed before the triggering event and a codicil executed after it and the effect of the "republication" by the codicil of the will:

1. OBSOLETE AREAS WHERE TIMING WAS IMPORTANT

a. Non-ambulatory Wills

Originally, a will "spoke as of the time of its execution" as to realty, i.e., it was sufficient only to pass realty owned at the time that the will was executed. Thus real property acquired after the will was executed was not passed by a devise (even if it stated "all my realty") unless there was a codicil executed after the additional realty was acquired. Now, wills apply to subsequently-acquired property unless the testator indicates an intention to the contrary.

b. Deceased Beneficiary

If a beneficiary was dead at the time a will was made, the bequest was void, as opposed to being "lapsed." Anti-lapse statutes which did not precisely cover the point sometimes were construed to apply only to bequests made to persons who died after the will was executed and not to apply to void gifts to persons who were dead at the time the will was written. Thus, if the chronology was (1) will and (2) death of beneficiary, the anti-lapse statute would apply, but if (3) execution of codicil was added, the republication of the will made the gift void, as opposed to a lapsed gift and the anti-lapse statute might not apply.

c. Mortmain Statutes

Treated here as obsolete because so few jurisdictions still have them, limit the amount which a testator may give to a charity in a will executed within a statutory period (often 30 days, 90 days or 6 months) of death. Thus, a testator who writes a will leaving his estate to charity (to the deprivation of relatives within the "protected class" of the particular statute) could live for a year or more and avoid the "time" limitation of such a statute. (Some statutes limit the percentage of the estate which can be given without regard to the respective times of the will and death.) If, however, the testator wrote a codicil which "republished" the will (even though not enlarging the gift to charity) and then died within the statutory period, the codicil might trigger the mortmain restrictions. Many jurisdictions construed the republication provision not to apply in this situation because the purpose of the statute (to restrain improvident death-bed bequests which were to the detriment of certain relatives) was not served by the republication theory.

2. CURRENT AREAS WHERE REPUBLICATION IS RELEVANT

a. In many situations, a revocation, exercise or bequest is required to be made by a will which was

executed "after" some other event. For example, a
gift causa mortis may be revoked by a will executed
after the gift was made, but is generally not revoked
by a will made prior to the gift. A power of
appointment may be created by an instrument
which provides that the power will be exercised only
by a will executed "after" the power was created.
A statute or a marital settlement agreement between the divorcing spouses may provide that all
bequests, powers and nominations made by wills
executed "prior to" the divorce or settlement agreement are revoked or renounced. Should a codicil to
the prior will republish it to revoke the gift causa
mortis, exercise the power of appointment or renew
the bequest, conferring a power or nomination as
personal representative or guardian of a former
spouse? It should probably be viewed as a matter
of the intention of the testator (combined with the
intention of the person creating the power in the
power of appointment situation). Should an otherwise unrelated codicil serve to revoke the gift causa
mortis if there is no clear intent? Here the issue is
more difficult. Courts could be expected to arrive
at different conclusions on that issue as well as the
issue whether the residuary clause of a pre-power
will is republished to be considered as "executed"
after the creation of the power. In this case, the
protection imposed by the creator of the power
might tilt the scale in favor of non-exercise, especially when the change made in the codicil is unrelated or minor. On the other hand, a pre-divorce
will with a post-divorce codicil probably should be

considered to be "re-executed" so that the bequests and nominations to the former spouse are preserved. Here, other factors (such as whether the alternate taker by intestacy is a new spouse or more remote relatives) might be considered by the court in a particular case, if it did not feel bound by prior cases.

b. Where there are multiple documents or contradictory provisions, the later provision is usually held to control. The concept of republication artificially gives a new date to an older bequest or other provision. If all the provisions concerned are in the testamentary documents, to say that each codicil republished both the will and the prior codicils would be to ignore the actual timing of the documents. In this area, the legal fiction should not be employed.

c. When pretermission applies only to children (or issue) born after the making of the will and in the post-will spouse situations, the pre-birth or premarital will can be republished by a post-birth or post-marital codicil. If the provisions of the codicil show that the testator contemplated the birth or marriage in making the codicil, republication is obviously appropriate. What effect should a codicil which makes some unrelated change have? For example, if T left his entire estate to his brother, married and had a child and then wrote a codicil which changed his corporate executor, who should receive T's estate?

d. Incorporation by reference often includes as one of its requirements that the document being incorporated "be in existence" at the time that the incorporating document is written. If T executes a will on January 1st and purports to include provisions in a letter to be written and dated on February 2d, can a March 3d codicil republish the will to make the incorporation complete? It probably should.

e. When there are changes in the beneficiaries, e.g., class gifts in which members could be added by birth or deleted by death between the date of the will and the date of the codicil, which date should the will's "now" refer to? The original date seems likely, but this may not carry out the intention of the testator, either because of a desire to include subsequent members or the operation of other policies of the law. For example, T provides "I make no provision for my children now living." in a will, has another child born and writes a codicil making an unrelated change in the will.

f. Where there are changes in the items bequeathed, e.g., changes which trigger the concepts of ademption by satisfaction or extinction, accretions, abatement or exoneration, does the bequest as of the time of the will or as of the time of the codicil pass by a will which is republished by the codicil?

Although the foregoing list may seem impressive, if not oppressive, the author has not had any other situation suggested to him which would trigger the

issue of "republication" or the relevance of the date
of the will or codicil. It is intended as an exhaus-
tive (if not exhausting) list.

M. INCORPORATION BY REFERENCE

It is common drafting practice to "incorporate by
reference" an existing writing into a pleading, contract or other legal document. Rather than copying
the exact words of the existing document, it is
described (and a photocopy is often attached to the
incorporation document). This standard practice,
however, encounters difficulty with statutory requirements for a will: If the will is holographic, the
attachment may not be "in the handwriting" of the
decedent. (Query: Are we positive that a photocopy of one's own handwriting "is" one's own handwriting?) If the will is formal, an attachment may
violate the requirement that the testator or the
witnesses "subscribe" "at the end" of the will. If
the applicable statute does not require subscription
at the end, it is possible that the incorporated
document may not be present at the time the will is
signed in which case the question arises whether
the testator has "declared" it to be a part of his or
her will.

The document which is incorporated is usually
not treated as a part of the will itself, but as an
external source from which the meaning of the will
can be completed. This maintains the distinction
between "integration" of pages which constitute
the will and "incorporation by reference" which is a

figurative, rather than literal, integration. It is treated *as if* it were integrated.

Fear of fraudulent substitutions is probably the basis for the legal insistence upon compliance with certain conditions in order to incorporate a document into a will by reference. The testator is not allowed to "waive" the protections of the statute of wills as to a document which does not have testamentary formalities. The requirements for incorporation by reference into a will are sometimes stated to be the following:

1. The document to be incorporated is in existence at the time the will is executed. This requirement is rigidly applied in order to obtain certainty, even though the will is not effective until death. The desire to dispose of property by a list "to be made later" is carried out only by the relatively unique provisions of Uniform Probate Code § 2–513, dealing with tangible articles of personalty disposed of by a written statement or list.

2. The incorporating document must manifest the intention to incorporate the provisions of the incorporated document. This essential requirement stresses the fact that it is the intention of the testator, within the bounds permitted by law, which governs.

3. The incorporated document must be sufficiently described to permit its identification. This is simply a variation on the theme that the intention must be discernible in order to be carried out. The descriptions could vary from lawyerlike preci-

sion (accompanied by inclusion of a photocopy) to the hopelessly vague. Some courts stress the reverse side of this requirement—that the incorporated document comply with the description—as a separate requirement.

4. Some, but not all, statements of the requirements for incorporation by reference include the requirement that the incorporating document refer to the incorporated document as being in existence (in addition to the requirement that it actually be in existence). This less understandable requirement is deleted from many decisional and statutory statements of the rule, such as Uniform Probate Code § 2–510.

Most states now permit incorporation by reference into wills, if the foregoing conditions are complied with. In the states which permit holographic wills, most of them permit the incorporation *by reference* of non-holographic material, even though *actual* incorporation (i.e., integration) would make the will invalid because not "entirely" in the handwriting of the decedent.

A specialized statute, designed to resolve problems encountered in the theories of integration, incorporation by reference and reference to facts of independent significance is the Uniform Testamentary Additions to Trusts Act, also found as Uniform Probate Code § 2–511. This provision authorizes "pour-overs" by will to trusts, without regard to the chronology of creation, funding and amendment.

N. INDEPENDENT LEGAL
SIGNIFICANCE

Uniform Probate Code § 2–512 summarizes the permissive nature of the doctrine of completion of the meaning of a will by reference to facts having significance apart from the testamentary scheme of the testator. That section permits a will to dispose of property "by reference to acts and events that have significance apart from their effect upon the dispositions made by the will. . . ."

Perhaps this doctrine is nothing more than a formalization of a common sense response to the abhorrence of the common law to attempts to "delegate the testamentary power" to oneself. The rigid insistence of the law that all of the provisions of the will be within the will's four corners and known at the time of execution has caused the defeat of many attempted bequests. Courts regularly accept a bequest of "the residue" of my estate (the extent and character of which is known only at or after death) to "my heirs" (who are determined at the time of death). In such a bequest, the identity of both the property given and the recipient is determined by reference to a fact having significance independent of the testamentary plan. Similarly, a bequest of "all automobiles which I own at my death" to "such of my children as survive me" will be resolved by reliance upon facts outside of the will. Going further, a gift of "the contents of my safe deposit box" to "the person with whom I dine on Christmas in the year before my death" is more difficult and may be ineffective. Few courts will give effect to a bequest of "the sum of money which I mentioned to my attorney" to "a certain person to be designated by me to my attorney." The attorney may be "independent" and "legal," but the dispositions have no significance apart from the testamentary scheme.

CHAPTER 5

BENEFICIARIES

A. INTRODUCTION: BENEFICIARIES WHO CANNOT TAKE THEIR BEQUESTS

Despite a valid, unrevoked will which is not lost and which contains a clear disposition of an existing part of a decedent's estate, the purported beneficiary may be unable to take or enjoy the property because of action by himself, the testator or both.

Action by the beneficiary alone includes the following:

• Inability to take because not a human, non-felon citizen.

• Death of the beneficiary before, with or after the testator.

• Renunciation (Disclaimer) by the beneficiary.

• Slaying of the predecessor in title.

Action by the testator alone may be the creation of a contract to make a will which binds the testator in equity to make a certain disposition; the enforcement usually involves a constructive trust being imposed upon the will beneficiary.

The joint action of the testator and the beneficiary is involved in the following situations:

116

● The testator inserts a "no contest" clause in the will which the beneficiary triggers by initiating a contest.

● The will sets up an "election" or imposes an equitable charge as a condition to the receipt of the bequest.

● A property settlement agreement between the testator and the beneficiary (or another) includes a provision by which the beneficiary contractually waives his or her interest in the testator's estate.

● The testator gives, and the beneficiary accepts, a gift during life which is intended as an "advancement" or ademption by satisfaction of the share which the beneficiary would otherwise receive at the death of the testator (or, in the case of advancement, the intestate).

● The beneficiary owes money to the testator which is unpaid at death, triggering a "set-off" or "retainer" right to be exercised by the personal representative of the testator.

B. BENEFICIARY'S OWN ACTION OR NATURE

1. FELONS, ALIENS AND NON–HUMANS

At common law a **felon** lost all civil rights, including the right to receive property by inheritance or will. Most states today permit a felon to inherit and deal with property (including the making of wills), but there are residual restrictions and exceptions.

Although restrictions on the ownership of land by **aliens** can be traced to feudal traditions, many states have enacted restrictions on alien inheritance only in the 20th Century. These restrictions have been severely limited (but not dealt a complete death blow) by Zschernig v. Miller (1968) which held an Oregon "reciprocity" statute (requiring the beneficiary to demonstrate that a citizen of Oregon could inherit in the foreign country the same as a citizen of that country before the beneficiary could inherit in Oregon the same as a resident citizen), as applied, to be an unconstitutional interference with the federal government's conduct of international relations. Subject to this and the further limitation that a treaty would prevail over such statutes, some states have retained statutory restrictions upon the rights of aliens to inherit. The statutory limitations are of the reciprocal ("You show me yours ...") or the impounding type, requiring the alien to "appear and claim" ("Come and get it."). In these statutes, drafting and construction to avoid problems raised by the equal protection clause of the XIVth Amendment usually draw a line between the resident and the non-resident alien, with the former being more constitutionally favored. Four states still prohibit aliens from inheriting any land (but do not so restrict personalty) while six others permit inheritance, but require a quick sale of realty by the inheriting alien. Uniform Probate Code § 2–111 provides that "No individual is disqualified to take as an heir because the individual or an individual through whom he claims is or has been an alien."

Non-humans encounter problems of limitations of gifts to **charities** (so called "mortmain" statutes) and the inability of corporations and animals to be will beneficiaries. For the most part, mortmain restrictions have been eliminated; those that remain are diverse in approach and complicated by judicial interpretation. The statutes restrict the amount (a set percentage or all) which a decedent can leave by will to charities. Often the statutes apply only to bequests in wills executed within a certain period of death (30 days, 3 months, 6 months) and only to the wills of decedents who are survived by certain classes of relatives. **Corporations** (including in some cases, municipalities, states and the United States government) have been held at various times to be ineligible to receive bequests because they are not "persons." Generally, this type of limitation has been removed by defining "person" as in Uniform Probate Code § 1–201(35) to include corporations. The non-human beneficiaries against whom the greatest restrictions exist are the "pet" **animals.** A direct gift to an animal generally fails, although many jurisdictions give the bequest practical effect through the concept of the "honorary trust" or construe it as a direct bequest to a human person who is named with or otherwise linked with the animal purported beneficiary.

2. DEATH OF THE BENEFICIARY

A beneficiary may die before the testator or at the same time (simultaneous death) or subsequently.

Except for the Uniform Probate Code § 2–104 requirement that an heir survive the intestate by 120 hours, there is generally no requirement that an *heir* (i.e., intestate taker) survive the decedent by more than an instant. The testator, of course, can attach any survivorship condition that he desires to any bequest.

Simultaneous death of the decedent and the beneficiary is generally handled by enactments such as the Uniform Simultaneous Death Act. That act, seeking to avoid the cost and delay of multiple probates, provides that, under circumstances where there is no sufficient evidence that two or more persons died otherwise than simultaneously, the property of each "shall be disposed of as if he had survived," i.e., the possible heir or will beneficiary is deemed to have predeceased the person whose estate is being distributed.

In intestacy, one must survive the predecessor in interest in order to become the "heir." What happens when a will beneficiary predeceases the testator? At common law a distinction was made between the will beneficiary who was dead at the time that the will was written (in which case the bequest was "void") and the will beneficiary who died between the time that the will was written and the death of the testator. In the latter case, the bequest was said to "lapse."

Almost all jurisdictions have enacted some form of "anti-lapse" statute which provides an alternate taker for a predeceased beneficiary. The following statutes show the range of anti-lapse statutes:

Uniform Probate Code § 2–603, the most common form of anti-lapse statute, was expanded to six times its prior length in 1990 and extended to nonwill transfers by Uniform Probate Code §§ 2–706 and 2–707. The statute is now both comprehensive and incomprehensible. Its basic parts are as follows:

UNIFORM PROBATE CODE § 2–603

... If a devisee fails to survive the testator and is a grandparent, a descendant of a grandparent, or a stepchild of ... the testator ... [and if] the deceased devisee leaves surviving descendants, a substitute gift is created in the devisee's surviving descendants....

While ten states narrow the deceased devisees to issue of the testator, another ten states broaden their anti-lapse statute to cover deceased devisees who are "kindred" (blood relatives):

CALIFORNIA PROBATE CODE § 6147

(a) As used in this section, "devisee" means a devisee who is kindred of the testator or kindred of a surviving, deceased, or former spouse of the testator.

(b) ... if a devisee is dead ..., the issue of the deceased devisee take in the devisee's place....

The broadest coverage is by the Maryland statute:

MARYLAND ESTATES AND
TRUSTS CODE § 4–403

(a) ... Unless a contrary intent is expressly indicated in the will, a legacy may not lapse or fail because of the death of a legatee after the execution of the will but prior to the death of the testator....

(b) ... A legacy described in subsection (a) shall have the same effect and operation in law to direct the distribution of the property directly from the estate of the person who owned the property to those persons who would have taken the property if the legatee had died, testate or intestate, owning the property....

———

A comparison reveals the areas in which statutes vary:

• The statutes admit what is probably the universal rule: The application of the anti-lapse statute is a matter of the testator's intention. A clear statement of intention, excludes the application of the anti-lapse statute.

• Some statutes expressly apply to class gifts; not all jurisdictions agree, especially if the statute is silent. To apply the statute to class gifts produces such seeming anomalies as including a niece (i.e., the daughter of a deceased brother) as a taker under a bequest to "my brothers."

• The group of deceased will beneficiaries ranges from the unusually broad Maryland provision for *any* beneficiary through relatives by blood ("kindred"), as in California, or a group of them, as in the Uniform Probate Code, to descendants of the testator. The earliest provisions were the narrowest and the Uniform Probate Code provision represents the middle stance most commonly found today.

• The group of alternate takers substituted by the anti-lapse statute is often limited, as by California and the Uniform Probate Code, to issue of the deceased beneficiary. Few statutes are as broad as the Maryland statute in substituting the testate or intestate takers of the deceased beneficiary. When the broader group of alternate takers is used, questions arise as to whether the creditors of the deceased beneficiary (including the testator's estate in its claim for set-off or retainer) can collect prior to the distribution to the alternate takers. Maryland, in a provision not quoted above, specifically denies creditors of the deceased beneficiary the right to proceed against the legacy.

The 1990 version of the Uniform Probate Code extends the anti-lapse coverage to will substitutes. The anti-lapse statutes are also available for use by analogy to two related fields: Failure of bequests for reasons other than death (e.g., a renunciation statute which phrases the alternate takers as "those persons who would take if the renouncing beneficiary were dead") and will substitutes. The application of anti-lapse statutes by analogy to will substitutes is a relatively new and unexplored field. Some courts have applied anti-lapse to revocable trusts. Use with life insurance policies is almost totally unknown. Application to powers of appointment creates problems of timing because the theory of "relation back" of the appointment (i.e., reading the appointment as if it were made at the time that the power was created) conflicts with the recognition of the death of the appointee between the time the power was created and when it is exercised.

3. RENUNCIATION (DISCLAIMER)

At common law it was possible to renounce a bequest or devise, but not possible to renounce an *intestate* succession. Many jurisdictions have changed this rule to permit renunciation of a testate or intestate bequest. Generally the renunciation was done in order to avoid creditors, minimize taxes or achieve some imperfectly executed, but known, intention of the testator.

The most intriguing question when there is a renunciation is the technique by which the alternate takers are selected. Often the courts use the fiction that the renouncing beneficiary predeceased the decedent whose estate is being distributed. This approach serves as a guide for other occasions when the beneficiary is not able to take the bequest or inheritance.

4. RIGHT OF THE SLAYER TO TAKE

The murdering beneficiary appears more frequently on examinations than in practice. It is more difficult to analyze the issue than to detect it. Three zones of variation exist: The legal theory, the type of slaying and the type of property involved.

a. Legal Theories

If the source of the law is a statute prohibiting the slayer from taking, the problem usually centers on whether this type of slaying and this type of property interest are within the statutory language and, if not, whether the statute should be extended by analogy. Statutes proceed in only one direction—prohibiting the slayer from taking, so the issue is whether this statute has extended this far.

If there is no statute which applies or can be extended by analogy, then the court will determine whether a slayer will be allowed to receive the property of his or her predecessor in interest. Three possible judicial approaches exist. The first approach is to allow the slayer to take. This is justified on the theory of legislative inaction. ("If the legislature had desired to prohibit such an inheritance, it could have so provided.") Although there is no constitutional "right" to inherit, some of the impetus for allowing the slayer to take has constitutional overtones of various provisions, including due process, equal protection, ex post facto, cruel and unusual punishment, and the dislike of forfeitures as in the bill of attainder provision.

The most direct approach for a court in the opposite direction is a prohibition of inheritance similar to, but without the authority of, a statute. Modernly, some courts have adopted this approach.

At the turn of the twentieth century, legal writers and courts were reluctant both to let the slayer receive the property of the victim and to admit that courts made, rather than "found," the law. Thus, the circumlocuting device of the "constructive trust" was utilized. The courts stated that the slaying heir or will beneficiary was entitled to receive by intestacy or will (thereby paying lip service to the absence of authority to the contrary), but many courts then imposed a "constructive" trust upon the slaying heir or will beneficiary for the benefit of the persons who would "otherwise" have received the property. This verbal fiction of a trust imposed by operation of law was used to achieve the same effect as if the inheritance or bequest was denied to the heir or will beneficiary.

If the slayer is denied or is held to be a constructive trustee, who takes or is entitled to the beneficial enjoyment? It is unlikely that one would draft a will with a provision revoking any bequest to a person responsible for the death of the testator. Provisions for the death of a beneficiary could be extended to cover the barred slayer—but should the anti-lapse statute be applied if the beneficiaries and alternate takers are within its terms? To extend the anti-lapse clause to theoretical deaths would allow one to take "through" a person who could not take, but to deny the application of the anti-lapse clause would be to visit the sins of the parent upon the child and revive a portion of the antiquated concept of "corruption of the blood."

Should other persons be allowed to benefit as a result of the slayer's action? If the slayer is married to the heir or if there are other persons who "benefit" from the "wrong" of the slaying, should they also be prohibited from taking? Normally, only the slayer is barred from inheriting.

b. Type of Slaying

The course in Criminal Law teaches that killing of a human being ranges in degree of culpability from justified and accidental through negligent to various degrees of manslaughter and murder. Obviously, the more culpable the killing (and the fewer sympathetic circumstances as in the so-called "mercy killing"), the more likely the court or statute is to deny the killer's right to take. When a statute demands a certain degree of murder or manslaughter or a certain burden of proof, it is difficult for the court to extend the purpose of the statute to a lesser amount. Some statutes, for example, require a criminal burden of proof (to be consistent in the findings of fault) and thereby are inconsistent in making the determinations of the criminal court conclusive on the civil court.

c. Type of Property

Although most statutes and court decisions are consistent between realty and personalty and between testate and intestate estates, many do not extend their application beyond the probate estate to will substitutes. The life insurance situation introduces another possibility: Relief of the insurance company from the obligation to pay to anyone when the beneficiary has murdered the insured. This would bring to the life insurance area the rule applied in the casualty insurance area: If an arsonist cannot collect fire insurance on his or her building, why should a murderer collect life insurance on his or her victim? Normally, however, the company is required to pay the proceeds and the only questions involved are whether the beneficiary should be allowed to take the proceeds and, if not, who is the alternate taker?

It is easy to apply the equitable doctrine of denying the slayer any rights under a trust, but generally it is more difficult to determine, under the typically complicated scheme of distribution of a trust, the identity of the alternate takers. Who should take when the trust instrument provides for distribution among persons "living at the time of the death" of a murdered life tenant? Similarly, if the slayer is one of the takers in default of exercise of a power of appointment, who takes his share if he is deprived because of his murder of the person possessing the power?

The most difficult of the will substitutes and the most likely to be encountered in practice is the joint tenancy situation in which one joint tenant slays the other. Once it is decided that the slayer will not be allowed to enlarge his or her share one encounters the problem that a killer cannot be deprived of his or her "own" property (except for attorney's fees) because of the murder. The two doctrines clash because of the common law (but not common sense) concept that each of the owners of joint tenancy property owns the entire property, subject to the right of survivorship of the other joint tenants. If a joint tenant slays another joint tenant and it is decided that the slayer cannot take the "share" of the victim, the possible alternatives include all of the following:

● Create a tenancy in common as if the slayer terminated the joint tenancy.

● Deprive the slayer of all interest in the property and thereby raise great problems of forfeiture.

● Retain the joint tenancy between the slayer and some alternate taker of the victim, e.g., the victim's heir.

● Deprive the slayer of all except a life estate (or a life estate in one half), thereby having a constructive resurrection.

● Deprive the slayer of all except the cash value of a life estate, adding a constructive sale to the constructive resurrection.

● Deprive the slayer of all of the joint tenancy which he or she did not originally contribute. This approach, taken from the death tax field, is usually applied when the victim contributed more than one half.

There are other variations in the fictions which can be applied in trying to resolve the knotty problems of the slaying joint tenant. Many of these involve the use of the constructive trust fiction.

C. TESTATOR'S ACTION:
CONTRACTS TO MAKE
A WILL

A contract to make a will is an agreement by one
party to devise or bequeath property to another,
such promise being made in consideration of a
promise or action by the purported beneficiary.
The contract to make a will is enforced by a court of
equity in appropriate cases. Normally, this enforcement is through the means of a constructive trust.
Two typical situations in which a contract to make
a will may exist are as follows:

EXAMPLE # 1: T induces F to move into T's
house and administer to T's needs for the balance
of T's life in exchange for T's promise to devise
the house and one-half of the residue of T's estate
to F.

EXAMPLE # 2: H and W, both having children
by prior (terminated) marriages, marry each other. They agree that the survivor should be entitled to use all of the property for his or her life
and that the balance remaining after the death of
the second of them should be divided one-half
each to the descendants of each of them.

If the contract is fully carried out by both parties,
the only difficulties are the tax treatment of the
amounts received in Example # 1 and the relative
priorities of the beneficiaries as opposed to creditors
of the estate. Normally, the creditors would be
satisfied prior to the gratuitous will beneficiary, but
in Example # 1, F is also a creditor. If F is unable

to enforce the contract, F may still be able to claim the value of F's services which were performed within the period of the statute of limitations.

A special provision of the Statute of Frauds may apply to a contract to devise realty (or both realty and personalty). Often an exception, such as full performance by the other party to the contract, is available. Additionally, a document which is ineffective as a will (e.g., because of lack of formalities or revocation) may be effective as written evidence of the contract or its terms. See also Uniform Probate Code § 2–514.

Performance by the party who is to make the will may be incomplete. If T in Example # 1 were to write a will with the provisions for F which were promised, but T then revoked the will, the court of equity might be called upon to enforce an "implied covenant of good faith and fair dealing" to enforce the contract by constructive trust upon the heirs of T. Note that the heirs are not being punished for their wrongdoing; the court is preventing their unjust enrichment. Similarly, in Example # 2, if H died having left all his property to W, W might be prevented by the court from giving away the property, although she might be entitled to use it for her necessary living expenses. W would therefore be like the owner of a legal life estate (who is not permitted to use principal), but W might have some of the rights of a beneficiary of a "discretionary trust" (in which so much of the principal as is necessary to maintain her standard of living can be consumed).

In Example # 2, the "Joint Will" form, in which both parties sign the same document, may be used. This form suggests that a contract was intended. If a contract is found to exist, certainty of disposition is obtained at the expense of flexibility. Another form which could be used in satisfaction of a contract (or which might not indicate a contract at all) is the "Reciprocal Wills" in which mirror image provisions are made. Thus, in Example # 2, H's will would give the property to W for life (with, perhaps, some power of invasion or appointment) and the remainder one-half to H's issue and one-half to W's issue. W's will, in turn, would make similar provisions for H and the identical disposition among the issue of H and W. The presence of a pair of reciprocal wills does not by itself prove a contract, but is consistent with the existence of a contract. The contract may also exist independent of the wills which were written. Thus, the wills of H and W might give a fee simple to the survivor, with or without a remainder over in the event of the prior death of the beneficiary. In the case of a will which purports to give a fee simple to the survivor (or any disposition which does not comport with the contract), the contract will be enforced, by constructive trust, if properly proved.

D.   JOINT ACTION OF TESTATOR AND BENEFICIARY

1.   "NO CONTEST" ("IN TERROREM") CLAUSES

A "no contest" clause attempts to punish any will beneficiary who participates in a will contest by forfeiture of the share which the beneficiary would otherwise have taken. A very simple "no contest" clause (too simple for effective usage) might state: "If any beneficiary contests this will, he shall take nothing under this will." No contest clauses are one type of conditional bequest. The condition— that the beneficiary refrain from instituting a contest of the testator's will—is generally regarded as "lawful" although strictly construed. "No contest" clauses are distinct from "disinheritance" clauses (attempts to avoid pretermission and post-will spouse provisions by providing "I intentionally make no provision for my heirs.") although they are commonly found together.

No contest clauses usually are ineffective for a number of reasons:

• Many assets are not in the probate estate. The clause only terminates the rights to the probate estate, not will substitutes, such as joint tenancy, life insurance etc.

• Not all challenges to a will are "contests" of a will. For example, pretermission and post-will spouse claims and the forced share of a spouse are not asserted in a "contest" of the will, even though they limit its effectiveness. Similarly, petitions to

construe or interpret the will or to deprive a beneficiary of his or her share for any of the reasons
described in this chapter are not "contests" of the
validity of a will *as a will*. The contest of a will is a
formal proceeding challenging the will as a vehicle,
i.e., the *external* validity of a will. There are also
all the problems of *internal* validity by which a
provision in an otherwise valid will is ineffective for
some stated reason. The particular challenge to
the will or its effectiveness must be proscribed.

• No contest clauses tend to be strictly construed
because they are in the nature of a forfeiture. The
particular act of the beneficiary must fall within the
terminology of the testator. This tendency toward
strict interpretation has led to longer and more
complicated "no contest" clauses.

• The clauses only work to deprive a beneficiary
of some portion of the estate which he or she would
otherwise have received. Thus, a disinherited child
will not be deterred by a no contest clause unless
the will makes a substantial provision for him if he
does not contest.

• An effective bequest to an alternate taker is
necessary in order to divert the bequest, especially
when there is an attempt to disinherit an heir. A
will which makes no dispositive provision except "I
give nothing to my heirs" gives the entire estate to
the heirs. (Some jurisdictions might claim an escheat to the ultimate heir, the state.)

• A successful will challenge defeats the will *and*
the no contest clause contained in it. Therefore,
only an unsuccessful will contest is punished.

● Even an unsuccessful will contest which clearly falls within the language of an unambiguous no contest clause may not be enforced in some jurisdictions, if the contest was entered into in good faith. The reluctance of the court to close its doors to legitimate inquiry and the court's dislike of forfeiture combine to justify a good faith questioning of the validity of the will.

2. CONDITIONAL BEQUESTS, EQUITABLE CHARGES AND ELECTIONS

a. Conditional Bequests

Any lawful condition can be imposed upon the will as a whole or upon any bequest within the will. In many cases the conditional bequest makes good sense; in others, the dead hand of the past is making an obscene gesture.

EXAMPLE # 1: T's will provides: "I give $1,000 to my friend, X, provided he survives me." Valid and usual.

EXAMPLE # 2: T's will provides: "I give $1,000 to my friend, X, provided he kills my wife." Invalid.

EXAMPLE # 3: T's will provides: "I give my automobile to my older son, provided he gives his automobile to my younger son." Valid and reasonable. Note that the testator sets up an election here and attempts to dispose of property which he does not own. It is more difficult when the election involves property which the testator may have believed he had the right to dispose of, e.g., joint tenancy property.

EXAMPLE # 4: T's will provides: "I give $1,000 to my son provided he never marries." Traditionally, this type of restraint upon future action (Contrast "provided he is unmarried at the time of my death") has been declared invalid, even if the son is a priest.

EXAMPLE # 5: T's will provides: "If my daughter is divorced or widowed, I give her an annuity of $12,000 a year." The validity of this bequest may turn on the motivation: Was it an (invalid) effort to induce divorce or murder or was it a (valid) desire to provide for the daughter if the wage-earning husband should not be available?

Many of the conditional bequests are similar to situations in which the question is whether there is any beneficiary, e.g., bequests to an animal, for a monument or to burn the money or raze a house. It is possible to phrase the same potential bequests as conditional bequests: "I give to X, provided he ..." cares for an animal, builds a monument, burns the other money or razes a building. Courts differ in their acceptance of these bequests in either form, but the conditional form is more acceptable in most cases.

b. Equitable Charges

Some bequests, such as Example # 3, above, attempt to dispose of property which the testator does not own, or attempt to carve out an interest of an unusual nature.

> EXAMPLE # 6: T gives his farm, Blackacre, to his son, "provided he pays his sister $500 a month for her life." The annuity which T attempts to create is not a trust. A court of equity will enforce the annuity by an "equitable charge" upon the farm. Note that the equitable charge may be a cloud on the title of the farm preventing the son from selling or refinancing it.

The equitable charge arises when a court of equity determines that it is appropriate to enforce the testator's scheme. Analysis of whether to impose such a charge must take account of a great many factors including the terms and duration of the charge, the reasons for it and alternatives to it and other difficulties (such as the cloud on title) which it may cause.

c. Elections

A more formal choice given to the beneficiary and enforced by legal, rather than equitable, rules is an election. The forced share of a spouse is an election set up by operation of law. An election may also be involved in conditional bequests (whether expressly made conditional or not) which attempt to dispose of property of someone other than the testator, as in Example # 3, above, including the attempt to dispose of property held in joint tenancy to someone other than the joint tenant. Must the joint tenant give the property which had been held in joint tenancy in accordance with the will in order to take the bequests under the will? In election situations, there is an offer which the beneficiary can refuse, but the refusal of the offer also involves a loss of all other rights under the will in most cases. Peripheral questions are whether the "right" to serve as personal representative is also lost and who are the alternate takers of the failed bequests.

3. PROPERTY SETTLEMENT AGREEMENT

Although divorce revokes a will in some jurisdictions by operation of law, the rule is not universal. In the other jurisdictions (and in all jurisdictions to the extent that a property settlement agreement is effective before the entry of the final decree of divorce), the rights to take under (or against) a will or by intestacy, including the rights to exempt property and family allowance and the right to serve as personal representative may be waived by a property settlement agreement. This is simply an offshoot of the renunciation doctrine, but it has the added contractual flavor.

Generally, property settlement agreements are strictly construed so that a waiver of each individual right must be included. The property settlement may not become effective because of the non-entry of a final decree of divorce before death. If it is final and effective, the agreement's terms are as enforceable as any renunciation.

4. ADVANCEMENTS AND ADEMPTION BY SATISFACTION

If an intestate "advances" the heir's share by giving it to the heir-apparent during the intestate's lifetime, the doctrine of "advancement" calls for an adjustment of the fractional share of the estate which the heir takes. (Naturally, the doctrine is inapplicable in sole heir situations; it is a doctrine for equalizing shares among co-heirs.) The adjustment calls for a figurative adding back of the value of the lifetime gift to the intestate estate to compute the figuratively enlarged estate for distribution and charging the heir who received the advancement with the value of the gift up to the total amount of his or her intestate share. It is not required that an heir return any excess since that would defeat the testator's intention to make the gift during lifetime.

The concept of the advancement (and also ademption by satisfaction) is to carry out the intention of the decedent that the lifetime gift be applied against the ultimate share of the heir or will beneficiary. Many jurisdictions require a greater amount of evidence of such intention, such as a writing, because of the possibility of misunderstanding. Some jurisdictions go to the opposite extreme and assume that a large gift to a child is intended as an advancement. In the middle are those jurisdictions which neither set up a presumption that there is an advancement in large gifts to issue nor require a writing to verify the intention of the testator that it was an advancement. See Uniform Probate Code §§ 2–109 and 2–609.

Ademption by satisfaction, sometimes simply called "satisfaction" to avoid confusion with ademption by extinction, is similar in theme to advancements. It is the testate analog: After writing a will, the testator makes a lifetime gift of the same property (or amount of money). Courts have made many distinctions concerning ademption by satisfaction, reaching diverse results on such issues as whether the doctrine applies to realty, residuary bequests or pro tanto satisfactions and whether a presumption arises when the amount given is to descendants of the testator. Generally, most courts apply the doctrine to one of the residuary takers; it is immaterial if the living gift is to the sole residuary taker. It is possible to have an ademption by satisfaction of a portion of a bequest, but both a *pro tanto* satisfaction and a satisfaction not in the same kind raise questions as to whether they were intended as satisfactions.

EXAMPLE: T's valid will devises Blackacre, now worth $100,000, to T's son, S, and the residue to a friend, F. T gives $50,000 cash to his son, S. Is there an ademption by satisfaction?

Without further evidence of intention, the differing amounts and types of property indicate that an advancement was not intended. Most courts state that the doctrine of ademption by satisfaction does not apply to realty. Of course, if the exact property was given to the beneficiary, there would be an ademption by extinction and the bequest would fail. On the other hand, some courts presume an advancement or ademption by satisfaction when there is a substantial gift from parent to child.

Two problems of timing are associated with advancements: Normally the gifts are valued at the time of the gift (as a matter of convenience, to avoid tracing) and the estate is valued at the time of death. The advancement (or the remaining estate) may increase or decrease in value. Thus, in the Example, Blackacre could decrease in value to $50,000 and the $50,000 cash given the son could increase or decrease. The other problem of timing is that the will must precede the gift in order for the issue of ademption by satisfaction to arise. Thus, in the Example, if T wrote a codicil to his will after the gift was made to S, the codicil might "republish" the will to make the doctrine of ademption by extinction inapplicable.

In situations in which the person who has received the putative advancement or ademption by satisfaction dies before the donor, it is obvious that there cannot be any "advancement" to the heir because the heir apparent did not achieve that status. It would be extremely unusual to charge an heir with an advancement made to another person who was the heir apparent, even when the heir and the heir apparent are closely related. Related difficult areas include heirs who, having received an advancement, renounce the bequest or murder the predecessor.

Often in a family situation it is difficult to tell whether the donor intended a normal gift, an advancement or a loan. This preliminary determination points toward the applicable doctrines.

5. SET–OFF (RETAINER)

If a will beneficiary owes money to the testator, most jurisdictions permit the personal representative to "set-off" the amount of the debt against the bequest. The doctrine is more likely to be applied when the debt is liquidated and the bequest is fungible. It is unlikely that the personal representative would be allowed to offset a personal injury claim against a bequest of copyright royalties and Blackacre, at least not until a court determined the value of each.

The difficult areas of this doctrine include instances in which the will beneficiary is not the one to take the bequest (e.g., because of death, renunciation or murder) and instances in which the debt is barred (e.g., by the statute of limitations or bankruptcy of the beneficiary). Jurisdictions vary in their treatment of both issues.

• When there is no legally binding debt upon the will beneficiary because of the bankruptcy of the beneficiary or the statute of limitations, some courts have reduced the bequest by the amount of the debt. This is generally defended upon general concepts of "fairness".

• When an alternate taker has been substituted by the anti-lapse statute for the original beneficiary, should the debt of the original beneficiary be off-set against the bequest? Conceptually, the alternate taker is said to take the share which the original beneficiary "would have taken". The problem with this approach is that it charges the debt of one person (the original beneficiary) against another (the alternate taker).

CHAPTER 6

CHANGES IN ITEMS
BEQUEATHED
A. TYPES OF BEQUESTS
AND DEVISES

All of the problems in this chapter deal with the division of a testator's estate among multiple takers. The guiding rule is that the testator's intention governs. The approach is first to seek the particular testator's intention; and, only if that cannot be determined, to determine what rule governs in the absence of an intention to the contrary.

A common approach utilizes the characterization of each bequest and devise into one of a number of categories—specific, demonstrative, general, annuity and residual. The technique of this approach is to classify the bequest by its wording and then have the consequences of the various doctrines flow inexorably from the classification. This approach is generally followed or at least paid lip service. An alternate approach would focus upon the function involved (abatement, accretion etc.) and decide whether the bequest is specific, general etc. for the purpose of this function. It is often difficult to tell whether a court is using the characterization or functional approach.

Acceptable definitions of the various classes of bequests and devises are as follows:

1. SPECIFIC BEQUESTS OR DEVISES

A bequest or devise of a particular and uniquely identifiable item is "specific." In the strictest definition of specific, the characteristic of uniqueness (as opposed to fungibility) is also stressed. Realty has a tradition of being considered "specific" both from the concept that each parcel is unique and the now-obsolete provision that a will did not pass after-acquired realty. A devise of "all the realty I own at the time of my death" is probably better classified as general or residual, rather than specific, even if the testator owned only one parcel of realty at all times. The dividing line between specific and other types of bequests has been obscured in many instances as courts sought to apply, or refrain from applying, certain doctrines which flow from such classification. For example, specific bequests are favored in abatement and exoneration, but disadvantaged in ademption and may grow (or shrink) under accretion principles. There is also some confusion and sloppiness in use of the term "specific." For example, one may "specify" a sum of money, e.g. $5,000, but that sum, although "specified," is technically not a "specific" bequest because the funds are fungible. On the other hand, a bequest or devise of the oil painting of Grandfather Hotchkiss or Blackacre is specific. The uniqueness of the asset suggests that its value is not a sufficient

replacement for it if it does not exist in the testator's estate at his death (or, stated another way, the
law infers that the testator wanted to give the
particular thing and not merely the value of the
thing).

2. DEMONSTRATIVE BEQUESTS

The demonstrative bequest (a demonstrative devise is quite rare) is characterized by a two-part
bequest: The testator bequeaths a sum of money,
but also indicates the source of the funds. If the
source is existent and is sufficient, no problem
arises. If, however, the source is nonexistent or
insufficient, the question arises whether the bequest can be distinguished from a specific bequest.
A specific bequest of an item which is not existent
causes an ademption, but generally the demonstrative bequest does not fail when the fund or property
from which the amount or quantity is to be paid
fails. Thus a bequest of "$10,000 from my savings
account at First National Bank" will generally pass
$10,000 from a solvent estate even if the savings
account is not in existence at the time of death; on
the other hand, a bequest of "my savings account at
First National Bank" would fail if no such account
existed. (A third possibility is that the bequest
might require interpretation; e.g., the testator had
certificates of deposit, but no savings account. Did
the testator mean "certificate of deposit" when he
said "savings account"?)

3. GENERAL BEQUESTS AND DEVISES

General bequests and devises is the catch-all classification of bequests. If a bequest is not specific, nor demonstrative nor residual, it is "general." Some jurisdictions also segregate other types of bequests and devises, e.g., annuities, but there does not seem to be any functional difference. To avoid the possible confusion of general bequests ("all other types of bequests") and residuary bequests ("all other assets"), bear in mind the difference between the pitcher and the baseball in the game of baseball. A bequest is the pitcher, so a general bequest is a classification of a bequest which does not fit conveniently into other categories of bequests. The assets of the estate are the baseball, the thing acted upon. Thus, the items not acted upon by other bequests (be they specific, demonstrative or general) are passed by the residuary clause.

At times the distinction between general and residual may be immaterial; e.g., a bequest of "my entire estate" is general, but will have the same effect as a residual bequest ("the balance of my estate").

A general bequest or devise is derived from the general (as opposed to specific) assets of the estate and is not dependent upon the existence of the particular thing bequeathed or devised.

EXAMPLE: Testator's will bequeaths "100 shares of American Telephone and Telegraph Company" to A and devises "160 acres of farmland in Washington County, Minnesota," to B.

Although testator's estate is solvent, it does not include any such stock or land.

If the bequest and devise in the example are interpreted as being "specific," the doctrine of ademption will apply. If, however, the bequests are construed as "general," they will be construed as instructions to the executor to purchase such assets, utilizing funds of the estate. Most bequests of money are correctly characterized as "general pecuniary legacies" if they are not demonstrative. It is common to treat bequests of a certain number of shares of stock to be general rather than specific; this appears to be the result of the desire to avoid the effect of some function, such as ademption.

4. RESIDUAL BEQUESTS AND DEVISES

The residual bequest or devise gives whatever assets are left in the estate after the satisfaction of all debts, expenses of administration, taxes and all other bequests. Although last in line, it may be the major part of the estate. The residual taker is like the owner of common stock of a corporation: As the size and net worth of the estate (or corporation) increases, the benefit is bestowed upon the residual taker (or common stockholder); conversely, as the size and net worth of the estate (or corporation) shrinks, the share of the residual taker (or common stockholder) decreases.

Bequests which fail for any reason (lapse, renunciation etc.) pass as the testator directs. In the absence of such provision, they pass as provided by statute, e.g., an anti-lapse statute. In the absence of a statutory provision, failed bequests fall into the residue. When the gift which fails is part of the residual bequest, the majority of jurisdictions state that the failed part of the residue passes by intestacy (rather than to the other residual takers) unless the testator provides to the contrary. A large minority of states by decision or by statutory provision similar to Uniform Probate Code § 2–604 permit the "residue of a residue" so that the remaining residual takers share the failed portion of the residual bequest (except in anti-lapse situations).

As the chart below illustrates, the dividing line of the functions is generally between "specific" and not specific or between "residual" and not residual.

CHARACTERIZATIONS AND FUNCTIONAL
ANALYSIS OF BEQUESTS

FUNCTION/BEQUEST:	SPECIFIC	GENERAL, ANNUITY AND DEMONSTRATIVE	RESIDUAL
ABATEMENT, TO PAY:			
—DEBTS, ADMIN. EXP.	Last	Used After Residue	First
—OTHER BEQUESTS:	Exempt	Not Used for Others	Used
(FEDERAL ESTATE TAX IS OFTEN PRORATED BY STATUTE.)			
ACCRETION	Takes	Does Not Take	Takes
ADEMPTION	Applies	Does Not Apply	
EXONERATION	Applies	Not Exonerated, But May Be Applied to Exonerate	

B. ABATEMENT

Abatement issues arise when the estate is not as generous as the testator's dispositive scheme and because the spouse, pretermitted issue, taxing authorities or creditors take their shares before the will beneficiaries. In all cases involved in this chapter, the estate must be solvent after the payment of expenses of administration, taxes and debts. If the estate is insolvent, there is nothing over which the multiple beneficiaries can fight. If there is only a single beneficiary, his or her fight is with the spouse, pretermitted issue, taxing authority or creditor, rather than other beneficiaries.

Unless otherwise provided by the testator or by statute, the residue of the estate (or any portion which would pass by intestacy) is used first to satisfy the various claimants against the estate, then the other bequests abate in proportion to their value, except that some (but not necessarily all) specific bequests may be spared the imposition of the burden if to do so would destroy their value.

EXAMPLE: T's will bequeaths an oil painting of Grandfather Yarrow, worth $1,000, to A, cash of $4,000 to B and the residue to C. The total gross estate is $10,000, including the value of the painting; there are expenses, taxes and debts of $6,000. Who receives how much?

In the example, the residual bequest to C is used first to pay the expenses of administration and debts. If there is federal estate tax, a statute may require that it be "equitably prorated" in accordance with the value of each bequest. Assuming no such proration, how is the remaining $1,000 of expenses and debts to be charged between A and B? Many courts would spare the specific bequest because of its indivisibility. The $1,000 value is coincidental; it is the item itself which the testator intended to pass and to charge a portion of the expenses of administration and debts to it might force a sale of the very item which the testator desired to give in kind. Thus, B would receive $3,000, C would receive nothing and A would receive the painting undiminished in value. On the other hand, some courts would apply abatement proportionately to the value (or such apportionment would be appropriate if A were also the beneficiary of a cash bequest, e.g., $2,000). Thus, in abatement, a specific bequest is the most favored and the residual bequest is least favored. The themes of abatement are avoidance of the destruction of the specific item, use of the residue (or portion of the probate estate not disposed of by will) and apportionment in accordance with value among the remaining bequests if further abatement is necessary.

C. ACCRETION

Accretion is the growth of an item bequeathed between the time the will was written and the testator's death. It is used here to include the possibility of shrinkage, as well as growth. There can also be a growth between the date of death and the date that the estate is distributed. In this latter case, the growth (or shrinkage) of a specific bequest clearly passes with it and the residual bequests receive the additional growth unless the testator or a statute provides otherwise.

The growth can be of various sorts. No account is ordinarily taken of shrinkage due to inflation.

Thus, a 1940 bequest of $10,000 by a decedent dying in 1995 will pass $10,000 in 1995 (or whenever distribution is made) purchasing power, not the purchasing power of 1940. Similarly, growth due to income separated and paid is not considered.

EXAMPLE: T bequeaths 100 shares of each of A, B and C Corporations to beneficiary in a 1989 will. Between the date of the will and T's death, each of the corporations has the same earnings, but they react differently. A Corporation pays $1,000 in dividends; B Corporation declares a 10% stock dividend in 1994 and C Corporation simply increases in value.

Specific bequests tend to carry their growth with them so that the 10% stock dividend might pass with a specific bequest of the B Stock. It is not certain that the bequest would be treated as specific, even if the number of shares owned coincided with the number bequeathed. Here, however, we are applying a doctrine which benefits, rather than destroys, the bequest (cf. ademption) and construction of the bequest as "specific" is more likely. Although general bequests do not ordinarily carry separated and reinvested income as in the case of B Corporation, the general bequest of C Corporation does carry the increase in value. Increases and decreases in value tend to be disregarded. If there were a two-for-one stock split, the specific bequest is more likely to pass 200 shares than the general bequest; it is also more likely that the bequest would be construed as "specific" in such a case. Mutual funds with the options of reinvesting the "capital gains portion" of dividends pose particular problems in this area: Can a testator vary his testamentary plan by choosing to reinvest the capital gains distributions (and obtain additional certificates of beneficial interest)? Generally, yes. The theme of accretion is to keep intact the item specifically bequeathed (but not necessarily its value, income or purchasing power) with any portions not given to (or taken from) the specific bequests being given to (or taken from) the residue. As far as growth is concerned, the specific bequest and the residual bequests are favored at the expense of other bequests.

D. ADEMPTION BY EXTINCTION

Ademption arises when the subject matter of a specific bequest is changed or not a part of the testator's estate at his death. A more elegant, but less understandable, definition is as follows: "The failure of a bequest or devise to pass as directed by the testator's will because of the legal or physical nonexistence of the thing bequeathed or devised in the estate of the testator at his death on account or its disposition, destruction, loss or substantial change subsequent to the execution of the will."

Possibly a majority of the states still follow the principle of "in specie" ademption enunciated by the English courts in the late 18th Century: If the item is not present in specie (i.e., exactly in the kind specified), the bequest fails, regardless of the testator's intention. Probably the better view and that held by a large minority is that the intention of the testator controls. This leads to a series of issues when ademption is possible:

• Is the bequest specific? Construing the bequest or devise as demonstrative or general may avoid the ademption issue, but be too broad a stroke because of the effect upon other functions, such as abatement and accretions upon the bequest so construed.

• Is it changed materially? A "mere" change in form or value may be deemed "immaterial" in order to avoid ademption.

• Is the item bequeathed traceable and identifiable even though changed? Tracing is similar to, but lacks the equitable flavor of tracing the trust res.

• Does the testator's intention govern? Here, the doctrinal split explained above must be dealt with. If the testator's intent does govern, the further issues arise:

• What was this particular testator's intention?

• As of when is the intention relevant? Often there are at least two points in time—the time that the will was written and the time of the change—and other possible times such as the time of codicils, further changes or death. Do we discern the intention only from the will or from the surrounding circumstances? This leads to issues as to what evidence is, or should be, admitted.

In approaching ademption issues, it is often helpful to consider the type of asset bequeathed (realty, promissory notes, securities, automobiles, etc.) and the type of change involved. For example, realty which is condemned represents the least volitional change in the asset bequeathed. Conversions or pay-offs of bonds, mortgages and other securities may occur without much participation by the testator. Realty could be sold with a mortgage taken back as security for a promissory note upon which the maker defaults. Upon foreclosure, what is the effect upon a devise of the property by the purchaser or by the seller?

The many possible changes in corporate securities create the issues mentioned under accretions, plus others: Stock redemptions, options and rights (which require the addition of cash), splits and stock and cash dividends all must be dealt with.

EXAMPLE: T's valid will makes the following bequests and the changes indicated occur after the will was written:

A. "To A, my pink Spode chinaware, 34 pieces." (Only 30 pieces have been found; there is no information concerning any other pieces.)

B. "To B, the oil painting titled 'Solitude.' " (T gave the painting to B two years ago.)

C. "To C, my John Hancock life insurance policy." (The company paid the proceeds to K, the beneficiary designated in the policy.)

D. "To D, my Mercury station wagon." (Two years after the will was written, T traded the Mercury and paid an additional $4,000 for a Dodge sedan.)

E. "To E, my Corvette sports car."
(T was killed in an accident which destroyed the Corvette; the automobile insurance company paid $7,000 to T's executor for the total loss.)

F. "To F, my AT & T stock."
(The 100 shares owned when the will was written split 2 for 1 and then had stock "warrants" which T exercised by paying $500 to obtain 10 more shares. T died owning 210 shares of AT & T.)

G. "To G, 100 shares of IBM stock."
(T owned 100 shares when the will was written, but sold them two years ago and purchased 200 shares of Xerox.)

H. "To H, the Smith $10,000 promissory note."
(The note, secured by a mortgage, had an unpaid balance of $9,500 when the will was written. Monthly payments of $200 have reduced principal $2,000 and paid $3,000 interest, making $5,000 which T received in cash and leaving an unpaid balance at death of $7,500.)

I. "To I, Blackacre."
(At the time the will was written, Blackacre was owned free and clear. T mortgaged the property and used the funds, plus $50,000 of additional funds, to build a small apartment house on Blackacre.)

J. "To J, the residue of my estate."
J gets what's left.

What does each beneficiary receive?

It is not unusual for a problem to include two or more variations of the same issue. The most efficient approach is to combine the aspects which are similar and then distinguish the dissimilarities.

Is ademption an issue for each of the bequests? Perhaps the 100 shares of IBM stock (G) is a general bequest which would be treated as a direction to the executor to purchase from the otherwise residual assets 100 shares of IBM stock. In the case of the oil painting (B) which was given during T's lifetime to the beneficiary, we have an ademption by satisfaction, rather than extinction. The will bequest will be, and should be, ineffective to pass the value of the painting to the person who already has the painting. The life insurance policy is not part of the probate estate; the will is probably ineffective to change beneficiaries, and there are no proceeds to which it could be traced. Thus, C's bequest is adeemed in all jurisdictions. In all the bequests except the residual there was a change so that the item in the estate was not the same item that T owned at the time that the will was written. The strictest application of the "in specie" test would cause all of the bequests to be adeemed, even those in which the value increased such as the AT & T stock (F) and Blackacre (J), because they have been disposed of, destroyed, lost or substantially changed. Ademption is less likely to be applied when there is a lesser degree of change, as with the chinaware (A), AT & T stock (F) and promissory note (H). In the last case, change is typical of the asset. There is an ambiguity concerning the change in form of the Corvette (E). If the death occurred before the wreck, ademption is not an issue. Rather, it is an issue of the executor's duty to insure and retroactive application of that duty

from the time the executor qualifies. It is more
likely that the damage occurred before the death.
There is little law on simultaneous death and destruction of the item bequeathed.

In the case of the chinaware (A), the 4 pieces are
adeemed, but it is unlikely that the remaining 30
will also be adeemed because the set is not exactly
as described. The change was material as to 4
pieces, but not as to the remaining 30. If the IBM
stock (G) is construed as a specific bequest, can the
conversion into Xerox stock be treated as a mere
"change in form?" The facts are unclear as to
whether there were additional funds invested as in
the cases of the Mercury wagon (D) and Blackacre
(I). It is easier to resist ademption when the funds
can be traced, undiluted, into another asset. Commingling of funds tends to defeat tracing. The
involuntary conversion of the Corvette (E) is the
best example of a substantial change which should
not cause an ademption of the item bequeathed.

A more formal approach to Blackacre (I), especially in a state with the "title theory" for mortgages,
treats the mortgaging of realty specifically devised
as an ademption. This seems unreasonable especially when the proceeds are reinvested in the property.

The promissory note (H) typifies many ademption
problems: The note itself has dropped in purchasing power and unpaid balance, but these changes
are immaterial. The monthly payments, even if
traced, are probably adeemed, even as to the princi-

pal portion. The interest paid before death would almost never be given to the will beneficiary, although accumulated and unpaid interest probably would pass with the note and mortgage. If additional amounts were advanced and a new note given for the new and old debts, then the accretion problems found in the station wagon (D), AT & T stock (F) and Blackacre (I) situations would also be involved.

The AT & T stock (F) bequest will pass the 210 shares owned at death. A more difficult situation arises when the bequest is worded "my *100 shares of* AT & T stock." In that case, the application of tracing forces the words of the will to take on new meaning: "100" means "210" just as "100 IBM" in G might become "200 Xerox" and "Mercury station wagon" in D becomes "Dodge sedan." The hardest case for determining the intent of T to mean something other than the words which were used in the station wagon (D) voluntarily converted with the additional investment.

It is suggested that you review the foregoing problem until you feel comfortable with the answers and are able to make the distinctions between the bequests outlined above. Review item I in the example and note that two different issues arise because the testator subsequently mortgaged realty which was specifically devised: First, is the net value of the property devised adeemed because of the mortgage? Second, is the value of the debt not a partial ademption, i.e., is the devisee entitled to have the property "exonerated" of its debt?

E. EXONERATION

A clear direction by the testator that a debt
secured by realty or personalty be paid from the
general assets of the estate will control so long as
there are sufficient assets. What provision should
govern in the absence of a clear indication of the
testator's intent? At common law, the heir or
devisee of realty was entitled to have the land
exonerated, i.e., delivered to her free from debt.
The doctrine did not apply as uniformly to personalty. When still applied, the doctrine is generally
limited to specific devises of realty, although at
common law all devises of realty were originally
considered to be specific.

The doctrine of exoneration does not have much
to commend it. It distorts the testamentary plan,
was based upon an economy less dependent upon
(and favorable to) credit acquisitions and causes
additional problems such as lack of liquidity, loss of
advantageous interest rates or pay-off penalties.
Some jurisdictions have abolished or limited it by
decision. The doctrine is said not to apply if the
testator was not personally liable for the debt secured by the mortgage.

Uniform Probate Code § 2-607 provides that, "A
specific devise passes subject to any mortgage interest existing at the date of death, without right of
exoneration, regardless of a general directive in the
will to pay debts."

The personal representative may find it advantageous to the estate to pay off some or all of the debt

secured by the property devised; e.g., it may be wise to continue the monthly payments on a promissory note secured by the property devised or bequeathed. If there is no exoneration, the beneficiary is placed in a position where he or she must contribute the funds necessary to reimburse the other beneficiaries. If there is exoneration, the source of the funds within the estate is the property not disposed of by will, if any, and if not, the residuary estate, if any. If there is no residuary estate, there is a split of authority as to whether general bequests can be used to exonerate. Specific bequests and devises are exonerated themselves and are not subject to abatement for the exoneration of other specific bequests or devises.

CHAPTER 7

INTERPRETATION

Interpretation of the terms of a will is a process which does not lend itself to facile explanation. For each trend or technique, there seems to be an opposing trend or technique. In some cases rigid rules of future interests dictate what the testator is deemed to have intended by a certain word. In other cases, typically when an "ambiguity" is found, words take on entirely new meanings.

Recall that the application of wills doctrines may give an unexpected meaning to words: Anti-lapse and ademption doctrines may cause a bequest of "My 100 shares of IBM stock to my brothers" to be interpreted "200 shares of Xerox to my nieces."

The Holy Grail of the interpretation process is the "intention of the testator." In search of that intention, various techniques have been used. Most words have varying degrees of clarity. Some words, especially "technical" words such as "heir" have precise meanings which will be attributed to the testator unless it is obvious that he did not intend them. (For example, a will which starts "This is my will if I die intestate....") The more usual legal approach to a word is Justice Holmes' much quoted assertion, "A word is not a crystal, transparent and unchanged, it is the skin of a living thought and may vary greatly in color and content according to the circumstances and time in which it is used." Beyond this approach is the circular and less helpful semantic approach by which the word is deemed to mean whatever the user intended it to mean.

A sampler of interpretation principles includes the following:

● All the testamentary writings should be construed together to be consistent, if possible. If they are inconsistent, the later will prevail.

● The will should be construed to avoid partial or complete intestacy, but the courts will not write the will for the testator.

● Words are to be taken in their ordinary sense and technical words are given their technical meaning, except that any contrary intention by the testator can be shown and given effect.

As an examination technique in this area, the presence of quotation marks or other indicia of direct quotation offers the material about which interpretation may be sought. Three typical areas for interpretation are as follows:

1. What passes under a bequest of "belongings," "bonds," "business," "cash," "contents," "dwelling," "funds," "household," "money," "personal" property, estate, effects or things, "possessions," or "securities"?

2. Who takes under certain descriptions such as "child," "first cousin," "devisee," "family," "spouse," "off-springs" or "relations"?

3. What is the effect of certain provisions? For example, a gift to a class which includes a person specifically excluded in another provision of the will, percentages which do not total 100, whether a fee simple or a life estate is given to a beneficiary, implied bequests, gifts over in default, bequests for "college education" or "maintenance" and gifts to the executor who does not so serve.

PART II

DECEDENT'S ESTATE ADMINISTRATION

CHAPTER 8

ESTATE ADMINISTRATION

The subjects of Wills and Trusts are both divisible into two parts: Creation and administration. No real effort is made, however, to describe probate administration in detail because of the great divergence in procedures among states. In the only area where there is some consistency, see The Uniform Probate Code in a Nutshell.

The administration of a decedent's estate involves a process of passing certain landmarks. The process may be "formal" use of a petition to the court, notice to the interested parties and a court hearing resulting from a hearing or it may be the "common" (informal) form of proceeding until someone objects.

The landmarks past which the process flows are the following, each of which is usually represented by a document:

1. **Letters.** The "letters" of the personal representative are the identification card by which the decedent's name is linked with the personal representative. Unless there is an emergency or a procedure by which letters can be obtained "ex parte" (without a notice of a hearing being served upon interested parties), the petition for letters is usually the opening round. Those who desire to contest the will usually must take action in a short period. If bond is to be required of a personal representative, the first occasion for posting it is upon "qualification" and the issuance of letters testamentary or letters of administration.

2. **Inventory and Appraisal.** Inventory of the decedent's assets is combined with an appraisal by either the estate personal representative or some officer involved with the tax determination process.

3. **Claims by Creditors.** The unusually short statute of limitations which can be, or is, invoked upon a decedent's death, requires that each creditor (with varying exceptions, such as secured creditors) present a formal statement of the amount of the claim within a specified period of a formal printing, posting or serving of notice. Often a creditor may be barred for failure to comply with the procedure.

4. **Death Tax Documents.** The federal estate tax is an elephant trap, catching only the largest of the estates; often the state death tax is more the octopus—interested in small and large prey and active in reaching out and attaching the assets of a decedent. For example, state death tax procedures

may require an inspection of safe deposit boxes, may impose requirements for transfer of bank accounts and securities and may have a local death tax lien on real property, any of which must be satisfied before particular property can be transferred.

5. **Accounting.** The personal representative, having reported the items initially received and their value in the inventory and appraisal, reports receipts, disbursements, sales and other changes during the period of estate administration (except changes in value) and shows the balance on hand for distribution.

6. **Receipts and Discharge.** Upon the authorized distribution of the assets of the estate to the beneficiaries, the receipt of each is obtained and filed with the court. The personal representative then traditionally seeks termination of his appointment and discharge of himself from any further liability.

*

PART III

CREATION OF TRUSTS

CHAPTER 9

OVERVIEW

A. TRUSTS CONTRASTED TO WILLS

The subject matter of Trusts, unlike Wills, is evenly divided between creation and administration. The creation portion of the Trusts course can be summarized by a definitional point of view; i.e., the elements of the trust (res, trustee, trustor, beneficiary and trust intent) cover the subject. Like the offer, acceptance and consideration elements of contracts, the elements of a trust serve as the overview of the creation part of the course. The administration part of the Trusts course, on the other hand, consists of a series of duties which can each be approached with the same technique used in discussing negligence issues in the subject of torts: Duty, Breach, Causation, Damages and Defenses.

Many parts of the Trusts course are purposefully vague; the courts left room to allow the subject to grow. Efforts to codify and make certain have resulted in a Restatement (Restatement, Second

169

and Third, Trusts) rather than a Uniform Code. While Wills was predominately based upon statutes, Trusts is based more upon case law. Trusts is the child of the Courts of Equity and shows the markings of that ancestry: A greater emphasis upon broad principles than upon specific rules, greater uncertainty at the border areas, and case-by-case determination of matters rather than a clear-cut dividing line drawn in advance to resolve all matters.

While Wills focuses upon what part of the estate is distributed to whom, Trusts focuses upon the duties of the person making the distribution and how distribution is achieved.

B. DEFINING A "TRUST"

A trust is an intentionally created fiduciary relationship with regard to property in which the legal title is in the trustee, but the benefit of ownership is in another person, the beneficiary. The trust relationship imposes "fiduciary" duties upon the trustee for the benefit of the beneficiary. These fiduciary duties are the life-blood of the relationship.

The center of the trust concept is easy to define and recognize; its margins are quite obscure. Among the problem areas are the following:

• There are other relationships which are similar in one or more ways to a trust—agencies, bailments, partnerships, personal representative status (executor, administrator, guardian, conservator, committee), third-party beneficiary contracts, assignments, mortgages, equitable charges and liens. Distinguishing these relationships from a trust helps one to see the general areas of the trust field, but does not clearly define what a trust is.

● There are other "fiduciary relationships" besides trusts. Agencies (including attorney and client), partnerships, directorships, personal representative status and trustees in bankruptcy are fiduciary relationships. In each of these relationships, various duties may be owed by one person to another. The origin of the duties is often the same as that of the law of trusts. Many of the "trust" concepts have crossed the line between these relationships and the ordinary trust.

● Terminology is not uniformly agreed upon. In this work, "trust" is used in the narrower sense and "fiduciary" is the broader, generic term which includes both trusts and other fiduciary relationships (agencies, partnerships, etc.). In many cases, "trust" and "fiduciary relationship" are used interchangeably for the more specific or the more generic situation.

● Even when the terminology is agreed upon, it is often overworked. For example, the term "trust" is used in the term "constructive trust," but that is not a voluntary arrangement. A constructive trust is an equitable remedy that uses only the terminology and the convenient theories of trusts. Constructive trusts are beyond the scope of this nutshell.

● "Trust" is a broad category, like the term "clothing." A particular trust may be designed for a particular purpose, but may be inappropriate for other uses, just as a pair of shoes protects the feet, but will not satisfy the dictates of modesty, and a pair of coveralls will protect from arrest for indecent exposure, but not keep the hands and feet warm. Both the coveralls and the shoes are "clothing." Similarly, a "charitable trust" and a "private (i.e., not charitable) trust" are both trusts, although opposites. The word "trust" may be modified by words indicating any of a great number of dimensions; e.g., a "spend-thrift" trust is one which contains certain provisions limiting the assignability of the beneficial interest; it could also be a "living" or "testamentary" trust. It could be "revocable" or "irrevocable."

A trust arises when the owner of property separates the benefits from the burdens of ownership by giving them to different people. Normally the benefits and burdens of property ownership are in the same person; for example, an owner of an apartment house would be entitled to collect rents (a benefit) and would be required to make repairs and pay taxes (burdens). The owner would then receive the net benefit (or have the net loss). If the owner wanted to separate the benefits and burdens, he could create a trust by delivering legal title to one person (the trustee) and the equitable (or beneficial) title to another (the beneficiary). The trustee would then have duties imposed upon her by the terms of the trust instrument and by general trust law. The beneficiary would have only the benefits (perhaps reduced slightly by the trustee's fees). The trustee would have the power (unless denied by the trust instrument) and perhaps even the duty (perhaps even if prohibited by the trust instrument) to sell the apartment house and reinvest the proceeds for the benefit of the beneficiary.

It is the separation of the legal title and the equitable title (i.e., the "ownership" which would have been protected by the respective courts of law and of equity) which provides the poles between which the "fiduciary duty," the electricity of a trust relationship, flows. A trust is a relationship which requires the existence of some property interest, the "res."

The elements of a trust can be visualized as an electrical plug. The two prongs are the negative aspects of ownership (the duties) which are assumed by the trustee and the positive aspects (the benefits of ownership) which are received by the beneficiary. The relationship is in regard to the property, the res, and is created by the intention of the settlor or trustor, the creator of the trust. Given these elements, the court of equity made them significant by imposing duties which are the electrical current or life of the trust. We examine those duties in the last portion of this nutshell.

THE PARTIES TO THE TRUST RELATIONSHIP

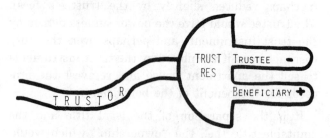

C. CONTRASTING A TRUST AGAINST OTHER RELATIONSHIPS

The edges of the trust definition can be explored by comparing and contrasting the trust with other relationships. In these marginal areas, the crucial facts are often unknown. Thus, the attorney must navigate utilizing incomplete and seemingly contradictory indications of the proper direction.

1. AGENCY v. TRUST

Both the trust and the agency are fiduciary relationships in which one person acts for another. Both may involve property, although an agency need not concern property while a trust always does. The practical consequences that flow from the distinction include the effect of death, consent and extending liability to another. An agency is terminated upon the death or incapacity of either agent or principal because it is a continuing consensual relationship. (A "durable" power of attorney, permitted by many state statutes, is an exception.) A trust, once created, exists as long as permitted by the trust terms (and the Rule against Perpetuities). The principal is liable for the acts of the agent done within the scope of the employment, but neither the trustor nor the beneficiary is liable for the acts of the trustee (although the acts may cause a diminution of the trust estate).

Both trusts and agencies come in a variety of forms and only the roughest guidelines for separating the two can be offered: An agency is more like a puppeteer (the principal) governing the acts and limiting the discretion of the marionette (the agent). The principal has greater control of the acts of the agent and is therefore liable for the agent's acts. On the other hand, a trustee is normally free of control by the settlor and the beneficiary, although a certain amount of control can be retained through the creation or retention of a power to terminate or revoke or to replace the trustee. The beneficiary need not consent to the acts of the trustee and does not have a day-to-day control.

The agent seldom has title, while the trustee always does. The range of acts permitted to the agent is smaller than the range of acts permitted to a trustee. Examination of the understanding of the parties as to the amount of control which the agent or trustee is to have is probably the best means for distinguishing the two relationships. Examples of agencies are the employer-employee relation, powers of attorney, escrows and most custodial arrangements.

2. CUSTODIANSHIP v. TRUST

The borderline between agencies and trusts probably runs right through the middle of the statutory creature known as a "Custodian under the Uniform Gifts to Minors Act." Most of the troublesome points are determined by the statute, but the concept carries elements of both a trust and an agency. It has indeterminate characteristics in that it involves property given by one person to a second to be held and managed under fiduciary principles for a third person. Like a trustee, the custodian can make broad decisions including the decision to sell the property involved and is totally free of any control by the donor who created the arrangement. Delivery to the custodian is a sufficient delivery to complete the irrevocable gift for property and tax reasons, whereas one cannot normally make a completed delivery to one's own agent (since the agent would be under a duty to return it, if directed by the principal). The distinction is less material in the case of the custodianship because most of the troublesome differences have been eliminated by the statutory provisions. Bogert Trusts & Trustees, 2nd ed. § 15 states that the custodian is an agent (rather than a trustee) with duties fixed by statute. The legal title, under the uniform act, is in the minor, but the custodian has full powers of management, sale and reinvestment. The absence of title may tip the scales toward agency, but the complete powers of disposal, indestructibility by death and non-consensualness (How can a minor consent? What if the minor directs the custodian to deliver it to the minor?) seem to point toward a trust rather than an agency.

3. PERSONAL REPRESENTATIVE (EXECUTOR, ADMINISTRATOR, GUARDIAN, CONSERVATOR, COMMITTEE, CURATOR, ETC.) v. TRUST

A person who is unable to act in his or her own behalf may have a "representative" appointed to care for his or her person or estate. The personal representative of the estate (whether or not the protected person is deceased) is a fiduciary dealing with the property of another, but none of the arrangements falls within the classic definitions of a "trust." Generally, the relationships are established in accordance with a statute. A deceased person may be represented by an executor (if chosen by the decedent's will) or administrator (if not so chosen) or the generic "personal representative" title used by the Uniform Probate Code. A living person may be unable to manage his or her property because of some permanent or temporary legal disability such as minority. Each state provides for the appointment of a representative of one or more names to manage the property of such minor, incompetent or conservatee. Normally the personal representative is appointed by the court (although nomination by will or the involved person is often permitted); supervision of the representative is by the court, with limited discretion; title is usually in the beneficiary rather than the representative; the historic derivation of the relationship is the court of law, rather than the court of equity.

4. BAILMENT v. TRUST

A bailment is the delivery of personal property by the owner to another for the performance of some act (shipment, storage, cleaning, repair) and return to the owner, subject to a possessory lien for the reasonable charges for the service. Like a trust, a bailment is involved with property. Unlike the trust, the bailment is not possible for real property, is very limited in scope, involves the possession (rather than title) to the personalty being in the bailee, is not a fiduciary relationship and has its origin in law rather than equity. Trusts tend to be longer-lasting and more formal than bailments.

A bailment is a contract in which arms-length dealing is permitted; a fiduciary relationship requires good faith and loyalty; therefore, a transaction may be permissible in a bailment which would be a breach of duty if a trust existed. Similarly, a bailee is responsible for only his own actions; if the subject of the bailment is lost, destroyed or decreased in value without fault on the part of the bailee, the loss is borne by the bailor. On the other hand, a trustee has a higher duty to preserve the trust property and may be liable for a loss which occurs without fault on his part.

5. POWER OF APPOINTMENT v. TRUST

A power of appointment is the power in one person to designate who shall be the owner or recipient of property. The power to give away is an attribute of ownership which can be separated out of the bundle of interests and given to another. If one decides to allow another to designate who shall receive or enjoy property, the person so chosen is said to be the donee of a power of appointment. (Do not confuse this concept with the "power of attorney" in which one can act for another, a form of agency.)

The power is an ownership right; it is not held subject to any fiduciary duties (although it can be limited and efforts to evade the limitation would be "in fraud" of the power). Like a trust, a power of appointment relates to property. Unlike a trust, it can be exercised only once as to any particular property. Powers of appointment deal with the ownership attribute of property; the donee of the power exercises it to appoint to one or more permissible appointees. Generally, there are no management powers associated with a power of appointment. A power is not a duty to appoint. Thus, it need not be exercised. If it is not exercised, the property subject to the power goes to (or remains in) the "takers in default of appointment."

Since a power of appointment is a right which exists in one person to divert the ownership, it is necessary that another person have the title until the power is exercised or eliminated. Often the holder in the interim is a trustee. Thus, a power of appointment is usually found contained in a trust although such an arrangement is not necessary.

A power could be "general" permitting one to appoint to oneself or "special" permitting one to appoint only to or among a certain group of persons (which usually does not include the donee of the power).

EXAMPLE # 1: T's will bequeaths "my entire estate to my son, John, to be used for my daughter, Ann." This sounds in management for another and is probably a trust.

EXAMPLE # 2: T's will bequeaths "my furniture to my children, my son John to pick who gets which item." John has a power of appointment and can appoint to himself, but there may be a question whether he can take all items or whether he is limited to equalizing the shares.

EXAMPLE # 3: T's will bequeaths "my entire estate equally to my children, my son John to manage it." John is a trustee, but is also entitled to an equal share as a beneficiary.

6. SECURITY ARRANGEMENT (MORT-GAGE, PLEDGE, LIEN AND EQUI-TABLE CHARGE) v. TRUST

Security arrangements are designed to provide protection to a lender. The title to the property which comprises the security may apparently or actually be given to a lender by a borrower, subject to a condition of repayment. The trust form is used as a security arrangement in the "trust deed" in which the borrower gives title to property to a third person as security for a debt.

Occasionally the exchange of money and title to property may be obscured by unclear language and preexisting relationships so that a sale cannot be distinguished from a security arrangement.

EXAMPLE # 1: A, the owner in fee of Blackacre, is financially pressed, but desires to retain ownership of Blackacre. B, a friend, suggests that A convey Blackacre to B in exchange for B's delivery to A of money which approximates the value of Blackacre. B tells A: "Don't worry, you can repay me and get Blackacre back." Perhaps A is permitted to remain in possession of Blackacre, paying "rent" to B. This may be a sale or it may be a security transaction. It may also be a fraud by B which would result in a constructive trust. The exact words used, the reasonableness of the price and the possession and rent are each relevant in determining whether this is a sale, security arrangement or fraud. A's belief that B would not convey the property without giving A the opportunity to repurchase (pay off the debt) may not match B's desire to help a friend while acquiring a desired parcel of property.

The law of mortgages contains both the "title theory" (in which the lender obtains title to the property) and the more prevalent "lien theory" (in which the interest of the lender is seen as "merely" a lien, a security interest with the borrower remaining the owner of the title to the property). Equity interacted with the law of mortgages to create the "equity of redemption" by which a mortgagor who had defaulted on the express terms of the mortgage was nevertheless entitled to title upon curing the default. This was, in effect, an equitable demotion of the borrower's breach from material to immaterial status.

Some security arrangements have their origins in equity and are therefore similar to trusts. The equitable lien (a lien recognized in equity even though not complying with legal formalities) and the equitable charge (a charge upon the property imposed by a court of equity) both give an interest related to the property, but not the property itself.

EXAMPLE # 2: T dies, survived by his two children. T's will provides: "I give my Blackacre to my son, S, provided he pays his sister, D, $5,000 a year for her life." The legal and equitable title to Blackacre has been devised to S, but D has an equitable charge upon Blackacre, a security interest, for the payment of the $5,000 annuity.

The distinction between a security interest and a trust is similar to the difference in a corporate organization between a bondholder and a shareholder. The bondholder has a debt, fixed in amount, which normally takes priority in payment. The shareholder owns the "equity" interest and benefits from or is burdened with any increase or decrease in value. After the debt is paid, the security holder no longer has a value in the property and the shareholder has the entire ownership.

The distinction between a debt and a trust is relevant when statute of limitations problems arise. After the period of the applicable statute of limitations has expired, a debt cannot be enforced. Trusts are not subject to the statute of limitations or may have a different statute or may, with the same statute, have a different starting time (the breach of the trust, as opposed to the time that payment was due). Because of these differences, lenders who have not enforced their rights may assert that the *borrower* is a trustee. Ordinarily, the assertion is that the *lender* was merely a trustee or that a purchaser was merely a lender.

The key to distinguishing a trust from a debt (or a contract or other relationship) is the intention manifested by the settlor. It is objectively determined by what the parties said and did.

7. CONTRACT v. TRUST

Trusts and Contracts in their classic forms represent the traditional differences between the enforcement and principles of the courts of equity and law. In equity, good faith was required; on the other hand, the court of law merely required compliance with the express terms of the promise. The growth of the law of contracts has been largely into areas of equity—third-party beneficiary contracts, assignments (partial or complete) to third parties of the chose in action represented by the contract, implied covenants and specific enforcement of contracts to convey land.

The distinction between a trust and various types of contracts is material for procedural reasons (the equitable jurisdiction over trusts possibly does not exist in certain law courts, especially small claims and conciliation-type courts), for the statute of limitations, for tracing of proceeds when the promisor-trustee is insolvent and for imposing the higher fiduciary standards of a trustee.

8.   IMPERFECT GIFT v. TRUST

A gift is a voluntary transfer of personal property, although gratuitous transfers of realty are generally similarly treated.   Gifts are made during the lifetime of the donor with the entire law of Wills and Intestacy governing gratuitous dispositions of personalty and realty at death.   A gift is normally irrevocable, although one species of gift, the gift causa mortis, is revocable.   In order to make a gift, there must be the intention to make a gift and a delivery.

Trusts and gifts interrelate in that a trust may be and traditionally is created by gift.   It is also possible to create a trust for consideration, such as the security transaction, the trust deed.   Trusts are capable of being revocable while many courts hold the characteristic of irrevocability is essential to the ordinary (as opposed to causa mortis) gift.   A gift is a one-time transaction, while the trust creates an ongoing relationship.   Thus, the gift is the door which leads in many cases to the trust's tunnel through time. Each could exist without the other, but they often overlap.

The essential elements of a gift are the intention to make a gift and the act of delivery. Delivery is normally from the donor to the donee, but can be to the donee's (but not the donor's) agent or a neutral third party. A relatively unusual situation arises when the donee is already in possession (e.g., as bailee or tenant) and the donor intends to make a gift. At that point, no further delivery is necessary. This situation is unusual except in the area of declaring oneself trustee of one's property for the benefit of another person. The self-declaration of trust is permitted and the sole trustor becomes the sole trustee by virtue of a manifestation of intention only; no additional act is necessary.

The desires of persons to hold on to property until death, but also to indicate who should have the property upon death have resulted in situations to which a two-headed aphorism has been applied. The aphorism is that "Equity will not transform an imperfect [usually because of a failure of delivery] gift into a trust, but if the gift is incomplete by reason of some technicality [e.g., delivery] and if the essential elements of a trust are established, the manifest intention of the donor may be sustained through a trust." The first part stresses the legal requirement of delivery; the second part permits a loophole in cases where the intention of the donor (usually dead at the time the controversy is to be resolved) is "clear."

QUIZ ON TRUSTS v. OTHER RELATIONSHIPS

1. A delivers his automobile to B and directs B to keep the automobile for one month and then to deliver it to C. What arrangement might this be? Why? What facts would change your decision?

2. A transfers by signed deed and registration certificates to B a commercial garage and lot, together with three automobiles with directions to B to sell the garage, lot and automobiles and to invest the proceeds and pay the income to C for life and, upon C's death, to deliver the principal to D. What arrangement is this most likely to be labeled?

3. A devises Blackacre to B "on the condition that B pay $1,000" to C. Would B commit a breach of trust by conveying to D without having made payment to C?

4. A employs B as her housekeeper. B hands over to A $1,000 of his (B's) savings in exchange for A's promise "to keep the money for" him and to pay him 6% interest. Is A a trustee for B? How would you determine the intention of the parties?

ANSWERS TO QUIZ ON TRUSTS v. OTHER RELATIONSHIPS

1. This is probably a bailment, rather than a trust. It is a delivery of personal property to be stored and then delivered. B does not seem to have any discretion to use, or duty to make productive, the automobile. Compare the situation if it were a

taxicab and all parties involved were taxi drivers. Had A given B the title documents, power to sell and directions to use the property and deliver the proceeds to C, a trust would have been created.

2.   Here the delivery of title, power to deal, longer existence of the relationship and broader powers of B indicate that he is a trustee. Additionally, the division of the equitable estate into life estate to C and remainder to D is a typical trust disposition. This case contrasts with question number 1 to show the effect of additional details in deciding what arrangement has been made.

3.   The fixed sum (as opposed to an ownership of the thing) payable to C sounds in debt and the means of creating the arrangement (a will) suggests that an equitable charge, rather than a trust, has been created.   Property subject to an equitable charge can be transferred; a bona fide purchaser for value without notice cuts off outstanding equities; if the conveyance was not to such a purchaser, then the charge remains on the property.   There is no breach of trust unless there is a trust (or other fiduciary relationship).   An equitable charge, although enforced in equity, does not impose equitable duties.

4.   Restatement, Second, Trusts § 12g is helpful in this situation.   After stating that the intention of the parties controls and is determined by the words and conduct in the light of the circumstances, the restatement suggests the following relevant factors: The presence or absence of an agreement to pay

interest, the amount involved, the time before repayment is due, the relative financial position of the
parties, their respective callings and the custom or
usage in similar transactions. The promise to pay
interest sounds in debt rather than in trust. The
larger the amount and the longer the period, the
more it sounds in debt (unless the period is measured by the life of a beneficial owner). Perhaps
the key to the relative position of the parties is that
when someone who needs money borrows it from
someone who does not, it sounds more in debt than
in trust. This is a borderline case, but probably is a
debt rather than a trust.

CHAPTER 10

ELEMENTS OF A TRUST

The elements of a trust are the transfer, the res, the settlor, the trustee and the beneficiary. A "key sentence" approach is possible: "The transfer of the res by the settlor to the trustee for the beneficiary's benefit creates a trust."

A. THE TRANSFER

The Restatement, Second, Trusts § 17, sets out five methods of creating a trust, of which the first three are the most commonly encountered:

1. Declaration by the owner of property that he or she holds it as trustee for another person;

2. Transfer during lifetime by the owner to another person as trustee for the transferor or a third person; or

3. Transfer by will by the owner to another person as trustee for a third person;

4. Appointment by the donee of a power of appointment to another as trustee for the donee or a third person. This is identical to number 2 or number 3, above, except that the donee of a power of appointment was not, technically, the owner of the property subject to the power;

5. Promise by one person to another person whose rights thereunder are to be held in trust for a third person. This is a contractual form of creating a trust; most trusts are gratuitous.

In summary, a trust could be created gratuitously or contractually during life or at death by the owner of (or possessor of a power of appointment over) the property.

Each method of creating the trust must comply with the formalities required by that method: A lifetime transfer by gift must have the elements of intent and delivery; an exercise of a power of appointment (whether during life or at death) must comply with the terms of its creation and the laws governing powers of appointment; a creation by will must comply with the requirements of the applicable statute of wills and be done with testamentary intent; a contractual creation must have the elements of offer, acceptance and consideration. Often trusts are classified by their method of creation and called "testamentary" (if created by will and therefore effective at death) or inter vivos (living).

Is a writing required to create a trust? It usually is for trusts of realty, but possibly the statute of frauds for a particular jurisdiction might not cover a declaration (i.e., creation by transferring the equitable title only to the beneficiary, the declarant-settlor being the trustee) of trust of realty. Writings are seldom required for a trust of personalty.

Lawyers who are preparing trusts for their clients generally prepare a formal trust instrument, deeds for realty and instruments of transfer for personalty. The trustee formally accepts the trust and the beneficiary is notified of the existence of the trust and furnished a copy of the trust instrument. This is the usual "lawyerlike" way of creating a trust; it is the maximum that is required. A trust could also be created by a minimum which might consist of a deed to the realty signed by the settlor and an oral discussion (if not barred by the parol evidence rule) of the terms and agreement between the settlor and the trustee, without the beneficiary even being aware of the existence of the trust. The deed might not have been recorded, or possibly not even delivered, yet the trust will be in existence. The execution of the deed and the oral agreement on the terms of the trust would be a sufficient manifestation of intention to transfer the legal title to the trustee and the equitable title to the beneficiary. That would create the trust. Local law might declare that a delivery to the trustee of the deed by the settlor (as opposed to signing it only) or a recording of the deed is necessary in order to create a trust, but the better view appears to be that delivery and signing are not essential to the creation of a trust. Naturally, a bona fide purchaser for value without notice would cut off outstanding equities or be given full title by a recording statute if the deed to the trustee had not been recorded, but finding a trust to have been created might give rise to the trustee's fiduciary duty to protect the trust property (including its title); breach of that duty would leave the beneficiary of the purported trust a possible right against the trustee.

The barest minimum of formalities for creation of a trust exist in the self-declaration of trust, since no transfer of legal title is necessary. All that is required is that the settlor manifest in some way that he or she holds the property in trust for another. One seeking to prove the existence of the trust, however, may have a difficult time without a clear manifestation of the settlor's intent.

In order to make a transfer during life or by will, a settlor must have the legal capacity required for the form of transfer. Thus a minor, incompetent or other person suffering under legal disability cannot form the intention to make a gift during lifetime and may, additionally, fail the more lenient rules for capacity to make a will to transfer the property at death.

The settlor must manifest the intention to create a trust in a way which can be objectively determined; the secret intention is insufficient if there is no outward indication of intent. Although the statute of frauds, recording statute or parol evidence rule may prohibit (or deem insufficient) some means of proof, there is no general rule indicating what is "minimum" proof except those three statutes or rules. It is not necessary to use the term "trust" but the use of the term tends to indicate that a trust was intended.

The use of "precatory" (if you please) language, usually in a home-drawn will, typically presents problems of whether the testator intended to create a trust with its binding duties upon the trustee or was merely suggesting without intending to make it a condition of the taking. The format is often the "2 × 4" ("to" by "for") often found in charitable trusts (e.g., "I give *to* the trustees *for* the charity.") The purpose, however, may be one which cannot be carried out except as a direct gift, e.g., a bequest to friend, A, "for my cat, Claude." 1 Scott, Trusts, 4th ed. § 25.1 and § 25.2 suggest that the earlier trend to find a trust in all such situations has abated and that a trust is less likely to be found in such a situation today.

In the following situations, the testator (T) devises the residue of his estate to the beneficiary (B) with the following additional language. Is a trust created?

EXAMPLE # 1: "... hoping she will keep Blackacre in the family." This is now generally held not to show an intention to create a trust; the uncertainty of the identity of the beneficiaries (other than B) is probably the key factor.

EXAMPLE # 2: "... desiring that she give it at her death to my son." Older cases held this to create a trust with life estate in B and equitable remainder to the son so that B could not make a contrary disposition of the property in her will. More modernly, this probably would not create a trust, but each case would be decided on its own merits.

EXAMPLE # 3: "... provided that she leaves all of her estate at her death to my son." Here, the language is stronger and would create a trust if T had the power to create a trust. However, the property which T attempts to dispose of ("*her* estate") includes property over which T does not have the power directly to create a trust. It may be treated as a bequest on condition or as a species of contract to make a will, imposing an equitable (if not legal) duty upon B to bequeath her property as requested if she desires to take the benefits of T's estate.

EXAMPLE # 4: "... so that he can go to college." Or "... hoping that he will buy a new home." Or "... suggesting that he devote himself to the service of mankind." Or "... recommending that he conduct himself like a gentleman." All of these bequests would probably be treated as outright bequests with surplus language to which no effect will be given. Note that what might be construed as a condition is ignored when it is in the nature of suggestions for self-improvement, unless the language is very clear, e.g., "; ... provided, however, that he refrains from drinking any alcoholic beverage for two years. If he does not so refrain, this bequest shall fail and pass instead to...."

EXAMPLE # 5: T purchases life insurance on T's life, naming B as beneficiary. T tells B of the policy and "suggests" that the money be used in a certain way. The facts of each individual case will tip the scale one way or the other and different courts might well find different results on what appears to be the same fact situation.

EXAMPLE # 6: In clause # 1 of the Will, T gives his estate outright to B with no language of condition or trust. In clause # 2, T purports to dispose of the same property "after B dies." Whether a life estate only or a fee simple was created in B is a matter upon which disagreement is likely. The intention of the testator is controlling, but two clear intentions make either result possible. The scale may be tipped by factors such as the relationship of the parties and tax consequences, but the intention of the testator to impose binding duties upon them is the determining factor.

B. THE RES

There must be some property interest upon which the trust relationship is imposed. Unlike other "confidential relationships" such as an agency or the attorney-client relationship, the trust exists only in relation to some specified and assignable thing. To name this entity, the simple term "res" (Latin for "thing") is used, thus avoiding problems of terminology involved in the distinctions between principal and income and problems of the sophisticated legal usage of the word "property."

The res may be any type of property, real or personal, tangible or intangible, so long as it is in existence, separated (although undivided interests can be placed in trust) and assignable.

The following quiz may be helpful in sorting out items which are not yet property, those which are not assignable and those which lack the specificity required for a trust res:

QUIZ ON THE TRUST RES

1. S declares in an otherwise effective instrument a trust of any and all profits he should make in the future from dealings on the stock market. Is there a valid trust?

2. Same facts as Problem # 1, above, except that S declared himself trustee of $100,000 to be used for trading in the stock market, the principal of $100,000 to be returned to S at the end of the year. The profits, if any, of the trading are to be kept in trust for S's children. Valid trust?

3. A theatrical producer, owning the stage and movie rights to the not-yet-produced "My Fair Lady," purports to transfer five percent of his share of the profits from the stage and movie rights as the sole asset of the trust. Is there a valid trust?

4. T executes a trust instrument, but does not act in relation to the trust res other than to sign an "Authorization" to the trustee to collect the assets of the trust. T dies before the authorization is acted upon. Valid trust?

5. T executes a trust instrument as described in Problem # 4, but adds the following clause to the "Authorization:" "I hereby transfer all my right, title and interest in the estate of my father to this trust." The father is still living, but has no spouse, no other children and no will.

6. Same facts as Problem # 5, except that the father died, intestate, last week.

7. If the only property transferred to the purported trust was the right to receive the proceeds of a life insurance policy (i.e., the policy itself was not transferred, but the trustee was named as the "beneficiary" of the life insurance contract), is there a valid trust?

8. If the only assets of the purported trust consisted of a leasehold interest and a patent or copyright, which is an intangible property right with a limited duration, would there be a valid trust?

9. If in Problem # 8, above, the lease contained a clause prohibiting the tenant from assigning or sub-leasing the premises, would the tenant of the lease be able to make a valid trust of the leasehold interest only? Would the landlord be able to do so?

10. Assume that the only asset of the purported irrevocable trust was the contract right to receive payments for an asset which was sold at a great gain, which the settlor elected to report on the installment method for income tax purposes, as permitted by Internal Revenue Code § 453. That section does not prohibit assignments, but requires that the election to defer payment of tax be termi-

nated upon transfer of the asset to an irrevocable trust. Thus, there is a tax disadvantage, but not an outright prohibition against assignment. Is there a valid trust?

11. D owes C money. D offers a novation by creating a trust for C's children. Is there a valid trust?

12. Same facts as in Problem # 11, above, except that C purports to create a trust of D's debt to C. Valid trust?

13. If S, the owner of an undivided one-half of certain realty and personalty (in which X owns the other undivided one-half), purports to establish a trust of his undivided one-half interest, is it a valid trust?

14. If S, being the owner of 500 cattle, purports to create a trust of 50 cattle from the herd, is it a valid trust if they are not separated, ear-marked or otherwise sorted out from the remaining 450?

15. If S, the owner of $5,000 in cash, purports to establish a trust of $1,000, but does not segregate a particular $1,000 of his cash, is it a valid trust?

16. S purports to establish a trust by writing his personal check for $1,000; when, if at all, does it become a trust? Will there be a trust if S dies before the check is "cashed"?

17. S, being uncertain of the amount of wealth that he has, purports to establish a trust of five percent of his wealth. Is it a valid trust? What if the attempt is by his will, to become effective on his

death, and therefore includes what will be future income, viewed from the time that the will is executed? Is it a valid trust? When? Will it include "future" income?

ANSWERS TO QUIZ ON THE TRUST RES

1. Brainard v. Commissioner (1937) held that there was no trust because property not yet in existence cannot be the subject of a trust.

2. Although next year's apple crop may not be enough of a property interest to be a trust res, the orchard, even for one year, can be. Thus, a valid trust exists.

3. In Speelman v. Pascal (1961), a close case, such an assignment of future profits was deemed to be a sufficient trust res. Delivery had been made by a writing reciting a consideration. Equity will enforce, in appropriate cases, assignments of a future interest, if supported by an adequate consideration; but a gratuitous assignment of future property would become effective only after it became a property interest and the settlor reaffirmed the original assignment. Restatement, Second, Trusts § 86 says that "An expectation or hope of receiving property in the future cannot be held in trust."

4. There is no valid trust until the res is transferred to the trustee. An authorization to the trustee to collect the trust assets was held to be an agency which terminated upon the death of the

settlor in Farmers' Loan & Trust Co. v. Winthrop (1924).

5. There is still no valid trust, even though the document is in form sufficient to effect a present transfer. There is no property interest to pass since "No one is the heir of a living person." The expectancy of an inheritance, bequest or devise is not sufficient property to be a trust res. (Contrast the contractual assignment in Problem # 3.)

6. A valid trust would be created, even in jurisdictions which hold that title to realty, or the entire estate, vests in the personal representative (the administrator here) and even though the administrator has not yet been appointed. The right of the heir is now vested and can be a trust res.

7. Possibly the designation of the trustee as the contractual third party beneficiary of a life insurance policy is sufficient property to be a trust res, but the issue has been resolved in many states by statute, expressly permitting such an "unfunded life insurance trust" with the incidents of ownership of the policy (or merely the beneficiary designation, as here) as the sole trust corpus. This is an extremely close case in the absence of a statute because of the similarity of life insurance to an inheritance during the life of the person insured.

8. A valid trust can be created even though the res has a short lifetime. These wasting assets create problems for the trustees because their cash return is not entirely income but a combination of

both principal and income. A portion of the cash return should replace the expiring asset.

9. An asset which cannot be transferred cannot be the trust res. The prohibition upon the tenant assigning would probably prevent a trust from arising. On the other hand, the landlord could create a trust of the underlying property, subject to the lease, or of the rights the landlord has under the lease. In the latter case, the trust res would be a wasting asset; it is doubtful that a court would transform the prohibition against assignment by the tenant into a mutual prohibition. If the lease called for prior landlord approval of the assignee, the trust would arise upon such approval (or actions which make the approval unnecessary, such as actions which give rise to an estoppel). If the lease called for an additional payment rather than imposing a blanket prohibition, the lease could probably be a valid trust res. The payment should probably be the responsibility of the transferor, but it is possible that the trustee would take the leasehold, subject to the obligation to pay the amount called for in the lease.

10. Mere difficulty or expense in transferring the interest, if not amounting to impossibility, will probably not prevent a trust from arising. The better thinking appears to be that the asset can be placed in trust, even though such an act is unwise. How far equity will permit one to make a mistake is not clearly defined. Other examples of nonassignable property include future salary (because of the potential of slavery), Series EE savings bonds, social

security benefits and other benefits the assignment of which is prohibited by federal or state law, pension and profit-sharing plans (because of almost universal non-assignability clauses) and the interest of a beneficiary in a Spendthrift Trust in a jurisdiction which permits such clauses. Note that in the last case, the interest of a beneficiary of a trust could be a trust res although it is, itself, only an equitable interest.

11. No trust is created because one cannot create a trust out of a debt which he or she owes. A debt is a liability, not an asset. The amount owed has not been segregated out and specified among the assets of D. See Molera v. Cooper (1916).

12. On the other hand, the creditor in a debt situation has an asset which can be a trust res. It is a chose in action against D.

13. A valid trust can be created of an undivided interest in a particular parcel even though it is not possible to say which part of the whole is subject to the trust. There is seldom any dispute about the presence of an undivided interest in trust; there may be a conflict of interests if the trustee is the owner of another portion of the property in the trustee's own right. Similarly, separate shares of a corporation, although not representing the entire ownership, could be a trust res.

14. However, the attempt to make a trust of "50 head out of 500 head" instead of an "undivided one-tenth of 500 head" may cause the trust to fail for want of specificity of the identity of the trust res.

If a cow dies, is it part of the trust or not? If there are five calves born to the 500 cattle, how many of the calves are in the trust? Note that if a trust is found (which is remotely possible), the trustee will have the immediate duty of separating and earmarking or otherwise identifying the cattle which are in the trust.

15. Classic trust theory says that a failure to segregate an identifiable portion of the trust will make the trust res too indefinite. Thus a trust of "$1,000 out of this $5,000" will not be effective. Cf., a trust of "one-fifth of this $5,000" which would probably be a valid trust res. Should the existence of a trust turn on the felicity of the phrasing?

16. The settlor's personal check is merely a direction to the bank to pay an amount; it is an authorization, as in Problem # 4 above. When the check is negotiated, the funds are separated and the trust has a res. Statutes permitting a bank to honor checks after the death of the maker are designed for the protection of the banks and possibly may not be sufficient to permit a post-death negotiation to create a trust.

17. A trust of 5 percent of one's fortune (whether 5 percent of each asset or the value of 5 percent) might well fail for lack of specificity, if made during lifetime. Contrast the 5 percent of certain contract rights in Problem # 3 and further contrast an assignment of "an undivided one-twentieth" as more acceptable, despite the same approach. A trust to

become effective on death is "testamentary" and
must conform to the statute of wills; if it does, it is
a valid will and the 5 percent value can be, and is,
determined. An attempt to create a trust to arise
in the future fails for want of a present transfer.

In the foregoing problems, future property is involved in Problems 1 through 7; Problem 8 dealt
with wasting assets; Problems 4, 5, 9 and 10 fo-
cused on problems of assignment. Problems 11, 12
and 16 dealt with a trust of one's own debt while
Problems 12 through 17 dealt with the specificity
required of the trust res and the acceptability of
undivided shares of a specified thing as a trust res.

C. THE SETTLOR

The settlor of a trust is of importance only until
he or she has transferred the trust res with the
intention to create a trust by imposing fiduciary
duties upon the trustee in relation to the res for the
benefit of the beneficiaries. After that manifestation and the transfer of the property, the settlor is
similar to any former owner—of historical interest
only. In this regard the settlor is similar to the
incorporators of a corporation. Once the corporation is formed, the incorporators, as such, have no
further role. Naturally, the same persons may be
directors or shareholders as well as incorporators,
just as the same person can be beneficiary or trustee in addition to being the settlor. The areas of
interest of the settlor's role therefore revolve
around his or her ability to transfer the property

and form the intention to create a trust. Thus, the following requirements must be met:

1. The settlor must be the owner of the property or otherwise legally qualified to transfer it. The donee of a power of appointment is legally qualified to transfer it, but not the "owner" of the property. Attempts to put the property of someone else into a trust typically arise between spouses or other close family settings. The principles behind the concepts of contracts to make a will and gifts on condition may permit one to put the property of another into a trust by contractual means.

2. The settlor must have the capacity necessary to make the transfer and form the intention to create a trust.

3. Although a trust can be created without communication of the settlor's intention to any person (including the beneficiaries and the trustee), the trust cannot be created without a manifestation of intention to create a trust. An outward expression of his intention, in writing or to a third person, is required. An undisclosed secret intention to form a trust is insufficient.

4. The settlor can retain some or all of the legal title or the beneficial interest, but not all of both, since the trust is created by separating the legal title from the beneficial interest. The retention of the legal title is involved in the self-declaration of trust; in that case, the beneficial interest, or a part of it, must be given to another person. The retention of a beneficial interest can be express or im-

plied. Any portion of the beneficial interest not
disposed of expressly is retained. The implied retention is reflected in the concept of "Resulting
Trusts."

5. The settlor can retain powers over a trust
which would not be permitted in a common law gift
and which do not make him a beneficiary, in the
strict sense, of the trust. The power of revocation
is the most obvious of these powers. At common
law, irrevocability is deemed such an essential element of gifts that an attempt to make a revocable
gift is unsuccessful. On the other hand, the equitable trust can be made partly or completely revocable
(or terminable by someone other than the settlor).
Thus, a donor wishing to retain control cannot do
so unless a trust is used. Related powers include
the power to amend the trust or to control the
trustee in certain areas, such as investment or time
or amount of distributions of income and principal.
The power of revocation, amendment or control
over the trustee reserved by the settlor does not
make him or her a "beneficiary" of the trust in the
strict sense, but the retained powers obviously can
have value. The situation is similar to that found
in powers of appointment in which the "ownership"
is in one person or group of persons while another
person has ownership-like attributes in the form of
a power. Trusts are presumed to be irrevocable
unless expressly stated to be revocable, although
three western states (Oklahoma, Texas and California) have reversed that rule by statute.

D. THE TRUSTEE

The appointment of an original or successor trustee is made by the settlor in the trust instrument. If the settlor does not provide for an original or successor trustee who is able and willing to serve, appointment will be made by the court having jurisdiction over the trust.

The trustee can be any person or entity capable of taking (cf., conveying) legal title including individuals, corporations and governmental units. Unincorporated associations such as lodges or social clubs, generally are incapable of taking or conveying title; therefore they may not serve as trustees. There are individuals and corporations which are capable of taking title, but not of conveying it. Minors, incompetent persons and corporations without trust powers can therefore receive title, but should be removed as trustee in order to allow proper functioning of that position. The ability to take legal title may be necessary in order to separate the legal and equitable rights in the property. Nevertheless, it is possible that a trust could be created with no trustee being named initially. If the settlor transfers the equitable title to the beneficiary, he has manifested the intention to create a trust. The settlor will retain the legal title for failure to convey it to someone else; if he is dead, the legal title is vested in his heirs or will beneficiaries, but the equitable title remains in the trust beneficiaries.

Equity will not allow a trust to fail for want of a trustee except in the very rare situation in which

the settlor manifested the intention that the trust
should not come into existence unless this particular person served as trustee. Such a personal trusteeship is seldom found.

It is not necessary for the settlor to inform the
trustee of the trust in order for the trust to arise,
but the failure to notify the trustee tends to indicate that the settlor had not yet finalized his or her
intention to create a trust; i.e., failure to notify is
an indication that perhaps the settlor did not yet
intend to create a trust.

A trustee can decline the original appointment.
Once accepted, however, a trusteeship cannot be
resigned except as provided in the trust instrument
or by permission of the court having supervision
over the trust.

Acceptance is necessary in order for the trustee to
be liable for his or her acts as trustee, but the
acceptance is often said to relate back to the time of
the creation of the trust. Normally acceptance or
disclaimer of the trustee position is an irreversible
decision. Acceptance may be express or may be
implied from the circumstances such as participation in the creation of the trust, failure to decline
after being made aware of the trust or dealing with
the trust property in a way that is consistent only
with the existence of a trust relationship.

Delivery of the legal title to the trust property
must comply with the legal requirements for transfer of that type of interest and the type of creation.
An imperfect transfer of legal title to the trustee

causes the legal title to remain with the settlor or his heirs or will beneficiaries, but does not prevent a trust from arising if the equitable title was transferred to the beneficiaries.

The trustee may be the settlor or may be a beneficiary or both. The only impermissible combination occurs if a sole trustee is the sole beneficiary. In such a situation, the legal and equitable titles are said to merge. Also, the imposition of a duty on oneself for oneself prevents any duty from arising. On the other hand, if there is another trustee (or another beneficiary), a trust is created; and the conflict of interests of the trustee-beneficiary is only a factor to be considered in examining the liability of the trustee for his or her actions.

Co-trustees normally have full responsibility for all of the trust and must act unanimously unless the trust instrument provides otherwise. It is possible that the settlor divided the tasks between two or more persons, e.g., Trustee # 1 to manage apartment houses and Trustee # 2 to manage a farm, both in the same trust. It is also possible to have persons who are quasi-trustees in the sense that they are advisors to the trustee in such matters as investment, but are not involved in the day-to-day operations of the trust. These advisors are also fiduciaries and are bound by the same principles as the trustee even though they have a more limited role. Although the settlor has the power to divide up the tasks of the trustee among co-trustees, the co-trustees do not have the same power. It would be an improper delegation of the trustee powers for the trustees to make such a division.

Co-trustees take legal title as joint tenants, even in jurisdictions which would not otherwise find the co-ownership to be a joint tenancy because of statutory requirements that a joint tenancy be expressly declared or because of the lack of the four unities required by common law. Thus, if one co-trustee dies, the other co-trustee automatically succeeds to the legal title. Upon the death of the last of the trustees, the legal title descends to his or her heirs or will beneficiaries, but there is no beneficial enjoyment involved. Therefore, the spouse or widow of a trustee has no dower (or statutory equivalent) rights in trust property.

A trustee can resign as permitted in the trust instrument, by the court having supervision of the trust, or with the consent of all the beneficiaries if they are competent. It is common drafting practice to include a provision permitting the trustee to resign. In the absence of such a provision, permission of the court must be obtained, and the court examines the situation from the viewpoint of the beneficiaries, not the trustee. A form of estoppel can be applied to the extent the trust beneficiaries are sui juris and consent to the resignation of the trustee; however, those who are not able to consent or who did not do so could impose liability upon the trustee for breach of trust duties.

A trustee can be removed as provided in the trust instrument or by the court having jurisdiction of the trust. The trust instrument may reserve the power to the settlor or give the power to third persons, including beneficiaries, to remove the trustee. If the power is absolute, the court will intervene only in rare cases where the court deems it necessary to protect the interests in the trust. Removal is considered a strict measure and is not lightly done. Breaches of trust duty, including those giving rise to a liability to the beneficiaries, will not necessarily be sufficient cause for removal of the trustee. Disagreements or conflicts with the beneficiaries are similarly not causes for removal. The trustee may have an adverse interest, as beneficiary or otherwise; but such an adverse interest, if known to the settlor at the creation of the trust, will not serve as a basis for removal. Contrast, however, the acquisition of an adverse interest after the trust is created. In that situation, removal of the trustee for conflict of interests is more likely. The original appointment by the settlor is deemed to be an acceptance of a conflict of interests then existing; therefore, the court will decline to remove a trustee under conditions which would prevent the court from appointing the same person or entity as successor trustee.

E. THE BENEFICIARY

Two mutually exclusive types of beneficiary exist: The charitable beneficiary and the private beneficiary. The two types differ in the following ways:

• Ascertainability and Enforcement: The beneficiary of a private trust must be ascertainable so that the trust can be enforced; a charitable trust can be enforced by the attorney general.

• Rule against Perpetuities and related doctrines: A gift over from a charity to another charity is exempt from the Rule against Perpetuities, thereby permitting a condition to be imposed and enforced indefinitely. A gift to a charity may be vested for Rule against Perpetuities purposes and may be exempt from limitations upon the duration of a trust under conditions which would make a private trust invalid, such as a direction to pay the income only "forever" without a disposition of the principal of the trust.

• The charitable trust may enjoy various tax advantages such as full exclusion from taxation.

• Charitable, but not private, testamentary trusts are subject to the "Mortmain" statutes in those jurisdictions which still have restrictions upon testamentary dispositions to charity. The relatively rare restrictions upon charitable ownership of land generally also apply to charitable trusts. Note that in this area only, it is disadvantageous to the trust to be a "charitable" trust.

• Charitable trusts have the ability to use the cy pres doctrine to carry out the general charitable purpose of a trust when the original purpose becomes impossible.

1. PRIVATE TRUST BENEFICIARIES

As previously noted, a beneficiary may also have other roles (settlor or trustee) in the trust with only one combination producing no trust: The sole trustee cannot be the sole beneficiary because duties would neither exist nor be enforced by the trustee-beneficiary.

Although notice to, and acceptance by, a beneficiary of a private trust is not necessary in order to create a trust, it is necessary that the beneficiary be capable of taking beneficial title and be ascertained or ascertainable.

a. Capacity

The capacity to be a beneficiary of a trust is like the capacity to take (as opposed to convey) legal title. A minor or incompetent can be the owner of a beneficial interest, i.e., be a beneficiary of a trust. Occasionally a state will limit ownership of property (or certain types of property, such as farmland) by aliens or corporations. In such cases, it is a matter of interpretation of the statute whether ownership in trust is prohibited, but generally the prohibition does extend to such indirect ownership also.

b. Unincorporated Association

A potential beneficiary which creates problems of both capacity to take and ascertainability is the unincorporated association. This entity occupies the ambiguous area between a formal corporation on one hand and a class gift on the other. A typical unincorporated association is the fraternal organization, lodge or "fund" which has not formally incorporated or established itself within any of the traditional forms of organization. The unincorporated association may have a formal constitution and bylaws and elaborate internal rules or it may be simply a group of persons with a common interest, such as a bowling league. Restatement, Second, Trusts § 119, states the premise that an unincorporated association has a capacity to be the beneficiary of a trust. Many jurisdictions have enacted statutes which eliminate the common law rule that an unincorporated association was not an entity capable of taking legal title. A few jurisdictions refuse to recognize an unincorporated association as a juristic entity; it does not legally exist. Therefore, in those jurisdictions, the beneficial interest belongs to the members of the association. If the settlor intended a gift in trust to the members of the group, the beneficiaries can be determined if the group is "frozen in time" (e.g., the members of the association as of the time of the creation of the trust or some other time). In the latter case, a problem may arise with the Rule against Perpetuities unless the property must vest within the specified period or there is some person who has the power to terminate the trust within the period, Restatement, Second, Trusts § 119, Comment d.

The fringes of the unincorporated association blend into the category of "class gifts." Both deal with groups of people who are identified by some common characteristic. Fraternities are clear examples of unincorporated associations (unless they have formally incorporated) while "my descendants" is a clear example of a class gift. The spectators at a specified sporting event could be viewed as an unincorporated association while the members of the teams could be considered as borderline between a class and an unincorporated association.

c. Class Gifts—Construction

It is extremely common that the beneficiaries of a trust be designated as a class, such as "my issue." A number of interpretation questions and unique rules of future interests arise whenever a class gift is involved. In addition to the question of whether anti-lapse statutes apply, class gifts need to be interpreted to decide as of what time the class is to be determined.

As of when is the membership of the class determined? A class gift could be viewed as a tube extending through time. The sides of the tube are the description of the class's common characteristics—"my issue" or "my employees." The tube is capable of being open at either end—new members can be added and older members can be dropped from the class. Sometimes an end is sealed by nature or the terms of the class gift: I will have no further "employees" after I cease any business. The class of "my children" (contrast "my issue") will have no additions after my death. (A child conceived, but not yet born, would usually be treated as "in being," especially if later born alive.)

A class gift therefore needs to be frozen in time in order to determine the identity of the particular members who are the beneficiaries. Just as it is not possible to say which particles of water form the

river unless it is frozen (actually or by a still photograph), it is not possible to say who the members of
a class are unless it is frozen (by the settlor's
express language, an inference of intention or a
combination). For example, the use of the term
"now living" or "then surviving" gives a reference
to some particular point in time. The point may be
obscured even when such words are used. "Now"
in a will could refer to the time of writing or to the
time of the testator's death. "Then surviving"
after multiple life estates is unclear unless expressly
stated to be "the last to die of" them. Does one
who dies, leaving issue, "survive" through the issue?

The vesting certainty for the Rule against Perpetuities requires that both ends of the class gift be
sealed—no further additions can be made and no
condition precedent (such as survival) can exist for
any member of the class.

Class gifts trigger a number of rules which properly fall into the Future Interests subject matter,
but are intertwined with interpretation of trusts: A
number of these rules are mentioned, but not thor-
oughly presented at this point. Familiarity, at least
to the extent the rules are described, is strongly
recommended.

● Gifts to an individual and a class: Generally
persons take equally and members of a class take
equally (except that "by right of representation" is
often used with gifts to "issue" of someone). If a
bequest were made to "My brother and his children

who survive me" and three children of the brother survived the testator, would the brother take one-half (i.e., equal to the class as a whole) or one-fourth (i.e., equal to one member of the class)?

● The Rule[s] in Wild's Case deal[s] with gifts to the "children" of someone with distinctions turning upon whether such children exist at a particular time or not.

● The Rule of Worthier Title and the Rule in Shelley's Case deal with gifts to "heirs" of someone.

● The Rule of Convenience closes the class to after-born potential members when one member of the class is immediately entitled to his or her share of the principal.

d. Class Gifts—Ascertainability of Members

Class gifts use categories ("my nephews" etc.) rather than names to identify people. These categories can be ambiguous because of particular circumstances (Does "issue" include adopted or illegitimate issue? Is an aunt's husband an "uncle"?) or because of the particular term used ("friend"). In Clark v. Campbell (1926) a trust for the testator's "friends" was held void for indefiniteness of beneficiaries even though the term could have been construed to refer to persons referred to in other parts of the same will as "friends." The next step up in definiteness is "relatives," a term which is sometimes construed to mean the heirs or next of kin, but could also be construed as too indefinite.

e. Class Gift—Partial Ascertainability

It would not have helped in Clark v. Campbell, supra, if one of the testator's friends could be determined with certainty. The beneficiaries of a trust must *all* be determined with certainty.

If all of the persons who comprise the class cannot be determined, the trust fails as to that class. It is still possible, however, that the attempt to pass property to the members of the class may be valid as either a power of appointment or an outright gift to the trustee. Thus, in the case of a bequest "to my friend, John Doe, to distribute among my friends" a valid general power of appointment may have been created. Even though a trust's binding obligations upon the trustee do not exist, the donee has the power to appoint to anyone, including himself, if the language is construed to create a general power of appointment. Similarly, a bequest "To my friend John Doe so that he can take care of my relatives, if necessary" may be construed as precatory language connected to an outright gift to John Doe (and therefore valid) rather than a trust (and potentially invalid for indefiniteness of beneficiaries).

EXAMPLE: T devises the residue of his estate to A "[a] in trust [b] for my relatives [c] as A may select [d] excluding himself." Without the language in quotation marks, or without the "in trust" the residual bequest might be construed as an outright bequest to A. By itself the "in trust" indicates (but is not conclusive) that no beneficial interest was intended to pass to the "trustee." If it is a trust, the beneficiaries shown in "[b]" may be too indefinite to constitute a class; often "relatives" will be construed to mean "heirs" or "next of kin." If too indefinite to be a trust, such a term, however, when combined with the clause in "[c]" indicates that a power of appointment was intended. The power would probably be general except for the language of "[d]" but that language is sufficient to change the power from general to special while reinforcing the power of appointment interpretation of the entire bequest. Probably the best interpretation of the clause as written is that it created a valid special power of appointment in trust with the legal title in A and the equitable title in default of appointment remaining in the heirs of the testator.

The Restatement tests for the ascertainability of the members of a class vary for direct gifts and powers of appointment. Restatement, Second, Trusts § 120 insists that *all* members of the class receiving a direct bequest must be ascertainable in order for any beneficiary's share to be valid. This makes sense since the share of each beneficiary is based upon the total number of beneficiaries. Although the numerator of the fraction can be determined, (It is "1/___".) the denominator is the total number of beneficiaries. Restatement, Second, Trusts § 122, dealing with powers of appointment, states that if *any* potential appointee could be ascertained (regardless of whether *all* could be ascertained), the power of appointment would be valid at the time of creation. At the time of exercise, the question becomes whether it can be determined that *this* appointee falls within the description of the permissible appointees.

2. INCIDENTAL BENEFICIARIES

Not everyone who benefits from a trust is a beneficiary of the trust. The test is the settlor's intention to benefit, not the economic benefit. The distinction is important for procedural reasons, since an incidental beneficiary often does not have standing to challenge the trustee's actions or inaction.

EXAMPLE: T creates a trust for the benefit of A and directs that the trustee shall invest in common stock of Texaco, Inc. The corporation does not have a beneficial interest in the trust sense and does not have standing to sue to enforce the terms including the express provision for investment of the trust.

Other examples of incidental beneficiaries are schools at which "true" beneficiaries are enrolled with tuition paid out of the trust, creditors of a "true" beneficiary for whom the trust will pay debts and governmental entities which would otherwise expend funds for the care of a "true" beneficiary.

The concept of "incidental" beneficiary is used to deny enforcement of trust terms by those only tangentially concerned with the trust; it could be viewed as the court's decision that the interest of the incidental beneficiary is too obscure or attenuated to be enforced. The concept probably should not be expanded further, but it does serve as an explanation and bridge to the concept that the recipient of largess from a "charitable trust" is not the "true" beneficiary; the public is the beneficiary and the recipient of the largess is "merely" an "incidental" beneficiary.

3. CHARITABLE TRUSTS

The subject of "Charities" is treated almost entirely within the Trusts course in law school although the tax courses acknowledge the existence of such a concept. The legal form of charities usually evolves from the unincorporated association into either a non-profit corporation or a trust. The "Foundation" or "fund," as such, is not a legal entity.

a. Charitable Purposes

Since a charitable trust is simply a trust for charitable purposes, consider what purposes are charitable. No comprehensive definition is possible without a generic catch-all such as "other purposes which are beneficial to the community." The idea of what is charitable may change from time to time and from place to place, but four specific areas—Poverty, Education, Religion and Government—can be described.

(1) Poverty

Relief of poverty is and has traditionally been a charitable purpose, even though the definition of poverty has varied considerably. It is obvious that some of the commodities and services considered to be basic today would have been luxuries of the rich four centuries ago; consider the diet, shelter and transportation differences. To the extent that anyone receives economic benefits as an individual beneficiary of a charitable trust, he or she is further removed from poverty.

Relief of poverty is probably one of the oldest of the charitable purposes. More modernly there has been a tendency for governmental units to assume the task of relieving poverty thus blending two charitable purposes and blunting both the need and the tendency toward private relief of poverty.

A trust for "the poor" is charitable, but a trust does not have to be exclusively for the poor in order to be charitable. A gift or bequest in trust for "the poor" (like a similar disposition "for charitable purposes") can be applied for purposes which fit within the designation. If the trustee is unwilling to go forward, the court will assist in "framing a scheme" for the charitable disposition. A trust which benefits the wealthy as well as the poor is still capable of being charitable even though it does not fall within the "poverty" classification.

Private individuals can be "incidental" beneficiaries and they need not be totally destitute in order for the trust which benefits them to be charitable, but both the recipients' identities and their degree of poverty affect the probability that the purpose will be found to be relief of poverty. If the persons who are to benefit are not a sufficiently large and indefinite class, in the words of Austin Wakeman Scott, "that the community is interested in the enforcement of the trust" it is not a charitable trust. A trust for named individuals who are poor is not considered a charitable trust, but geographic, age and gender limitations ("poor, old women of Roseville") are permitted. On the border line is a trust for "my poor relatives" which might be upheld as a private trust if the beneficiaries can be ascertained, but is not considered a charitable trust *because* the members of the group can be ascertained, i.e., the group is too small. Perhaps the non-charitable nature can be explained in terms of the settlor's charitable intent being less than the intent to keep the economic benefits within his or her blood line.

(2) Education

Aid to any of the elements of the traditional learning process—institution, teachers or students—is an educational purpose, as are the creation of programs (research, dissemination of information etc.) and the creation of allied institutions (museums and libraries). The line between permissible education and non-charitable propaganda, if such a line exists, permits much to fall into the "education" side and eliminates only extreme cases of promoting one's own point of view.

Some testators overestimate the value of their personal writings, works or collections. An otherwise valid charitable trust to publish unpublishable writings or preserve the home of an undistinguished person as a museum will generally fail as a charitable trust because it is not of sufficient value to the community as a whole. It appears to be best that the court err in favor of allowing even the most divergent viewpoint to be represented, rather than imposing its own concept of what is suitable for public consumption. Although clear cases at the extremes can be visualized, a broad area of permissible taste should exist.

(3) Religion

Generally trusts for the advancement of religion of all types are upheld in the United States today. The advancement may be in the form of direct payment to a church or rabbi, minister or priest or it may be associated with religious work (missions, pamphlets etc.) or accessories (choir, organs etc.). A close area is a religious purpose which is connected to the personality of the testator, e.g., saying of masses or maintenance of a grave. In some cases, the predominant purpose may be interpreted to be the charitable portion; in others, the trust may be upheld as an "honorary trust;" if neither is applied, the trust is not charitable. If it must be valid as a private trust, if at all, it often fails because the beneficiary cannot be ascertained.

Established churches have had less difficulty in gaining acceptance as being for charitable purposes than newer religions. Some denominations such as the Church of Christ, Scientist (Christian Scientists) and the Church of the Latter Day Saints of Jesus Christ (Mormons) have evolved entirely within the United States from small initial groups. It is not a simple task to separate those churches in their initial years from other sects which were less successful (such as that of Joanna Southcote who declared that she was pregnant by the Holy Ghost and would give birth to a second Messiah). Generally, trusts for the benefits of such religious groups are upheld as charitable purposes unless the court decides that the religion is so absurd as to be irrational. Such a course of conduct pits the preconvictions of the judge against the religious convictions of the settlor of the trust.

(4) Governmental

Governmental purposes which are considered to be charitable include direct gifts to the governmental unit and gifts for creation or maintenance of public works (streets, libraries, bridges, firehouses etc.) as well as more intangible purposes such as fostering peace or preparing for war.

Trusts seeking to change the law (or the identity of the persons who administer it) walk the borderline between the permissible governmental function of peaceful and orderly change of the law and the impermissible "political" function which is not deemed to be charitable. Federal income tax law denies a charitable deduction for income of or contributions to an organization which seeks to influence legislation. Rarely will an individual's political campaign be deemed charitable, although the individual may be the leading spokesperson for some particular governmental policy. A guide in this area is the extent to which individual personalities are not tied to the cause. Tax rules, of course, do not necessarily determine what the trust law should be.

Increasingly, governmental functions are tending to include most of the other charitable functions (relief of poverty, education, public health etc.) except religion. Whether such a public approach will exclude or expand private charity has not been fully determined.

(5) Generally Beneficial to the Community

Potentially charitable trusts require analysis to fit them within any category of charitable trusts. Although many cases are clear, there are an equal number of instances in which the purposes have difficulty fitting the previous categories (Poverty, Education, Religion or Government). If analysis does not permit such labeling, there is still the further potential charitable purpose that the trust purpose is one which will benefit the community generally. Into this category fit (or attempt to fit) trusts for the protection of animals generally (including anti-vivisection, protection from cruelty and birth control of animals), promotion of sports and promotion of health, among other purposes. Not all of these purposes will be deemed to be charitable. The following guidelines may assist both in this general category and in the more specific categories already described:

• Generality of purpose is not fatal. The court will enforce, at the instance of the attorney general, a trust for "charity" as well as a trust for "education" or "relief of poverty."

• Private profit is generally fatal to a charitable purpose. Thus, a non-profit hospital is a charity while a proprietary hospital is not a charity (even if it does not, in fact, have a profit).

• Taint of personal interest, as opposed to personal attitude, tends to result in non-charitable classification. A trust for the relief of poverty of the grantor or his or her relatives will tend to be deemed non-charitable unless the group encompassed by the term "relatives" is extremely large. Often, it is permissible to give a preference to one's own relatives, e.g., by establishing a scholarship for education with such a preference. So long as it is not entirely limited in terms, expectation, reality or practice, the purpose will tend to be treated as charitable.

• Smallness of the number of potential recipients of largess, while fatal only if the group is absolutely limited, tends to indicate that a private benefit was sought. An award could be established which honored only one person at a time, but which potentially would honor a great number over a period of time. Such an award would be for a charitable purpose.

• Social utility is measured to some degree. Thus amateur sports (e.g., fox-hunting or yacht racing) are less likely to be held to be charitable purposes than the preservation of animals or the study of boat design. Professional sports, of course, involve proprietary institutions and therefore seldom, if ever, will be found to be charitable. Contrast the governmental role of providing a stadium for the same sports.

• The language used may build a stronger case, but is not determinative by itself. For example, a contribution to "improve the breed" of race-horses which in fact is designed to support professional horse racing will probably be deemed to be non-charitable. A skilled draftsman can aid interpretation but cannot transform every idiosyncrasy into a charity. A trust for the "education and relief of poverty of Antarctic penguins" (if not interpreted to make better sense) should fail no matter how diligently the draftsperson evokes the terms of charity.

• Uniqueness or unpopularity of the cause generally must be rather extreme in order for the trust to fail. Individual courts differ on what is a wholly invalid purpose.

b. Cy Pres

The cy pres ("as near" [as possible]) doctrine permits preservation of charitable trusts by seeking the nearest practical alternative to a charitable trust which would otherwise fail or be ineffective. The "key sentence" of the elements of this doctrine is as follows: When [1] a trust [2] evidencing general charitable intent [3] which was initially valid [4] becomes illegal, impossible or impractical to administer as directed, then the court will permit a change in the dispositive provisions to accomplish the general charitable intent as near as possible to the original intent.

The classic example of the cy pres doctrine is Jackson v. Phillips (1867) in which a testator who died in 1861 attempted to create a trust for the purpose of putting an end to slavery. The trust corpus was ultimately used for the education of former slaves to render them more capable of self-government.

Consider the elements of cy pres:

(1) A Trust

The cy pres doctrine arose in trusts and remains in that field predominantly, but there has been an occasional expansion beyond the pure trust situation, especially when non-trust charitable dispositions are involved. A similar but unrelated doctrine of flexibility which also exists in trust law is "deviation" which permits a change in the administrative provisions of a trust (as opposed to a change of the dispositive provisions which is involved in cy pres).

(2) Evidencing General Charitable Intent

If the charitableness of the settlor is narrowly construed to be limited to the impossible purpose only, the trust will fail. The principle of construction here is to carry out the settlor's charitable intention unless it does not contain a general charitable intent. The court is, in effect, asking itself: "Given the circumstances and the language used in the instrument at the time the trust was created, would the settlor have desired that the property be diverted to another charitable use of a similar nature if the exact use specified could not be complied with?"

Students tend to underestimate the need to consider this aspect of the cy pres issue.

(3) Which Was Initially Valid

There has been some weakening of this requirement so that cy pres has been applied in a few cases when the trust's charitable purpose was illegal, impossible or impractical at all times, but the traditional phrasing remains.

(4) Becomes Impossible, Illegal or Impractical

This is the triggering event for the cy pres doctrine. The difficulty may be insufficient funds for the purpose directed, a total change in the laws or the elimination of the disease or problem involved. Examples include large centers for the treatment of tuberculosis or poliomyelitis or smallpox, seeking to get the vote (or equal rights) for women or to relieve crowding in public elementary schools.

Impracticality is the difficult area here. If it is merely difficult, the court is reluctant to change the settlor's objective which is still possible. A detailed examination is required of a purpose which is possible but difficult.

Currently the cy pres doctrine is invoked in situations in which the testator-settlor imposed a racial, religious or other "suspect category" restriction upon the incidental beneficiaries who receive trust benefits.   In Evans v. Abney (1970), the Georgia trial and Supreme Court decided that the impossible function of maintaining a public park for white persons only was the sole charitable intention of the settlor; the park reverted to his heirs when those courts and the United States Supreme Court refused to apply cy pres.

c. Enforcement of Charities (Standing)

Traditionally the overworked staff of the attorney general is charged with the enforcement of both charitable trusts (sometimes under the Uniform Supervision of Trustees for Charitable Purposes Act) and corporations. The significance is more in the exclusion from standing of persons or organizations which might otherwise be willing to supervise the trust, e.g., an existing charity with similar purposes. The trustees and an occasional very direct incidental beneficiary (e.g., the professor for whom an endowed chair has been created by charitable trust) may also have standing to enforce the trust. Others (including the settlor unless such rights are expressly reserved) do not have standing to challenge the administration of the charitable trust.

4. MIXED CHARITABLE AND NON-CHARITABLE PURPOSES

A favorite examination area is the mixed trust. The variety of potential situations, absence of precise guidelines and consecutive issues provide a good opportunity to demonstrate the presence or lack of understanding of the issues involved.

One possible analytical approach is as follows: (a) Bearing in mind the differences between charitable and private trusts, (b) examine each purpose to see whether it is charitable. (c) If both purposes exist, can they be separated? (d) If not, something must yield. (e) If so, who receives the "trust" property? Let's examine these steps individually.

a. The Distinction

The distinction is relevant only when there are differences between private and charitable trusts, e.g., Mortmain statutes, Rule against Perpetuities or indefiniteness of private trust beneficiaries. On an examination, the presence of a potentially charitable purpose ("Poor" or "education" might be the triggering word.) should cause a search for failure due to the Mortmain statute. Of course, unless the statute is given, the potential failure cannot be said to have occurred with certainty. Thus, the trust must be treated both as if there is such a statute (a relatively rare likelihood) and as if there were none. Similarly, when problems of the Rule against Perpetuities or indefiniteness of private trust beneficiaries arise, it should be kept in mind that those rules apply only to non-charitable trusts. Thus, we must take the next step:

b.   Is Each Trust Purpose "Charitable?"

This question requires analysis of *each* trust purpose to fit within the traditionally accepted charitable purposes. Recalling that a purpose may be for a combination of purposes (e.g., to promote the health of poor missionaries), the examinee should specify exactly why this purpose is charitable.

Often it will be difficult to determine how many purposes are involved. Construction of ambiguous clauses is necessary. In Morice v. The Bishop of Durham (Engl.1805) a bequest directing that property be distributed "to such objects of benevolence and liberality as the Bishop of Durham in his own discretion shall most approve" was construed not only as not being a power of appointment but also as having two purposes, only one of which was charitable. In that leading case, "benevolence" was construed as charitable while "liberality" was construed as non-charitable. The trust therefore failed because it did not satisfy all the requirements of both a charitable trust and a private trust; specifically, the identity of the beneficiaries of the private trust could not be ascertained.

In Morice v. Bishop of Durham, one construction device was not used: The two purposes "benevolence and liberality" were linked by "and." It was therefore arguable that the object must be both, i.e., that "liberality" merely limited objects which were concededly charitable and the trust should be upheld. A similar situation exists when the trustees are directed to provide for "my poor relatives." The limitation to "relatives" by itself may be narrowly construed to be the heirs of the settlor, in which case it is valid as a private trust; the word "poor" might be disregarded as surplusage or a patronizing comment. On the other hand, a broad construction of "relatives" would encompass a group too broad to be ascertainable as a private trust. Relief of poverty is a charitable purpose; therefore "my poor relatives" might be a charitable trust limited to relatives who are poor. This mixed trust is not separable into "poor" and "relatives" and therefore would be upheld as a charitable trust only if the group of "relatives" was large enough that a broad social purpose would be so served. Probably a trust "for the relief of poverty, with preference to my relatives who are in need" would be entirely charitable. Contrast a trust, the income of which is to be divided between "the poor and my relatives."

Similar combinations blend into the area of honorary trusts, discussed later: "To the church [charitable] for the saying of masses for my soul [probably classified as non-charitable]," "to the city of St. Paul for the maintenance of my grave" etc.

c. If Both Purposes Exist, Can They Be Separated?

The easy cases of separation are those expressly stated as separate items—e.g., "One half for the poor of my city and one half for my relatives."

Despite the settlor's intent that there be one trust, two will be created to preserve validity. An unusual case could be conceived in which the settlor stressed a preference for a single invalid trust rather than two valid ones, such a preference would be given effect; i.e., the undivided trust would fail.

Another easy trust to divide is the life estate to an individual (non-charitable) and remainder to charity. Each portion would follow and be subject to the respective rules for private and charitable trusts. More difficult is the concept of capitalizing enough of the fund to satisfy the lesser of the two purposes (e.g., purchasing an annuity for an individual or providing enough funds by which the charitable purpose can be accomplished from the income of the fund) and delivering the balance of the trust assets for the other purpose (e.g., the charity or named individuals).

d. If Indivisible, Something Must Yield

If both charitable and non-charitable purposes exist and are inseparable, the trust must conform to all the requirements for each type of trust. Although Mortmain or Rule against Perpetuities or other problem areas exist, the most likely problem lies in the identity of the beneficiaries. To be valid as a private trust, the beneficiaries must be ascertained or capable of being ascertained within the period of the Rule against Perpetuities but a trust in which all the beneficiaries are ascertained is not likely to be a charitable trust. A trust can be charitable if it benefits one person at a time, but not if it benefits only one person. The one-person-at-a-time rule raises questions concerning the Rule against Perpetuities.

Normally, all parts of the inseparably mixed trust fail. One alternative, rarely used, is to strike the lesser portion, usually the non-charitable part because the charitable trust is generally treated more advantageously. Thus, a trust to build a public library (charitable) and to publish the settlor's undistinguished treatise on "Law and Apes" might be allowed to disregard the second, otherwise inseparable, purpose. In this area cy pres blends into construction. The charitable portion may be saved by construction, but it is not strictly cy pres (because the initial validity of the trust is not conceded), nor is it strictly construction of the terms used, since they are disregarded in order to obtain as much as possible of the charitable (or main) purpose.

If the problem is the Mortmain statute, it is possible either to strike the charitable portion or to construe the non-charitable portion as an alternative gift so that the charitable portion will be upheld.

e. If So Who Receives the "Trust" Property?

In the usual case of inseparably mixed charitable and non-charitable trusts in which some rule is violated by a part of the trust, the entire trust fails. It may be possible to construe the trust so that only a portion fails. Obviously, if the trusts are separable and the charitable trust violates rules applicable to it or the non-charitable trust violates rules applicable to it, that portion of the trust fails. A third possibility is to ignore the defective portion of the trust, but to allow the entire property to pass to the other portion of the trust; this technique is rarely used; it seems to be reserved for situations in which the ignored purpose is insignificant or the settlor specifically gives an order of preference.

Any failed portion of a trust passes to alternative takers if effectively so directed by the settlor. If there is no direction, it returns to him by resulting trust. If he is dead, it passes to his will beneficiaries (the residual takers if not specifically provided for in the will) or heirs.

Only in rare cases is the purported "trustee" allowed to keep the property personally. This result is more possible if the word "trust" is not used properly by the settlor and there is no strong indication of trust intent. The "precatory" trusts are the most likely area for this result with the "honorary" trusts being the second most likely.

To review these principles, consider the following example:

EXAMPLE: T dies bequeathing the residue of his estate "To my friend X so that he can use the income as chief executive officer of the American Legion Post # 75 and promote the spirit of Americanism in today's youth."

An analysis of the problem might proceed as follows:

Is a trust intended? The reference to "use" of "income" for specified purposes indicates a trust while the "friend" status of the potential trustee (as opposed to a trust company), the non-use of the word "trust" and the vagueness of the provisions indicate the possibility this is a gift with precatory language. Additional facts, such as whether this is an instrument drafted by one not skilled in the law, would be relevant. From a result-oriented approach of trying to carry out the intention of the testator, the potential failure of the bequest as a trust might tip the scales towards this being an outright bequest rather than a trust.

Does the bequest violate the Rule against Perpetuities? The principal of the trust fund is not specifically given to anyone. It is possible to construe this unlimited gift of income from personalty (assuming "bequeathed" to indicate personalty rather than realty) as tantamount to a fee simple, but this stretches the point. If not so construed, the basic Rule against Perpetuities is not violated because the property "vests" immediately; there is no contingency. However, the analogous rule limiting the duration of private trusts could be violated because there is no time set for distribution of the trust principal. If the jurisdiction applies the rule limiting the duration of trusts to private trusts only, one distinction between charitable and non-charitable (private) trusts is found.

Who are the beneficiaries of the trust? If it is not an outright gift to X, is the American Legion Post (which is possibly an unincorporated association) the beneficiary of the trust?   If the jurisdiction permits an unincorporated association to be the beneficiary (as advocated by the Restatement, Second, Trusts § 119) *or* if the group is incorporated *or* if the bequest is construed as a gift to the present members of the unincorporated association, the private trust has ascertainable beneficiaries and is valid.   If construed as a bequest to the membership from time to time, the Rule against Perpetuities is probably violated.

Are there multiple purposes?   While it is possible to say that the spirit of Americanism could be promoted by either an outright gift to X or the American Legion Post and that the "promote the spirit" clause is linked by "and," it is also possible that to "promote the spirit" is a separate purpose. If so, that purpose is probably "charitable" because it generally promotes patriotism.   Additionally, the "in today's youth" suggests both a separate purpose (since the American Legion members tend to be older) and an educational function, which is also charitable.

Assuming that the bequest for the American Legion is not charitable (even though it may be exempt from taxation under a separate test for charities) and that the bequest to "promote the spirit of Americanism in today's youth" is charitable as patriotic or educational, can the two purposes be separated?   No allocation has been made by the testator between the two purposes;   there is no suggestion that a life estate for the life of X is intended. Therefore, the charitable and non-charitable purposes are inseparable.

What must yield? Neither of the purposes is clearly superior to the other; neither can be easily disregarded as surplusage. The entire trust will fail.

Since this was the residual bequest, the property would pass by resulting trust to the heirs of the testator unless there was an alternate disposition set out by the testator in the residual clause.

Perhaps the final question is the result-oriented one which appeared at the beginning of the analysis: If the bequest would fail as a trust, would the testator's intention be better carried out by construing the bequest as an outright gift to X and hope ("trust"?) that he will use it for the purposes designated?

5. HONORARY TRUSTS

The term "honorary" trust is used to describe a purported trust which is invalid as a private trust because there are no ascertained human beneficiaries and which is invalid as a charitable trust because the number of incidental human beneficiaries is too small or non-existent. England, some of the United States and the Restatement, Second, Trusts indicate that no enforceable trust is created but the transferee has a power to apply the property for the designated purpose (within the bounds of the Rule against Perpetuities) if it is not capricious. The most common areas of the honorary trusts deal with honoring or remembering a dead person or caring for specific animals or things.

Dead persons are traditionally honored by burial or cremation, with monuments and graves or tombs and with a ceremony (including flowers) within a reasonable time after death. If a testator wished to provide for perpetual care of his grave, he could do so in most states because permitted by statute. In the absence of statute, a trust for care of a grave would violate the Rule against Perpetuities. If the trust were for the preservation of a public cemetery or the grave or tomb of a notable person, a valid charitable trust probably exists. A wide latitude is often allowed in monuments and other markers for graves, but the monument must be proportional to the wealth of the decedent and conform both to his preferences and to some sense of appropriateness. In honoring a deceased person, the saying of masses is often considered to be a charitable purpose. In jurisdictions where a trust for the saying of masses is not considered to be a charitable trust, the purpose could be allowed as an honorary trust.

Animals, especially pet animals, are often the intended recipients of the benefits of a trust. The dual problems of no human beneficiary and no human measuring lives for the Rule against Perpetuities period highlight the difficulties of a trust for particular animals. A trust for the care of animals (or some species of animal) is generally upheld as charitable. When the testator narrows the benefited animals down to one cat or dog or even "my horses and hounds," the group is too small for a charitable trust and too inhuman for a private trust.

Honorary trusts are not permitted in many states. The attempt to create a trust fails in such jurisdictions. The technique suggested by Restatement, Second, Trusts § 124 is to permit the "trustee" to carry out the "trust" (which is really treated as a power of appointment), but not to allow the trustee to retain the property. Thus, if the trustee does not fully expend the funds for the purpose allocated, the funds return by resulting trust to the settlor, if living, and if not, to his estate. The problem with such a technique is the same problem that causes many private trusts to fail—an ascertained beneficiary is necessary in order to enforce the trust. Again, the need is not satisfied. (The attorney general, of course, has the obligation to enforce charitable trusts.) One English court established a generally-unfollowed precedent of requiring a bond from the "trustee" of an honorary trust to secure performance (or at least guarantee the surrender of property subject to the power).

Capricious purposes will generally not be enforced, even by honorary trust. What is "capricious" varies from case to case. Skillful wording may change results. For example, a trust to sell all the assets and burn the money would fail as capricious, whereas the same trust to distribute the money to the United States of America is permitted as a charitable trust. A trust to brick up or raze a building is probably capricious, but some courts have permitted the demolition of a building. A trust to keep a clock in repair has been deemed capricious, but a similar trust for a clock in a museum might be permitted. One lady successfully insisted that she be buried in her aged sports car, coupling the request with a condition upon a bequest of a substantial amount of money. The beneficiary chose to honor the request rather than contest it. Some requests for monuments on graves can be capricious, e.g., the court struck down a bequest to pay for a band to play music at the testator's tomb on the anniversaries of his death.

F. EXPLANATION OF TRUST CLASSIFICATIONS

The term "trust," like the term "clothing," is a generic term covering many sub-categories. Just as clothing can be classified by color, purpose, where worn on the body and protectiveness, trusts can be classified by the manner in which they are created, revocability, voluntariness, special purpose, legality and type of beneficiary. Often the classification is only one attribute, so that the same item may fit a number of classifications. Just as a black work shoe combines color and function, so a testamentary charitable trust combines method of creation and type of beneficiary. The following classifications provide some—but not all possible—types of trusts:

1. PASSIVE AND ACTIVE TRUSTS

A "passive" trust is one in which the trustee has no duty except to transfer the property to the beneficiary. This type of trust was the historical starting point and most common type of trust until the enactment of the Statute of Uses which "executed" (i.e., carried out, not killed) the passive trust by stating that the beneficiary was given the legal title which then merged into the equitable title, destroying the trust. The only significance today is that a trust in which the only duty of the trustee is to convey title to the beneficiary becomes "passive" and may be deemed to have been carried out by the English Statute of Uses. Almost all trusts which we will encounter are "active" trusts in which the trustee has some additional duty.

2. RESULTING (IMPLIED), CONSTRUCTIVE AND EXPRESS TRUSTS

In the classification of trusts by the degree of voluntariness of their creation, the only three categories are the "resulting" (implied) trust, the "constructive" trust and the "express trust." The resulting or implied trust arises when there has not been a complete and effective disposition of the beneficial interest. For example, S transfers property to T in fee in trust to pay the income to L for life. The remaining undisposed-of portion of the equitable interest (an equitable reversion) remains in S by virtue of an "implied" or "resulting trust."

Similarly if there is a transfer to a trustee without a designation of the intended beneficial interest, it is presumed that a resulting trust was intended. In a few jurisdictions, this rule has been changed by statute for realty so that a conveyance to "T as trustee" without further indication of the trust may be construed as an outright transfer to T.

Constructive trusts are remedial devices, belonging in the Remedies rather than the Trusts course. The common paternity of equity is reflected in the "trust" terminology, but the siblings are very dissimilar. The Trusts course ordinarily ignores the constructive trust (although it may be a remedy to correct fraud upon an express trust).

The "express trust" is the type most commonly dealt with in the Trusts course. All the following classifications are types of express trusts.

3. LEGAL AND ILLEGAL TRUSTS

All the classifications of trusts in this book deal with "legal" (as opposed to "illegal," not as opposed to "equitable") trusts. Illegal trusts are non-trusts. The major reasons for illegality are illegal creation, violation of the Rule against Perpetuities or related rules or illegal purpose.

Illegal creation has already been examined.

The Rule against Perpetuities deals with "vesting" of interests at too remote a time, commonly beyond lives in being and twenty-one years. The same period is often used for related rules such as the Rule against Accumulations, the rule limiting the duration of trusts and rules limiting the suspension of the right of alienation or the absolute ownership of property. The Rule against Perpetuities and its related rules are beyond the scope of this work and the comprehension of most lawyers (but not the apprehension of malpractice insurers).

Illegal purposes extend from those which seek, induce or tend toward breaches of law or public morals, through illegal consideration and attempts to defraud others to the capricious. Breaches of the law could be as flagrant as a direction to furnish weapons to prison inmates. Attempts to defraud others could consist of transferring the property in order to avoid creditors, qualify for welfare or clothe another with indicia of wealth. Capricious purposes include such items as destruction of the property.

A difficult area of the potentially illegal trust is that involving non-marital sex—the mistress, unmarried couple or illegitimate child. If denied the protection of law which is given the married couple, the non-married couple (or group) may attempt to achieve the same economic interrelationship through the use of a trust. Traditionally, a trust executed in contemplation of future non-marital sexual relations or illegitimate children has been classified as illegal because it had an illegal consideration or because it defeated, or tended to defeat, public morality and was therefore contrary to public policy. If the trust was executed after the termination of the relationship or the conception of the illegitimate child, it did not induce future conduct and was generally not considered illegal. Changing social trends may lead to greater acceptability of such arrangements for couples who do not (or cannot) marry, but the traditional tide of decisions would make such trusts illegal.

Attempts to defraud others (typically the spouse or other creditors) may lead to the invalidity of the trust. In the case of the attempt to defraud the spouse's claim, a line is sometimes drawn between present claims for alimony and future claims for the spouse's share of a decedent's estate, with the latter being less protected. The more interesting aspect of this type of illegal trust is the decision as to the alternate taker. Ordinarily, the transferee is allowed to keep the property because equity will not protect those who do not come into it with clean hands. In some cases, the transferee has participated in or solicited the attempted fraud and the transferor has died leaving innocent representatives, so that a return of the property to the transferor's representatives is a fairer result.

Motivation of the settlor may be the dominant factor in determining whether a trust conditioned upon marital or religious restrictions is valid. As general matters, the law favors family harmony, religious freedom and freedom to marry whom one chooses. The following are examples of situations in which the validity of the trust may be questioned:

EXAMPLE # 1: T leaves life estate to his widow, so long as she remains unmarried. Upon the earlier of her death or remarriage, the remainder goes to S.

In this example, the life estate and remainder arrangement is valid, even though it might incite S (but not a reasonable person) to kill W in order to hasten S's possession. The restriction on remarriage would tend to be upheld, especially if it could be shown that the purpose was to provide for W as long as there was no source of economic support available to her. Perhaps (but probably not) the trust provision concerning remarriage might be stricken as a restraint on marriage.

EXAMPLE # 2: A trust provision "to C so long as he does not marry."

This provision, by itself, would probably be invalid since it totally prohibits marriage. The concept of encouraging family growth may be less important today. Other facts (such as C being a Roman Catholic priest) may influence the result.

EXAMPLE # 3: T conditions the share of a beneficiary as follows: "provided he marries, within three years of my death, a person of the Lutheran faith."

This type of condition has received mixed treatment by the courts. In Matter of Liberman (1939) in which the determination was to be made by the alternate takers, the condition was stricken. Other courts have upheld single-faith restrictions, at least when the faith offered a reasonably large choice to the beneficiary. The time limitation, requiring an early marriage, may also be unreasonable.

In all of the cases in which some illegality is found, a series of additional issues arise: How much of the trust fails? Will the condition alone fail or does the gift to which it is attached fail or does the entire trust fail? As to the failed portion of the trust, to whom should it be distributed? In some cases (e.g. attempts to defraud creditors), return to the settlor is not permitted generally. Allowing the property to remain with the beneficiary may tend to encourage the very act which the illegal trust declaration sought to avoid.

4.   CHARITABLE AND PRIVATE TRUSTS

Note that the first three categories are used mostly to exclude "trusts" of certain types from consideration. Thus, all the remaining trusts are subspecies of Active, Express and Legal trusts. The active, express and legal trusts are further subdivided by the type of beneficiary—charitable or private (non-charitable). The distinctions for which this division is relevant (Rule against Perpetuities, Ascertainability of Beneficiaries and Mortmain in addition to tax) have already been examined.

The remaining classifications are of trusts which are active, express, legal private trusts:

5. TESTAMENTARY AND INTER VIVOS (LIVING) TRUSTS

Trusts are further divided by the manner of their creation. Those created by will and effective at the time of the testator's death are called "testamentary" trusts while those created during lifetime are called "inter vivos" or "living" trusts. The significance of the distinction is mainly found in the formalities for creation (a valid will if testamentary, a valid gift or contract or exercise of a power of appointment if inter vivos) and the recipient of property if a resulting trust arises for any reason. Failed portions of a testamentary trust will pass as directed by the decedent's will, whether by specific alternate gift or the residual clause. If the failed trust itself was the (and usually even if only part of the) residual clause, the failed residuary material passes by intestacy. A failed portion of a living trust goes by resulting trust to the settlor if still living. If he has died between the time of creation and the time that the trust is declared to be partially or completely invalid, the failed property passes by resulting trust to the settlor, through him to any subsequent unrevoked disposition (e.g., a quit-claim of any interest in the property) and, if none, to his estate for distribution in accordance with his will, if any, and if none, to his heirs.

6. REVOCABLE AND IRREVOCABLE TRUSTS

A trust may be partly or completely revocable or irrevocable. Since the power of "revocation" is one which is reserved only by the settlor of a trust, the distinction between revocable and irrevocable exists only for living trusts. (Until the settlor's death, the testamentary trust has not yet been created, although the will creating it is revocable. After his death and the creation of the trust, there is no living person who can "revoke" the trust.) A similar power to terminate the trust given to one other than the settlor is either a power of termination (if all that is done is to terminate the trust status with the trust property being distributed as provided in the trust instrument or by resulting trust) or a power of appointment (if the person can both terminate the trust *and* direct who shall receive the trust property).

The settlor can declare a trust to be revocable or irrevocable. In the absence of such a declaration, most jurisdictions will deem the trust irrevocable unless expressly made revocable. The opposite rule exists in a few states by statute. The power to revoke is usually considered to contain the lesser power to amend. If the settlor expressly provides for amendment, but does not provide for revocation, it is a question of interpretation of the power to amend as to whether it can be extended to encompass a complete revocation. An unlimited power to amend probably should be so interpreted.

7. SPENDTHRIFT, SUPPORT, DISCRETIONARY AND BLENDED TRUSTS

Active express legal private trusts (which typically are also testamentary and irrevocable) may contain one or more of four optional methods of limiting access to the trust assets by the beneficiary and his creditors:

• **Spendthrift trusts** (typically of an equitable life estate) contain express restrictions upon the voluntary or involuntary alienation of the beneficiary's share. Most jurisdictions, but not all, permit such restraints upon alienation, but there has been a tendency to limit the scope of the exemption by statute. The most difficult creditors to ignore are the (usually former) spouse and minor children who are seeking to enforce court orders for support. It is clear that the settlor cannot establish, directly or indirectly, a spendthrift trust for his own protection from creditors. The attempt to do so would probably create a valid trust with an invalid spendthrift clause, since such clauses are not a vital part of the trust. The creditor of the beneficiary usually attempts to reach the beneficiary's interest by a number of equitable analogs to the legal process of attachment; these equitable means include (in various jurisdictions) creditor's bills, garnishment, attachment, sequestration or trustee process.

• **Support trusts** tend to have the same effect as a spendthrift trust (and are valid in jurisdictions which do not allow beneficiaries to hide behind a spendthrift clause). Both support and discretionary trusts protect the beneficiary by giving no vested interest to him or her. In the support trust, the trustee is directed to pay so much of the income or principal or both as, in the trustee's discretion, is necessary for the support of the beneficiary. Naturally, disagreements can arise as to what is encompassed in the term "support" and the intention of the settlor is sought in the trust instrument and surrounding circumstances. Again, the spouse and issue present the hardest issues—is their support part of the support of the beneficiary? Should it make a difference if the beneficiary is male or female?

● **Blended trusts,** only rarely recognized by courts, are trusts in which the beneficiaries are a group. The share of any individual is not ascertainable in advance, but is "blended" with the share of the others. This category could be considered to be another way of looking at the "support" or "discretionary" trust.

● **Discretionary trusts** extend beyond the support trust. Not only is the beneficiary not entitled as a matter of right to the income (the usual situation), but the beneficiary is also not entitled to anything, including enough for support. The trustee, in the trustee's discretion, decides exactly how much, if any, income or principal or both should be used for the benefit of the beneficiaries. This blends the duty to pay into a power of appointment. Such a trust is best used when a trusted family member can supervise the distributions.

This area of trust law is one of the muddiest battlefields. Decisional law has tended to go to one extreme or another (striking down spendthrift provisions as unreasonable restraints upon alienation or upholding all such provisions because the trust form permits the trustee to convey the property and thus keep it in commerce). Statutory law is both diverse and typically incomplete. Practicing attorneys have inserted spendthrift provisions into most trust instruments without regard to the practicality of such insertion. (Such a valid provision may prevent the beneficiaries from terminating a useless trust, even though they all agree to the termination.) Since the luxury of certainty is not available in the area of spendthrift trusts, it is a favorite examination area. An ability to handle the competing concepts and language involved in spendthrift trust considerations is an important part of the Trusts course. Distinctions often turn on the type of clause (Spendthrift, Support or Discretionary, as outlined above), whether the clause applies to both voluntary and involuntary transfers (although the restraint on one may be construed to include the other), the nature of the beneficiary's interest (life estate, term for years or other), the real or personal nature of the trust assets, the precise terms of an applicable statute and standards set by it (e.g., amounts for "support" as used in a statute tend to indicate a "station in life" test by which the person who has traditionally overspent may be allowed more than one who has been frugal), whether the claim is for "necessaries," and the type of creditor who is attempting to reach the trust (spouse and issue, Governmental, contract creditor, etc.).

Among the related issues involved in spendthrift trusts, are the effect of consent or participation by the beneficiary or the trustee and the effect of transfers (or claims by) the trustee to a third party or against the beneficiary.

8. FUNDED AND UNFUNDED LIFE INSURANCE TRUSTS, LAND TRUSTS

Trusts can be classified by the assets which they contain. The "ideal" trust assets to administer from the viewpoint of professional fiduciaries are the most liquid forms of investments—cash, marketable securities, etc. The ease of management and conversion of these assets is unequaled by other types of investments. The least desirable trust assets to administer are the high risk or thin equity assets—especially businesses and multiple-unit slum dwellings. It is common to classify the trust by the type of assets because of the relative desirability. Good drafting also requires that the trustee powers and duties correspond to the type of asset included in the trust.

Insurance Trusts are trusts which contain insurance policies upon the life of the settlor or another person (such as the settlor's spouse or parent) as their only (i.e., an unfunded trust) or principal but not only (i.e., funded trust) asset. The trusts are primarily designed for tax features and the funded

v. unfunded and revocable v. irrevocable features are therefore the most important. Elaborate provisions of the Internal Revenue Code (and comparable state income tax laws) govern the taxability of the transfers into and from the trust, the payment of premiums and the income and deductions of the life insurance trusts.

A "land trust," as such, simply indicates that the corpus of the trust is partly, predominately or completely realty, as opposed to personalty.

9. MASSACHUSETTS BUSINESS TRUSTS AND ILLINOIS LAND TRUSTS

The law of a particular state may permit a variation on the usual pattern of trusts. The lawyer's penchant for labeling is exercised and another classification of trust is born. Examples of classification by particular state law are the Massachusetts business trust and the Illinois land trust.

The Massachusetts business trust is simply an extension of the trust concept into the field of business organizations. Instead of organizing as a partnership or corporation, the trust form is used. Many so-called "mutual funds" are organized as Massachusetts business trusts. An investor, instead of being issued a "share" of stock received a "certificate of beneficial interest" which is approximately the same thing.

The Illinois land trust is used to convert realty into personalty on paper only. Equitable conversion of realty to personalty occurs when one who contracts to sell the realty is regarded as having sold the realty, even though the sales transaction is still in the form of an unexecuted valid contract. Thus, if the seller dies before completing the paperwork which he is legally required to do (i.e., sign and deliver a deed and accept money in exchange) the court of equity will regard the decedent as the owner of personal, rather than real, property. Most states treat an immediate duty upon the trustee to sell realty as being similar to a contract to sell the realty; the duty to convey is regarded by equity as having been performed. Illinois, however, carries this principle to a logical extreme and regards many long-range duties to sell as if they were immediate duties to sell. Thus, in Illinois, it is possible to convert realty, on paper, into personalty by placing the realty into trust and imposing an ultimate duty upon the trustee to sell the land.

The distinction between personalty and realty is important for a number of reasons. The distinction generally governs the proper jurisdiction to administer the decedent's estate, but does not do so in the case of a trust unless the trust is terminated by its own terms upon the death of the settlor. Because the property is managed and distributed in accordance with its terms, the property is not subject to probate administration. This distinction can be important for state death tax purposes.

Both the Massachusetts business trust and the Illinois land trust are rather obscure and unlikely objects for examination purposes, but they illustrate both the tendency to label trusts with many catego-

ries and the tendency for local law variations to
permit a great variety of trusts.

10. TOTTEN AND FARKAS
v. WILLIAMS TRUSTS

Some trusts of particular nature derive their
name from the cases in which they were found to be
valid. (A finding of invalidity tends to reduce the
repetitions.)

Totten trusts, derived from Matter of Totten
(1904) (also called "tentative trusts" because of
their hesitant creation and more accurately called
"bank account trusts") are purported trusts in
which a depositor in a savings account executes a
writing filed with the bank which declares that he
or she is the trustee of that account for another
person, but retains the passbook and, typically, does
no other acts indicating trust intent. Matter of
Totten considered the trust to be valid, but held
that it had special rules as to revocability. It was
deemed to be revocable unless acts or statements to
the contrary were done or made. This, of course, is
the opposite of the general rule that trusts are
irrevocable unless stated to the contrary. The New
York justification included the concept of "tentative" status as a trust.

The importance of the Totten trust is that it
permits a means of indicating a successor to the
particular asset (the savings account, a very commonly owned asset) without the expense, bother
and formality of a will (i.e., it is a "will substitute")

and without the disadvantages of joint tenancy (requiring a present gift of an undivided interest,
thereby losing control, flexibility and revocability).

The presence of a Totten trust raises the issue of
its validity; although most jurisdictions permit such
a trust (and a number further validate the practice
by statute), some decisions have considered such a
trust to be too tentative or violative of the purposes
of the Statute of Wills. If the Totten trust is valid,
additional issues may arise such as whether the
revocation can be by will and, if so, whether a
residual clause of the will revokes the trust.

Farkas v. Williams (1955) validated what is probably the "thinnest" possible trust. Capitalizing on
the fact that no particular trust attribute is essential (revocability, independence of trustee, trustor
and beneficiary of each other, independence of the
trustee, etc.) a trust was created in which the
settlor retained, in one capacity or another, virtual-
ly every bit of control over the property. The trust
was revocable by the settlor; he was also the life
beneficiary with right to direct the trustee to sell
the assets of the trust and distribute the proceeds to
him and he was also the trustee with a power to sell
the assets and terminate the trust. Only if none of
these terminating powers was exercised did the
remainder pass to another person. The Illinois
court upheld the trust and it served as the model
for other trusts (predominately for securities) urged
upon consumers as a means of "avoiding probate."

*

PART IV

TRUST ADMINISTRATION

CHAPTER 11

TRUSTEE POWERS AND DUTIES

A. IN GENERAL

Trustee powers, duties and liabilities are interrelated. A power is the negative form of a duty (one is not under a duty not to do the act) and may be derived from a duty. For example, the power to sell and the power to invest are natural outgrowths of the duty to make the trust corpus productive. Liabilities of the trustee arise when a duty is breached.

The primary source of trustee powers and duties is normally the trust instrument, but a writing is only required by the Statute of Frauds for dealings in real property. The settlor's contemporary (but not subsequent unless the trust is revocable or amendable) statements of intention are admissible unless barred by the parol evidence rule. The trust terms may expressly or impliedly give or impose the powers or duties. Additionally, the law will infer additional powers and duties from the particular trust instrument's provisions or from the general law (decisional or statutory). See Uniform Probate Code §§ 7–301 and following.

The historical trends in court and legislative imposition of trustee duties are as follows: Originally, the passive "use" neither imposed duties nor gave powers to the trustee. As the active use, the "trust", became more common, a series of duties was imposed upon the trustees by the courts. Professional trustees appeared on the scene and sought both broader powers and narrower duties in order to carry out the remaining duties imposed. The courts gave mixed responses to this trend. The professional trustees had greater success with the legislatures. Statutes were enacted permitting a number of practices which would otherwise constitute breaches of strict trust duties—registering securities in the name of a nominee rather than the trustee, combining investments in a common trust fund etc.

A related fiduciary, the personal representative of a decedent's estate, was more heavily regulated by statute. It has become very common for legislatures to spell out in great detail the powers and duties of the executor or administrator of a decedent's estate. The Uniform Probate Code is the leader in permitting the exercise of powers without direct court supervision when there is no objection by those interested in the estate administration.

When there are multiple fiduciaries, unanimous action is required unless the trust instrument permits otherwise.

B. POWERS OF THE TRUSTEE

1. SALES, LEASES AND MORTGAGES

Normally a power of sale of trust assets is found in the trust instrument. If not expressly given, a power may be inferred from the duty to make the property productive, unless there is a specific prohibition against sale. Normally, a prohibition against sale will be given effect, but the court may allow a deviation in the administrative provision prohibiting a sale, if the circumstances warrant such a deviation. An intention that the property not be sold may also be inferred from the trust instrument, the surrounding circumstances such as the character of the property (e.g., realty or family corporation stock originally belonging to the settlor) or the purposes of the trust (e.g., a funded life insurance trust, in which a sale of the life insurance policy may be unreasonable). An authorization to retain is not necessarily a direction to retain the property.

The power of sale is not a completely unfettered discretion. The trustee must still act in a reasonable and prudent manner, obtain a fair price, seek broad exposure to the market, accept only cash or terms which are reasonably secured and not sell to himself or his own close relatives.

Usually the power to lease also exists. For unimproved realty, the power to lease is a reasonable alternative to sale. For other tangible personalty and improved realty, the leasing raises problems of depreciation; with existing leaseholds, patents and copyrights, there is a problem of depletion. In all cases of leases, there is the problem of whether the trustee has power to lease the trust assets for a period longer (or potentially longer) than the trust duration. The typical trust arrangement involves a life estate and remainder. Can the trustee lease for a period which is different than the life tenant's life? Few lessees could be found for the period of the trust, and the power to lease for a longer period is therefore generally conceded by the court.

Often prospective tenants request that an option to purchase be included with the lease. Generally options to purchase are not permitted to be given by the trustee because of the one-sided nature of such an option. The tenant would ordinarily exercise the option only if the property has increased in value between the times that the option was given and exercised. The trustee has, therefore, abandoned the possibility of getting a higher price by giving an option. In order for an option to be a proper exercise of the trustee's duty of care, it would have to be shown that the option and lease terms, individually, constitute arrangements which could not otherwise have been made, i.e., the lease would not otherwise have been possible and the sale would not otherwise have been possible at the same terms.

Mortgages or other pledges of trust property in order to secure a loan to the trust are rarely permitted—or wise. Normally, such a power will not be inferred, even if a power of sale is given. Possibly a pledge may be allowed if there is an emergency and court supervision or approval of the mortgage or pledge cannot be obtained in advance. Generally, loans to the trust are not permitted, even if unsecured. If secured, the probability is that the amount borrowed is less than the probable sale price of the same property. The difference between the mortgage and the sale price is the amount which the trustee has "spent" in order to have the right to restore himself to the status before the mortgage or pledge was given. Contrast the situation where the property is received in the trust subject to a mortgage. In that event, the trustee has the option of investing additional trust capital into the asset by paying off the debt secured by the mortgage or of selling the asset which is subject to the mortgage. Although it is common business practice to buy property subject to a mortgage, such investments are often considered improper for a trustee in the absence of specific trust provision authorizing or directing them.

2. INVESTMENTS, IMPROVEMENTS AND EXCHANGES

Investments are not only permitted but are required by the trustee's general duty to make property productive. In making investments, the trustee must exercise due care, be loyal, diversify the investments and earmark the trust assets. These duties are analyzed below. The power to "manage" the trust assets is normally sufficient to imply the power of investment, even if it were not inferred because of the duty to make trust assets productive.

Improvements are often distinguished from repairs on the basis of the greater cost and lifespan of the improvements combined with their tendency to increase the usable lifespan of the asset improved. While the duty to repair is easily inferred, the power to improve is dependent upon express trust language or the need to make the improvement to carry out the purposes of the trust. The power to improve is not so readily found, but may be granted by the court even if not given by the terms of the trust instrument. An improvement can be viewed as an additional investment in the property being improved; as such, it is necessary that the improvement comply with all the duties of a trustee concerning investments. The duty to diversify is the most likely duty to be breached by the improvement of a trust asset; there may also be a breach of the standard of care.

Exchanges are within the power of a trustee who has the power to do the two things which constitute an exchange—sell asset # 1 and purchase asset # 2. At times, an exchange may be a better (e.g., for tax reasons) or only (e.g., a corporate reorganization) way of acquiring the new asset. Each of the two parts is examined separately for conformity with the duties required of a trustee; if all are satisfied on both aspects, the exchange is permissible.

3. DISCRETIONARY POWERS

The more common situation in professionally drafted trust instruments is not the absence of a power but the fact that the trustee has been given broad discretion in his, her or its exercise of the power. If discretion is expressly given to the trustee in the exercise of the power, the court will not ordinarily interfere with the exercise or non-exercise of the power unless the action or inaction is beyond the bounds of a reasonable judgment or is the product of dishonesty or improper motive. Improper motives include spite or the furthering of interests of persons (either the trustee or third persons) other than the beneficiary.

The trust instrument which confers the discretion will either impose a standard by which the reasonableness of the exercise can be tested, or it will not. In either case, the court will interfere with the exercise of a valid discretion only when the trustee acts beyond the bounds of reasonable judgment. The imposition of a standard by the trust instrument will aid the court in determining what is beyond the bounds of reasonable judgment. The court will ordinarily allow the trustee full discretion within those bounds even though the court might have acted differently if it were determining the same question.

EXAMPLE: S bequeaths a fund in trust to T to pay so much of the income and principal as T, in his judgment, should deem necessary for the support, maintenance and education of A. The amount necessary to maintain A in the style of living to which she is accustomed is reasonably between $1,500 and $2,000 a month. T may expend any amount between $1,500 and $2,000 a month; deviations from that acceptable range are subject to revision by the court. If T expends only $1,500 a month, but is the remainderman who will receive unexpended amounts, T's action may be revised by the court.

The standard imposed upon the trustee may be more specific—e.g., in the Example, above, if the standard used was "as is necessary to maintain the standard of living enjoyed by her immediately before my death, having regard to the other assets and the income from them that is available to assist her." The standard could also be so vague as to be no standard whatsoever, e.g., "whatever she wants," "keep her happy" etc.

4. DEVIATION

Changes in the administrative, as opposed to dispositive, provisions of a trust are a "deviation" from the trust. Such a deviation is required in cases where the terms are not lawful or are impossible to comply with. The trustee may also ask the court for permission to deviate from other administrative provisions when they do not appear to be in the best interests of the trust or its beneficiaries or were not in the contemplation of the settlor. Note that the deviation is concerned with the administration of the trust and does not (except incidentally) change the shares of any of the beneficiaries. Contrast the charitable trust doctrine of cy pres which changes dispositive provisions from one charity to another.

The closest that the doctrine of deviation comes to a change of beneficial interests is an acceleration of the vested interest of the beneficiary, usually a minor, despite a direction to withhold the property until a given age. The pressing present need of the minor for the funds or other property is a sufficient change of circumstances to permit the court to order earlier payment of part or all of the trust property to the needy beneficiary. One limit to this doctrine is the requirement that the interest of no other beneficiary be impaired by the earlier payment to this beneficiary. Thus, a contingent trust interest which requires, for example, survival in order to take the principal, would not be a proper subject for this deviation from the instruction to withhold the funds until the beneficiary attains a certain age.

C. DUTIES OF THE TRUSTEE

1. AN APPROACH TO TRUST ADMINISTRATION PROBLEMS

Many trust administration problems can be approached as if they were an unintentional tort— duty, breach, causation, defenses and damages:

a. Duty

A "breach of trust" is a breach of a trust *duty*. The nature, extent and source of each of the trust duties should be known. Often an old, vague duty may take on new meaning in new situations. The

pages which follow describe the major trust duties—
Loyalty, to Administer, Make Productive, Earmark,
Account, Nondelegation, Diversification, Impartiality and Accounting. Some duties have both positive
and negative phrasings; for example, the duty of
loyalty includes the duty not to self-deal, and the
duty to earmark includes the duty not to commingle.

b. Breach

Because of the higher standards imposed by the
fiduciary duties, breaches can more easily be found.
The trustee seldom has a de minimis defense. It is
usually sufficient to explain how the act done is
inconsistent with the duty imposed.

c. Causation

Slight, and in some cases nonexistent, causation
likens many breach of trust cases more to strict
liability than to negligence. For example, a trustee
may be liable for the loss in marketable securities
which were an appropriate investment, but which
declined in value if the trustee failed to earmark the
securities. Although earmarking the securities
would not have prevented the loss, it would have
made it more difficult for the trustee to shift the
trustee's own loss securities into the trust portfolio.
This aspect of the liability of the trustee for breach
of trust is less important than in Torts.

d. Defenses

The exceptions and defenses to charges of breach of trust generally come from one of four sources:

(1) An exculpatory clause in the trust instrument may relieve or reduce the trustee's duties, but the trustee cannot be relieved of liability for reckless, intentional or bad faith acts. Some duties (e.g., to account or loyalty) are so basic that attempts to relieve the trustee of the duty raise the question whether a trust was intended.

(2) Statutory authority for deviation from traditionally required fiduciary practices. Statutes may permit corporate trustees to hold securities in the name of a nominee (thus breaching what would otherwise be the duty to earmark) or to use a common trust fund (thus violating the duty to be impartial and loyal to each trust and the duty to keep the trust assets separate). Generally, these statutes are valid. They seldom relieve individual trustees of liability.

(3) Specific permission from the court to do the particular act. Although prudence dictates that prior consent is wiser, some technical breaches may receive retroactive validation. Nevertheless, it is necessary to explain to the court the reason why the general rule should not apply to this situation of this trust.

(4) Express consent of all beneficiaries when they are both fully informed and able to consent. The presence of any beneficiary who is not sui juris

deprives this exception of full force. The requirement of a complete and honest explanation in a
noncoercive setting tends to make the consent even
rarer. Many factual variations on this theme are
available. Some beneficiaries may be barred by a
knowing consent while others, not having consented
or not able to consent, will not be barred. The
settlor of a revocable trust can also consent.

e. Damages

The analogy to strict liability holds true in the
area of damages. The trustee is liable for money
damages which often have no relation to any gain
made by the trustee. Additionally, other equitable
forms of relief may be imposed, such as rescission of
a transfer or setting aside some other act or requiring positive action on the part of the trustee. In
severe cases, the breach may lead to additional
damages in the form of removal of the trustee and
perhaps denial of compensation in part or wholly.
A related issue which often arises is the ability to
offset gains made on one transaction against losses
on another with the touchstone being that the court
does not want to encourage further gambling by the
trustee and therefore, the court will not allow "separate" transactions (an equitable conclusion) to be
offset against each other.

This "tort" approach should be kept in mind in
examining the various trust duties which follow.

2. LOYALTY (DUTY NOT TO SELF–DEAL)

The greatest duty of a fiduciary is the duty of loyalty. The duty is inherent in the fiduciary relationship, i.e., it will attach because of the fiduciary relationship and is not derived from particular wording in the trust instrument. This concept of loyalty extends to all fiduciaries, not merely trustees, but is examined here primarily in relation to trustees. The duty is both positive—the duty to administer the trust solely for the benefit of the beneficiary—and negative—the duty not to deal with the beneficiary on the trustee's behalf without full disclosure and fair dealing.

The duty of loyalty is very strong in the trust setting. For example, in Magruder v. Drury (1914) a breach of trust was found when one of two trustees was also one of two partners in a real estate brokerage which regularly charged ordinary commissions on purchases and sales of notes secured by mortgages. The decedent-settlor had engaged in similar business with the co-trustee during his lifetime. The trustees invested trust funds through the partnership. The commissions charged by the partnership in the ordinary course of business were no larger than it charged others and the trust could not have purchased the investments at a lower price elsewhere. The court stated that although no wrong was intended and none was in fact done to the trust, the co-trustee could not profit from the trust. He was, accordingly, required to return one-half of the profits made by his two-man partnership from the business with the trust of which he was co-trustee. Note the absence of both causation and actual loss to the trust in this situation. The trustee was required to disgorge profits not because he had done wrong, but because his acts had the appearance of doing wrong. The salutary concept of loyalty requires an extreme disinterest. Perhaps this is a carryover of the concept of having the harem guarded by eunuchs.

This concept of disallowing ("requiring the trustee to account for") any potential profit by the trustee is logically extended to all cases in which the trustee sells or buys anything or renders any service (except as trustee) to the trust. Trustees who are casualty insurance salespeople or commission securities salespeople and who sell to the trust face a dilemma because they are required by trust law to return the commission and often forbidden by insurance or securities law from giving discounts. Attorneys who perform legal services such as defending a lawsuit or giving tax advice may not make a profit from such services. A trustee who serves as his or her own lawyer does not have a choice of which capacity he or she will be compensated in. The only position for which compensation can be claimed is the trustee position. To permit payment to himself or herself as attorney would be to allow him or her to profit from the trusteeship. The only profit permitted is the fee for serving as trustee, even though it is lower than the rates ordinarily charged by the same person when serving as a lawyer.

The trustee who purchases trust assets is similarly placed in the worst possible position by the options which are available to the beneficiaries: They can insist upon a return of the item sold (if it has not been sold to a bona fide purchaser) or claim any profits made by the trustee (whether or not resold) or can confirm the sale. The trustee is entitled to the return of the purchase price, often with interest, and the amount (or perhaps only the value) of any improvements made to the property if the trustee is required to return the property. Any changes in value of the property between the time of the sale and the time that the beneficiaries are allowed to take action is at the expense of the trustee: If the property goes up in value, the beneficiaries can seek return of the item itself or an accounting of the profits; if the item drops in value, the beneficiaries can ratify the sale.

Good faith of the trustee does not prevent the imposition of liability for the breach of trust, although it is relevant in determining whether further action (such as removal as trustee or denial of commissions) should be taken. The trustee breaches the duty of loyalty simply by buying, directly or indirectly, trust assets. The price paid by the trustee may be as high as, or even higher than, the price which could be obtained from others, but the court insists that a breach has occurred. One rationale for the strictness of this approach is that the trustee has such control over the manner and advertising of the sale that even a subconscious desire that no other buyer be found must be defended against.

It is not a defense to an action by the beneficiaries that the sale was fairly conducted by third persons or conducted by auction, since the third persons and auctioneers were chosen by the trustee.

The trustee cannot do indirectly that which he or she is forbidden to do directly. Thus, the purchase through an intermediary does not prevent liability of the trustee. However, in certain cases, if the trust connection has been broken, the purchase by the trustee is permitted. Thus, if the trustee is no longer trustee or if he or she purchases from one who purchased from the trust, the sale will not be set aside or otherwise subject to attack unless it can be shown that the trustee used information gained while serving as trustee or had prearranged the purchase prior to the resignation or sale to the third party.

The self-benefiting may be the purchase from the trust, the sale to it or an incidental profit or commission on either sale. Sales to the trust pose problems of determining exactly what constitutes the "profit" of the selling trustee. For example, assume that the trustee purchased an asset at $1,000 in year 1 and then, in year 2 when the asset was worth $3,000, sold it to the trust for $4,000. It is obvious that the excess of the purchase price over the value at the time of sale ($4,000 minus $3,000 = $1,000) should be returned to the trust. Should the difference between the price paid by the trustee in year 1 and the value in year 2 also be recovered? Some authorities say that the issue should be decided by whether the trustee purchased the asset with an intention to sell to the trust and that in the absence of such an intention, the trustee is not required to surrender the "profit." Consider further, in the same situation, if the selling trustee, in year 3, when the asset was worth $4,000 sold it for $5,000 to a third person or the trustee himself or herself. Are there two breaches or none? What is the measure of damages?

Corporate trustees, unless exempted by statute, have great difficulties with the duty of loyalty. Many of the things which could be done more efficiently by a bank with trust powers pose potential problems of loyalty. Use of a checking account in the trustee bank is a breach of the duty of loyalty, but going to a competitor to open an account for the trust is wasteful and embarrassing. Larger banks often participate in stock offerings which may be attractive trust investments, but the duty of loyalty is breached if the trust purchases any of the securities offered. Similarly, various departments of the bank are in a good position to evaluate and make loans on real property. The process of evaluation is often done by the loan department (in which case the bank as trustee would be purchasing services from itself) or by the trust department (in which case any loan not made by the trust department, but made by the loan department would be subject to the charge that the bank had taken a trust opportunity for its own profit). Often a loan would be too large for a particular trust, but could be shared by a number of small trusts. Mortgage "participations" by which one loan is made by a number of trusts raise a number of problems—earmarking, loyalty and propriety of investment being among them. Investment of the trust assets in stock of the trustee bank may be a breach of the duty of loyalty because other shareholders (and particularly the large shareholders who often control the bank) would not want the market value of the stock to drop. Thus, there would be pressure to continue to hold the trust stock even when there is knowledge in the corporate hierarchy of factors which would cause the value of the shares to drop. The problem is aggravated when the principal trust asset is the controlling stock interest of the trustee bank, for example a testamentary trust of the bank's founder.

As indicated above, the rigors of the duty of loyalty can be eased by statutory provisions (as is often the case for corporate trustees), exculpatory clauses in the trust instrument, court order or beneficiary consent. Such provisions are seldom inferred. For example, in Magruder v. Drury, described above, the trustee was merely continuing a course of conduct done during the lifetime of the settlor. Post-death sales of real estate mortgages were breaches of trust even though the trustee had made similar pre-death sales to the settlor; the pre-existing business arrangements were not considered to be an inferred exculpation from breaches of the duty of loyalty. On the other hand, an inference of an exculpatory provision is found in distinctions made between initial and subsequent trust investments. If the settlor placed assets, e.g., stock of the corporate trustee, in the trust, the trustee is not necessarily under a duty to sell the assets even though they might be an improper investment if purchased by the trustee.

One who is a trustee for a number of trusts may purchase from one trust for the benefit of a second trust, but the purchase and sale must be fair to both trusts. The thin line of such absolute fairness and the subjectiveness of what is "fair" combined with the devastating effect of hindsight suggest that it is an unwise experiment.

The concept of loyalty in fiduciary situations has been extended to require fairness in dealings with business opportunities by partners and corporate fiduciaries, e.g., directors. The concept of "corporate opportunity" is directly derived from the theory that a trustee should not profit from his trust.

The duty of loyalty also extends to the purchase of adverse interests. For example, if the trust property is subject to a lien or other encumbrance and the trustee acquires the claim in the trustee's individual capacity, it is a breach of trust. On the other hand, a debt owed to the trustee at the time the trustee assumes the office is not necessarily a breach of the duty of loyalty. Naming someone as trustee is not properly used as a means of compromising just debts. Another example of a trust opportunity is a renewal of a lease in which the trust is tenant; the trustee cannot renew in his or her individual capacity.

Trust ownership of a controlling interest in a corporation poses (in addition to problems of proper investment) problems of loyalty in the voting of shares for director and corporate officer positions. If the trustee uses the trust voting power, alone, to elect himself or herself to a compensated position in which he or she had not previously served, there is a breach of the duty of loyalty even though the compensation is earned. It is more difficult when the voting power is merely added to that which was already possessed by the trustee and most difficult to find liability when the individual was in the corporate position prior to becoming trustee.

3. DUTY TO ADMINISTER

The duty to administer is the generic duty imposed upon a trustee of an active trust by virtue of the trust relationship. It is a positive duty to go forward which arises without specific language in the trust instrument. The trustee should do what is necessary for the good of the trust and those who are interested in it. The duty to administer applies to both the terms of the trust and to the assets held by the trust. Thus, the trustee is liable for knowledge of and compliance with the terms of the trust (e.g., notifying beneficiaries of their rights and making distributions when required) and is also liable for errors and omissions in the management of the trust property (e.g., failure to maintain properly).

The general duty to administer is the well-spring of many other, more specific duties: The duties of loyalty and impartiality are aspects of proper administration of a trust. The duties to make productive and to account also can be traced to the generic duty to do that which is correct.

The trustee's duty to gather the assets of the trust, preserve and make them productive and distribute them in accordance with the terms of the trust may pose problems which are not specifically dealt with by the trust instrument or other trust duties. The trustee can seek the advice of the appropriate court if the trustee is in doubt, e.g., as to the wisdom of abandoning a valueless asset or maintaining or defending a claim in litigation.

4. DUTY TO MAKE PRODUCTIVE INVESTMENTS

The duty to make productive is express or implied in most trusts, but is not an essential trust duty. The trustee may be appointed for the purpose of preserving real or personal property in its present form and delivering title or possession upon the happening of some event, e.g., attaining age 21 or the payment of a debt. The trustee's duty to delivery realty, chattels or intangibles in kind negates a duty to make productive.

The duty to make productive is generally applied in a practical and reasonable manner. If the assets of the trust include an unproductive asset, e.g. undeveloped land, and the duty to make productive exists, e.g., by express provision or implied from trust terms such as a long-term trust with a direction to pay "income" to the beneficiary, the trustee will be allowed a reasonable time to make the property productive. In the case of undeveloped realty in which there is no duty to deliver the realty title to a beneficiary, it may be possible to rent the property in unimproved condition, e.g., as a farm or city parking lot. If not, the trustee would normally sell the property rather than build upon it. If the unproductive property is money on deposit in a checking account, (as opposed to undeveloped land), the time to invest would be less since the trustee does not have to sell in order to reinvest.

It is not necessary to make every penny of the trust funds productive. A reasonable amount of money can be retained in a checking account in order to pay current trust distributions and expenses. How much is "reasonable" is, of course, a matter of judgment.

Although a trustee may be liable for the (net?) income which should have been produced but was not actually produced, it is more difficult for the aggrieved beneficiary to hold the trustee liable than it is to seek apportionment of ultimate profit if the unproductive property is sold at a profit. The issue of trustee liability is second to the question of the rights of the beneficiaries among themselves. The trustee will not be liable except in egregious cases: There are issues of reasonableness of the amount reserved for anticipated future expenses and distributions, the reasonableness of the amount of time necessary in order to reinvest and possibly only a case of underproductiveness, as opposed to unproductiveness. The liability of the trustee, if any, is usually only for the income which would have been produced. Absent bad faith, there is not reasonable cause to remove a trustee (or deny compensation) for failure to make a trust asset productive.

On the other hand, a few depression-era cases held trustees liable for failure to make property productive when funds were left too long on deposit, without interest, in banks which failed. Presumably the same rule would be applied today to the extent the amount on deposit exceeded recoveries under federal insurance plans for banks and savings and loan associations. The absence of causation did not bother the courts in imposing liability. A strict penalty was imposed upon the failure to make the property productive. This line of cases does not seem to be consistent with either the general test of "reasonableness" of the duty to make productive or the tendency to seek causation for imposing penalties upon trustees except in cases of failure to earmark.

The pattern for permissible investments consists of an overlay of the trust provisions superimposed upon statutory patterns which are in turn superimposed upon case law. The absence of total certainty in this portion of trust law is the price of case-by-case determination of appropriateness of particular investments. Except when impossible, illegal or impractical due to a change in circumstances, the dictates of the settlor—whether expanding or contracting the permissible investments—must be followed. These provisions can change even statutory restrictions upon investments. Statutory provisions usually either contain a list of investments which in turn are either permissive (allowing trustees to make other types of investments) or restrictive (considering no other investment to be proper), or the statutory provisions may consist of a "prudent man" rule which is probably the most common statutory and judicial approach.

The prudent man rule for investments as phrased in Harvard College v. Amory (1830) stated that a trustee "is to observe how men of prudence, discretion and intelligence manage their own affairs, not in regard to speculation, but in regard to permanent disposition of their funds, considering the probable income, as well as the probable safety of the capital to be invested." This test stressed two contradictory points—probable income and probable safety. The amount of income which a given amount will produce increases as the degree of risk increases. Thus, a highly speculative investment such as a new business or vacant land purchased as an investment, might produce a great (though uncertain) gain (income) but it also imposes a substantial risk upon the capital. At the same time, federal governmental bonds tend to be as secure as the monetary system, but produce a very low income because of the small risk. Thus, in the ordinary case neither investment is a proper investment for the entire trust corpus. The bonds might be a proper investment for a portion of the trust, but the new business would generally not be considered proper because it is "speculative".

The prudent **man** rule is being subjected to changes which are more than politically correct gender-neutral terminology. The Restatement, 3d, Trusts introduced the prudent **investor** concept and renamed the restatement to emphasize it:

Restatement, 3d, Trusts (Prudent Investor Rule) § 227

The trustee is under a duty to the beneficiaries to invest and manage the funds of the trust as a prudent investor would, in light of the purposes, terms, distribution requirements, and other circumstances of the trust.

(a) This standard requires the exercise of reasonable care, skill, and caution, and is to be applied to investments not in isolation but in the context of the trust portfolio and as a part of an overall investment strategy, which should incorporate risk and return objectives reasonably suitable to the trust.

(b) In making and implementing investment decisions, the trustee has a duty to diversify the investments of the trust unless, under the circumstances, it is prudent not to do so....

The Restatement, 3d seeks to modernize trust investment law and "to restore the generality and flexibility of the original doctrine." The rules are "intended to reflect the lessons derived from modern experience and research, without endorsing or excluding any particular theories of economics or investment." This flexibility would permit expert trustees to pursue "non-traditional strategies when appropriate to the particular trust" while providing other trustees "reasonably clear guidance to safe harbors that are practical, adaptable, readily identifiable and expectedly rewarding."

In examining investments, no particular investment is always inappropriate or always permissible. This relative validity of investments leads naturally to examination questions in which the student should be able to identify probabilities, reasons for the probabilities and then proceed on the alternate theories that the investment(s) is/are proper or improper.

Certain trends in acceptability can be identified:

Government obligations of the United States, the state in which the trust is administered, other states (if no history of default and if adequately secured) and cities and governmental bonding districts (within certain limits) are generally the most acceptable traditional trust investments, in the order of preference stated. Note that such items, almost always found on statutory lists, favor the remainderman over the income beneficiary by being more safe than income-producing and have no protection against inflation.

Debt obligations secured by a first mortgage on real estate which has a value with a good margin over the amount owed is another traditionally first-quality investment. There are dangers that the property may drop in value, that the improvements may be destroyed and the title might be defective.

The percentage of value which commercial lenders will lend today (between 70 and 90 percent and up to 97 percent with federal insurance programs) is so high that trusts (unless protected by the federal insurance) cannot compete in the investment market. Second mortgages are considered to be improper investments in most cases, but the amount of the first mortgage might be so small that a second mortgage would not be an improper investment.

Corporate bonds, especially for utilities or quasi-governmental organizations are also highly regarded. It is still possible for the bonds to be a poor investment, e.g., in a railroad which has gone through bankruptcy reorganizations in the recent past.

Equity securities (stock of corporations) are investments which have met increasing approval. Although an investment in a new business is too speculative to be a proper investment in most cases, there are now greater safeguards in the security industry and more established and supervised corporations than at the time that trust investment policies were being formulated. Today, most states permit investments in the common or preferred stock of established companies.

Another investment which has met increasing approval because of federal protection is the unsecured loan to a banking corporation represented by a savings account of certificate of deposit. The latter item usually has a time restriction on withdrawal of funds (backed by forfeiture of income) and is therefore less desirable in a short-term trust. Federal insurance of deposits in banks and savings and loan associations has tended to make proper one part of an otherwise improper investment— unsecured loans.

New businesses and land remain the least appropriate investments. The speculative nature of both makes income uncertain and may risk the principal. A farm or an apartment house requires more skill and attention than the average trustee would possess or be able to devote. Trades and businesses, speculative investments and investments for capital gains are also generally considered improper, although they might be permitted in particular cases.

The "mutual fund", a trust or corporation which carries on the business of investing in other businesses, may be an improper investment because of the nature of the companies in which it invests even though it does accomplish a diversification. The presence of a mutual fund in the trust portfolio also raises questions of potentially improper delegation of the investment power and, more importantly, raises difficult questions of allocation and apportionment of the ordinary income and capital gains distributed by the mutual fund.

In examining the propriety of investments, it should be kept in mind that an otherwise proper investment might be improper because it breaches other duties of the trustee such as the duty to diversify, to be loyal, to be impartial or not to delegate. This point can be highlighted by dividing questions concerning investments into two parts: (1) Is this a proper investment generally? and (2) Is this a proper type of investment for this trust now?

Courts are not always uniform in examining each investment in the context of other investments; in some cases, the investment must stand on its own. Similarly, there are questions of off-setting one investment gain against another investment loss that are not completely answered by the approach of considering them as being either separate transactions or one transaction.

The trustee must use the care and skill of a reasonable person (even if the trustee does not possess such care and skill) and commentators and some courts attempt to impose higher degrees of care and skill upon those professional trustees which advertise expertise in the field of trust management. See Uniform Probate Code § 7–302.

The time for determining the appropriateness of an investment is the time that it is made. (Of course the litigation process is such that almost all contested cases of investment judgment involve items which time ultimately proved to be poor investments.)

5. DUTY TO EARMARK (NOT TO COMMINGLE), NOMINEES

There are two duties involved in "earmarking": First, the trust assets should be separated from all other assets. Second, the assets should be clearly identified as belonging to this trust.

The trust assets should be physically separated from assets belonging to the trustee personally, third parties or other trusts. The non-separation most likely to impose liability upon the trustee is the commingling of the assets of the trust with the trustee's personal assets. If done with the intention to misappropriate, the commingling is embezzlement. It is a breach of trust whether or not the intention to appropriate is present. The court is strictest with this type of commingling because the appearance is the same whether or not the intention to misappropriate is present. The presence of that intention is somewhat subjective and the presence can be determined only after the fact has occurred. Thus, as a matter of preventive law, the courts impose strong penalties upon trustees who commingle trust assets with their own assets.

Assets belonging to third persons, especially other trusts, also need to be kept separate, but the possibility of misappropriation is less severe. The most difficult cases in this area concern multiple (or potentially multiple) trusts created by the same settlor. The strict rule is that the assets of the trusts must be kept separate. Often it is difficult to tell whether a combined trust for many beneficiaries (e.g., children) is intended or whether separate trusts are intended. For income tax purposes, separate trusts are usually desirable. However, if the trusts are separate, the assets need to be separated and unambiguously earmarked for the individual trusts. A technical breach may occur if the trustee does not realize that separate trusts are involved.

A situation in which potentially separate trusts can exist, but which is usually treated as one trust, occurs when there are additions or "pour-overs" to an existing trust. The settlor may reserve and exercise the right to make additions to his trust while living or by will. Others may contribute to the trust, e.g., a spouse may contribute to the trust created by the other spouse or a grandparent may contribute to a trust established by the parent. The terms of the addition (and sometimes the original trust) dictate whether a separate trust using the same terms is intended; normally the total amount is treated as one trust.

The need to keep trust assets separate is felt most by the person attempting to trace trust assets. Other fiduciary relationships such as attorney-client or the husband-wife situation in community property states involve "tracing" an asset through changes in form to its present status (e.g., realty sold, converted to cash which is used to acquire stock certificates). If a fiduciary mixes the "trust" property with his own, the court may require the fiduciary to separate the interests or to become the guarantor of the value of the fiduciary portion or the court may subject the entire mass to the fiduciary relationship. Equitable principles are involved in such tracing; therefore many factors are relevant: the degree of culpability in commingling, the ownership of the portion commingled, the good faith of the fiduciary, the relative values of the amounts commingled etc.

The "duty to earmark" involves the obligation of the trustee to mark the asset, as appropriate, with the indicia of ownership by him or her in the fiduciary relationship for the benefit of this particular trust. The method (which takes its name from one method of marking cattle) varies with the type of asset involved: Realty should have record title in the name of the trustee as trustee for the particular trust. Properly recorded trust ownership indicia is notice to prospective purchasers. The registration should be complete, however. Some states permit, by statute, a purchaser to ignore a designation of the record titleholder "as trustee" if there is not a fuller description of the trust.

Earmarking of intangibles which are represented by a document in registered form should be accomplished by the same means as registration of title to land—by describing the trustee "as trustee for the XYZ Trust under the will of John Jones, deceased" or "as trustee under the John Jones Trust created by instrument dated July 1, 1994." Tangible items should be "earmarked" in accordance with their nature. If there is documentation involved with the ownership, such as motor vehicle registration or bills of sale, the trust status should be clearly shown. Bearer bonds present the most difficulty: By theory, such bonds should not be a proper trust investment because the "bearer" (i.e., any person who has possession of them) is the owner. In practice, however, such bonds have traditionally been permitted and used as trust investments. Thus, no actual problem of earmarking is involved with bearer bonds—but the duty to keep separate (and secure) is more critical for such assets.

The duty to separate and the duty to earmark pose difficult, but not insurmountable, problems for professional fiduciaries. The traditional response of the banking organizations has been not to conform the industry's practice to the law, but to conform the law to the industry's practice. Statutes excuse many of the practices of combining trust assets and registering assets in the name of the bank without showing trust status or in the name of nominees (often bank officers), thus showing neither the name of the trustee nor the trust status. These "nominee" statutes are almost universal, but they are not uniform. Some statutes permitting registration of trust assets in the names of nominees are restricted to the type of fiduciary (corporate only or some or all trustees, executors etc.) while others are restricted in the type of investment which can be so registered (mortgages, stocks or other named investments or all investments).

When the duty to earmark exists (i.e., it has not been excused or eliminated by the trust instrument or statute) and it has been breached, there is a further question whether causation should be relevant. The older (and therefore most) cases did not require causation between the failure to earmark and the loss suffered by the trust. Thus, the trustee who failed to earmark became a guarantor of the principal (and often the income) of the trust. A loss occasioned by general economic conditions and which would not have been charged to the trustee in the absence of the technical breach of the duty to earmark was often charged to the trustee. This strict liability was justified as penalizing the trustee for being careless or ignorant of the proper methods of administration and thereby unnecessarily subjecting the beneficiaries to risks (even though such risks did not come to pass). The Restatement, Trusts and Restatement, Second, Trusts § 179 advanced the position that the trustee should be liable only for bad faith failure to earmark. There is some trend to follow the Restatement position and ease the punishments inflicted upon the ignorant, but good faith, trustee.

6. DUTY TO ACCOUNT

The terms "account" and "accounting" are used in two senses. First, the "account" is the table of figures which show the financial condition of the trust, sometimes accompanied by a textual explanation. Second, the action of "account" is an equitable form of action by which fiduciaries (including resulting and constructive trustees) are called before the court to explain their actions as fiduciary. In the barest form, the account is simply financial statements—balance sheets showing the beginning and ending points and a profit and loss statement showing the changes between the two points. The beginning point of the first account is a statement of the assets received in the trust, which is usually part of the trust instrument for living trusts or the decree of distribution for testamentary trusts. For subsequent accounts, the beginning point is the ending point of the prior account. The account should show all receipts and disbursements, additions and subtractions and gains and losses on sales, exchanges and distributions. When rights of successive beneficiaries are involved, a breakdown of the items as principal and income is usually included. Finally, the account should end with a "Balance on Hand" which agrees mathematically with the prior balance as adjusted for the intervening action and which can be verified by examination of ownership certificates of the items claimed to be on hand. The trustee should obtain, preserve and have available for inspection by concerned parties documentation (e.g., receipts, canceled checks etc.) for each item. The trustee should also permit examination of the trust assets and the trust books. See also Uniform Probate Code § 7–303(c).

The duty to account has a number of subsidiary duties which can be enlarged or diminished by the trust terms or by statute. Actions of the trustee should be noted by writings which are preserved and available for inspection. The trustee should furnish the beneficiaries information concerning the trust and their shares in it. Any beneficiary can request that the trustee present an accounting. The trustee has a duty to verify facts upon which distributions are made such as death, remarriage, birth, age etc.

The importance of the duty to account, however, is that it is the opening round in resolving intra-trust disputes. As to matters presented in the account, the beneficiary is given notice by an account whether presented formally through a court or informally, directly to the beneficiary. Failure to object when able to do so constitutes acceptance. On the other hand, items not in the account (or items falsely presented) do not bar the beneficiary nor the court from examining them at a later time. If the beneficiary seeks to impose liability upon a trustee for something not shown in the account, the technique is to require the trustee to account for that item, e.g., secret profit by the trustee on dealings with the trust property, whether or not the duty of loyalty is also breached. The beneficiary's response to the trustee's account is to "object" to the inclusion (e.g., trustee expended trust funds for a contested purpose) or exclusion of the particular item. The trustee then has the burden of going forward, but generally makes a prima facie case by presenting receipts or other documentation or testimony in support of the contested items.

Because the duty to account is used as the procedural entry to the court, the duty to account traditionally could not be waived by the settlor of the trust. Some modifications are permissible to the duty, but the attempt to relieve the duty completely is inimical to the trust concept. However, the beneficiaries, if legally competent, may waive an account.

There is great diversity in statutory patterns concerning trust accounts. The variables focus upon whether the settlor can vary the requirement, the manner of creation of the trust (living or testamentary or both) and the desires of professional trustees to limit their liability by securing court approval of their actions. Statutes are more likely to require accounts from testamentary trustees, often continuing the jurisdiction of the probate court in order to do so. When accounts are required by beneficiary request or statute for living trusts, the court of equity generally is the proper court for the accounting action. The advantage of a court account in which a beneficiary is not required to take the initiative is sometimes offset by the cost, delay and lack of privacy involved in any court action. Some fiduciaries render private accountings to the beneficiaries thus barring later claims by beneficiaries who were sui juris.

The court which hears the account and the objections to it may wholly or partly approve or disapprove the account, order corrections, "surcharge" (i.e., state that the trustee is liable for an amount greater than the liability shown in the account), allow or deny trustee's compensation and expenses (including court costs and attorneys' fees) or remove the trustee. Approval of an account settles all matters truthfully presented in it, and possibly all misrepresentations which the beneficiaries, if competent, could have discovered with reasonable inquiry. The decree, like all decrees, can be reopened if there was fraud, concealment or mistake in the account or the order settling it.

The traditional phrasing of expenditures by the trustee is that the trustee "is entitled to reimbursement" from the trust, but actual practice is to pay the items from the trust and seek approval of the expenditure in the account. Thus, an account which shows disbursements is the occasion to challenge the nature, purpose or amount of the expenditure, but the hypocrisy of the phrasing is normally left untouched.

The amount of information which the trustee is required to supply the beneficiary varies. The fiduciary standard requires more than the arms-length dealings of persons contracting with each other. (Theorists insist that a trust is a conveyance which incurs fiduciary duties rather than a contract with or for the benefit of the beneficiary.) In ordinary dealings, the fiduciary is held to the standard of fairness in which all errors should be in favor of disclosure to the beneficiary (except, of course, information concerning other beneficiaries and their interests). Two situations in which an even higher duty is required are as follows: If a beneficiary is contemplating the sale of his or her interest in the trust, the trustee has a positive duty to give information which will assist the beneficiary in determining whether the price is fair. (The same duty does not extend to the prospective purchaser, apparently, until the sale has been completed. Then the purchaser is in the position of the beneficiary and is entitled to the information.) The other situation involves the marginal areas of the duty of loyalty. If the trustee is dealing with the beneficiary for the trustee's own benefit, the most complete and full disclosure is required. The logical extension of this principle is that attempts by the fiduciary, as fiduciary, to reduce or eliminate liability by submitting an account directly to the beneficiary (i.e., not through court proceedings) border on the self-interest field in which a fuller disclosure should be required. Computer printouts submitted directly to beneficiaries by corporate fiduciaries may be inadequate because of complexity or abbreviations.

7. DUTY NOT TO DELEGATE

A derivation of the duty to administer is the duty not to delegate the administration of the trust to others. When phrased in terms of the entire administration of the trust, the duty is absolute (unless expressly excused by the settlor in the trust terms, e.g., a trust in which the trustee holds only legal title and the beneficiary is allowed possession and management of the trust assets).

The duty not to delegate can be breached by delegation to other trustees—either co-trustees or successor trustees. Unless the trust instrument provides otherwise, the trustees must act unanimously. Any trustee who does not participate in the decision is therefore delegating the decision to the other trustees. A more subtle delegation is involved when a trustee attempts, unsuccessfully, to resign and delivers the trust assets to his "successor" (or resigns but delivers to an improperly appointed successor).

The damages for the breach of trust are both those which flow directly from the breach—liability for the negligence or other improper conduct of the delegate—and, in many cases, an additional penalty, without true causation, in the form of liability for all losses suffered during the period of delegation, even though if no breach were involved, the trustee would not have been liable for the damages.

Partial delegation, i.e., delegation to do particular acts, is permissible if prudent. A trustee can consult with others (and may have a duty to do so in particularly complicated matters) and may take advice from others, but the ultimate decision (and liability for it) remains with the trustee. The advice of counsel is a mitigating, but not an excusing factor in determining whether a trustee is liable for breach of trust. The more critical the decision (e.g., major sales and investments), the more important is the decision by the trustee.

No hard and fast rule is available to validate any delegation. Restatement, 3d, Trusts (Prudent Investor Rule) § 171 states that the trustee is under a duty to the beneficiaries to exercise fiduciary discretion and to act as a prudent person would act in deciding whether, to whom and in what manner to delegate fiduciary authority in the administration of a trust.

Among the factors to be considered in determining the appropriateness of a delegation of authority are the following: The nature and degree of discretion involved, the amount or value involved, efficiency and cost considerations in view of the property and activities involved, the relationship of the activities to the trustee's professional skills and the fairness in relation to the compensation of the trustee.

Restatement, 3d, Trusts (Prudent Investor Rule) § 171 is more accepting of delegation in situations in which "a prudent person might delegate those responsibilities to others."

The central theme of the duty not to delegate is that a trustee cannot seek to hide behind self-selected professional assistance. Having accepted the position as trustee, the trustee must carry out all of the functions except those which are dismissed as being "ministerial" rather than "discretionary."

8. DUTY TO DIVERSIFY

The duty of diversification was upgraded by Restatement, 3d, Trusts (Prudent Investor Rule) to be
part of the prudent investor rule: In the exercise of
the care and skill of a prudent investor, the risk of
loss should be spread among various types of investments. Placing the entire trust corpus into one
investment (or debts by one obligor) may not be
prudent under the circumstances. An easy example
of a breach of the duty to diversity (among other
duties) would be the deposit of funds in excess of
the maximum amount of federal insurance in a
bank or savings and loan association account.

Not all courts recognize the duty to diversify as a
separate duty. In jurisdictions which decline to
recognize the duty to diversify as a separate duty, it
is a factor in determining whether an investment is
prudent. The theoretical difference is important in
determining the appropriate measure of damages.
The failure to diversify calls for damages in the
amount by which the investment is excessive. If
the duty breached is the prudent investor rule, the
entire investment (rather than part of it) is improper and the damages are the entire loss.

Circumstances which are relevant in determining
both whether the duty to diversify is present and
whether, if present, it has been breached, include
the following:

• The approach of the particular jurisdiction as to
whether there is a separate duty to diversify.

• Language of the trust investment concerning the making and retention of investments. The duty to diversity, if it exists, can be expressly or impliedly waived by the settlor.

• Identity of the person who made the investment. An investment made by a trustee is more likely to be subjected to the duty to diversify than is an original investment by the settlor. Many jurisdictions have statutes which permit the retention of the assets in the form in which received in the trust; those jurisdictions eliminate both the broader duty of care and skill of the prudent investor as well as the subsidiary duty to diversify.

• The extent to which a single investment is, itself, diversified. If the entire trust corpus is invested in one mutual fund or one common trust investment fund, there would be diversification at the level of performing investment, but no diversification at the level of management immediately below the trustee level.

EXAMPLE: T invests, as trustee, the entire trust fund in Spread Mutual Fund, a diversified investment fund. The Fund suffers a large loss because of employee embezzlement. If the jurisdiction recognizes the duty to diversify, the trustee is liable to the beneficiaries to the extent of the loss suffered on the excessive investment. Thus, if a 30% investment would have been proper, 70% of the loss is charged to the trustee. If the duty to diversify is not a separate duty, the trustee may be liable for failure to exercise the care and skill of a prudent investor. If the embezzlement loss was the same amount to the trust, but occurred in one of the investments by the mutual fund, the duty to diversify is not so obviously violated.

9. DUTY OF IMPARTIALITY

Unless permitted or directed by the trust instrument to do otherwise, a trustee must act for the benefit of the trust as a whole and not favor the interests of one beneficiary over another.

The typical trust arrangement consists of a life estate and remainderpersons. The life tenant is benefited by the higher return of riskier investments and the remainderpersons are benefited by greater safety. Protection against loss due to inflation is more important to remainderpersons.

An instance in which the duty of impartiality is tested occurs when a trustee is requested to take certain action by one of several beneficiaries (either consecutive or concurrent). It would appear to be appropriate for the trustee to seek and obtain the approval of all other beneficiaries before doing any act which the trustee would not have done absent the beneficiary request. It may, however, be impossible to seek and obtain approval of unknown or contingent or minor beneficiaries. The trustee thus acts at the trustee's risk when the trustee follows the suggestions of some, but not all, beneficiaries. The requesting beneficiaries may be estopped from imposing liability upon the trustee for any breach of trust arising out of the requested transaction, but non-consenting beneficiaries are not estopped. The other duties imposed upon a trustee may create a dilemma. For example, the duty to make productive may conflict with the duty to preserve. Indeed, the concept of the prudent investor is one which balances income against preservation.

QUIZ ON TRUSTEE DUTIES

1. What approach is suggested by the text as an approach to problems involving potential breaches of trust duties?

2. What are the major trust duties described in this text?

3. What are the four methods of obtaining a defense to liability for an act which otherwise would be a breach of trust?

4. Which are the duties of a trustee that are least capable of being eliminated by the settlor?

5. Which duties are potentially breached by a banking corporation, as trustee, if the trust assets include a controlling block of the bank's shares and stock rights are issued by the banking corporation and exercised by it as trustee of the trust?

6. A corporate trustee acquires a mortgage in its own name for the purpose of holding various parts of the debt and mortgage in various trusts of which it is trustee. How many duties are potentially breached by this mortgage participation?

7. What potential trust problems are created by the existence of shares of (or certificates of beneficial interest in) a mutual fund as part of the trust assets?

ANSWERS TO QUIZ

1. The elements of an unintentional tort problem—duty, breach, causation, defenses and damages.

2. Loyalty (Not to Self–Deal), Administer, Make Productive, Invest, Earmark (Not to Commingle), Account, Not to Delegate, Diversify and Be Impartial.

3. Exculpatory clause in trust instrument, statute, court permission to do the act, informed consent of all beneficiaries.

4. Account, Loyalty (except that some self-dealing may be specifically permitted by the trust instrument) and Administer (as to active trusts).

5. The duties of loyalty, diversification and due care in making investments. Other facts would be necessary to raise issues of impartiality or duty to make productive.

6. Loyalty, duty to earmark, propriety of investment (possibly including diversification).

7. Problems of allocation of capital gains distributions between the life tenant and the remainderperson raise the issue of the trustee's duty of impartiality. In addition, the investment may not be on the statutory list of approved investments (or may

not be an exercise of due care in investment) and may raise issues of delegation of the investment power and diversification of investments.

CHAPTER 12

OTHER TRUST
ADMINISTRATION PROBLEMS
A. SUCCESSIVE BENEFICIARIES
(PRINCIPAL AND INCOME)

The most common division of beneficial ownership in trusts is into a life estate and a remainder,
e.g., life estate to the settlor's widow and remainder
to their issue. This is not necessarily the wisest
division, nor is it a continuation of the method
which the settlor used during life. The "life estate
and remainder" trust requires the beneficiary to fit
the trust. Another technique is to have the trust
fit the beneficiary by creating a "support" trust in
which both income and principal, as necessary, are
used for the support of the life beneficiary.

If we assume that the purpose of the life estate is
to ensure an orderly flow of income without bunch-
ing or accumulation in the hands of the beneficiary,
the life estate is an imperfect device. First, there is
generally no correlation between the net income
paid by the trust and the amount of expenses incurred by the beneficiary. Second, in testamentary
trusts composed of the residue of an estate, income
accumulates during the administration of the estate, but is not given to the trustee or otherwise

available for distribution until the estate administration is completed. (Those dependent upon the
decedent-settlor are usually entitled to probate family allowance, but it is unusual for probate family
allowance to be charged against accumulated trust
income.) Third, whenever there is a change among
successive income beneficiaries, a portion of the
income is usually in process in the sense that it has
been received by the trustee but not yet distributed
to the income beneficiary. Thus, the estate of a
deceased life estate beneficiary is entitled to the
income which was accumulated and unpaid at the
time of the life tenant's death. The life tenant
derived no benefit from the income, and administration of the life tenant's estate may be necessary for
the accumulated income.

Assuming a division of the beneficial interests
into a life estate and remainder, we encounter all
the problems of dividing principal and income.

1. PRINCIPAL AND INCOME GENERALLY

Principal is the property given to the trust by the
settlor, and amounts received in exchange for that
property. Income is the return in money or property from the use (as opposed to exchange) of the
principal. Typical examples of income are rent,
interest, regular cash dividends and receipts from
business.

"Receipts" and "Disbursements" can be "allocated to" principal or income or "apportioned be-

tween" them. In resolving problems of apportionment or allocation, the following steps should be
taken in the order presented:

a.   The trust instrument is controlling. The settlor could provide that all income and principal is to
go to one beneficiary (thus eliminating problems of
allocation and apportionment of principal and income), that one beneficiary is to be favored over
others or leave the entire question unsettled by
providing that "income" is to be paid to one beneficiary for the beneficiary's lifetime.

b.   Legislation has been enacted to resolve many
questions concerning the allocation or apportionment of principal and income. The Uniform Principal and Income Act (1931 Act) is in force in 8
states; and the Uniform Principal and Income Act
(1962 Act), has been enacted in an additional 34
states. Familiarity with the provisions of those two
acts is necessary for an understanding of the principal and income area of trusts.

c.   If the trust instrument gives the trustee discretion to determine what is income or principal (or
if the trust instrument and underlying law are
silent or obscure), the trustee is required to make
the allocation or apportionment in a prudent manner consistent with the duty of impartiality between
beneficiaries.

2.   EXPENSES

Some expenses can be directly allocated to income
(e.g., collection fees on interest income) or to princi-

pal (e.g., capital gains taxes on a sale of the asset).
These expenses are characterized by their relationship to either principal or income. Another group
of expenses can be allocated or apportioned based
upon their recurring or nonrecurring nature. Generally, periodic expenses such as utilities are allocated to income (or apportioned between different income beneficiaries) while nonrecurring expenses
such as estate taxes of the settlor are allocated to
principal. Some periodic expenses (e.g., the trustee
commissions, attorneys' fees, court costs) are for
the benefit of both the principal and the income.
The uniform acts simply divide these expenses one-
half each between income and principal. Extraordinary expenses, such as lawsuits to defend the title
to assets, are generally charged to principal.

Expenses which are periodic (such as interest or
taxes) are usually apportioned. Interest poses few
problems, since daily calculation is relatively easy.
Taxes, on the other hand, are more difficult to
apportion. In the income tax area, it would appear
that regular taxes on income should be charged to
income while capital gains taxes on gains allocated
to principal should be paid from principal. It is
sometimes difficult to reconcile tax and trust laws
concerning taxation. For example, if neither the
capital gains nor the ordinary income, alone, would
result in income tax being payable, but when both
are received in the same taxable year a tax is
payable, to which should the tax be allocated? If
not allocated, how should it be apportioned? Similarly, real property taxes may be a lien and payable

at one date (thereby being a "debt" payable from
principal) or be apportioned over the fiscal year for
which imposed.

3.   PROBATE ADMINISTRATION INCOME

A testamentary trust of the residue of the settlor's estate necessitates the allocation and apportionment of all of the receipts and disbursements
during the probate administration of the settlor's
estate.   Generally, the principal of the trust is the
net principal after the payment of administration
expenses, death taxes, debts (including accrued expenses), funeral and burial expenses, family allow-
ances, exempt property and the spouse's forced
share.

The income earned during the administration of
the trust, if not payable to the specific devisees, is
treated as income of the trust by the Uniform
Principal and Income Act (1962 Act.)

4.   INTEREST, BOND PREMIUM
AND DISCOUNT

The apportionment of interest on a daily basis
presents practically no problems. At common law,
interest was deemed to accrue on a daily basis.

Bond premium and discount, however, posed specific problems. Although there are "Series E"
United States "Defense," "War" and "Savings"
bonds in which the bonds are sold at a discount and
increases in redemption price are slated at semi-

annual periods, these bonds are not the type with which trusts are concerned. Rather, a trust would typically own bonds in $1,000 increments to which semi-annual coupons are attached. The coupons reflect a fixed interest rate payable until the maturity date of the bonds. The price of the bond fluctuates as the bond's interest rate is more or less desirable. Thus, a $1,000 bond paying 4% interest when prevailing interest rates are 8% would be sold at a discount. The amount of discount would vary with the length of time until the maturity date of the bond. Thus, a 4% bond maturing in 1996 (at which time the corporation would pay $1,000) would be worth more (i.e., would have a higher price) than a 4% bond maturing in 2006. At the same time, a bond paying 12% interest would have a higher value and would probably sell for a premium. Regardless of the price for which the bond was purchased, it would generally be redeemed at "par," i.e., its face value. Unless the amount received upon redemption is adjusted, the principal account would have a windfall when bonds are purchased at a discount and the income account would have a windfall when bonds are purchased at a premium.

In the absence of legislation, courts did not require amortization of bond premium or discount for bonds which were initial trust investments, but did often require amortization when the trustee purchased the bonds at a premium or discount. The rationale was that the settlor was probably contemplating only the interest, without adjustments, as belonging to the income beneficiary, while the trustee would have to apportion the premium or discount in order to avoid favoring one beneficiary over another. The Uniform Principal and Income Act (1931 Act) § 6 attempted to simplify administration by stating that no adjustment was necessary. That section was changed in many jurisdictions which adopted the act. The Uniform Principal and Income Act (1962 Act) § 7 retained the same concept that no provision should be made for amortization of bond premiums nor accumulation for discount, but clarified that bonds issued at a discount with a fixed schedule of appreciation created income to the extent of the appreciation in value.

5. DIVIDENDS AND OTHER CORPORATE DISTRIBUTIONS

Ordinary cash dividends are clearly income and a single liquidating distribution in exchange for the stock of a corporation is clearly principal. The difficulties come with the items in between those two poles. Additionally, there may be problems of successive beneficiaries in deciding when cash dividends were earned or whether a liquidating distribution includes any income element.

Many theories have been advanced as to the best method of allocation of dividends between life beneficiary and remainderperson.

● The "Massachusetts Rule" divided dividends on the basis of the form in which paid: Stock dividends were allocated to principal (on the theory that it

was merely a readjustment of the corporate struc-
ture) and dividends paid in cash or other property
were allocated to income.

• The "Kentucky Rule" declared that all types of
dividends, cash and stock, were income if paid from
earnings of the corporation, without regard to when
the funds were earned. This was a convenient rule
because it turned on the time that the dividend was
declared (an event which the trustee could easily
determine).

• The "Pennsylvania Rule" probably was the
closest to fairness, but the most difficult to administer. It required a comparison of the value of the
stock at the times when the trust was created and
when the dividend was declared. The value of the
trust's holding of the stock should not be impaired
by allocating a dividend (even an extraordinary cash
dividend) to income. Principal would be preserved
first, then income would be paid.

• The Uniform Principal and Income Act (1931
Act) § 5 and Uniform Principal and Income Act
(1962 Act) § 6 provisions adopt the Massachusetts
view of allocation by type of dividend: Stock of the
issuing corporation is principal; cash and other
property (including stock of other corporations) is
income, regardless of when earned by the corporation. This may result in a windfall to an income
beneficiary if there is a corporate "spinoff" by
which the shares of one corporation are distributed
by another. In such a case, there is an impairment

of the value of the principal and the income beneficiary is unduly benefited.

Rights to subscribe to additional stock of the
issuing corporation pose difficult problems of allocation or apportionment. They are generally of relatively low value (thereby being similar to ordinary
cash dividends) and can be "sold." They can also
be "exercised" by combining with other trust cash
(which would be principal cash) to purchase additional shares. The purchase might raise problems
of due care or diversification of investments. The
uniform acts distinguish between rights to subscribe to additional shares of the issuing corporation (which are principal) and rights to subscribe to
shares of another corporation (which are income).

Corporate distributions which are the results of
mergers, consolidations, acquisitions, reorganizations or liquidations are almost always principal. It
may be difficult to determine whether a particular
distribution is a partial liquidation or an extraordinary dividend.

6. RENTS, DEPRECIATION RESERVES

An initial problem with rental income stems from
the common law concept that the entire rent accrued on the date that it was due, rather than being
apportioned on a daily basis. Despite the existence
of the rule for determining rights between landlord
and tenant, proration among trust beneficiaries
tends to produce fairer results than allocating the
entire rental income to the beneficiary who was

entitled to the income on the date that the rental was due or was paid.

It is clear that the net rental received for the use of trust property should be allocated to the income beneficiary. In arriving at the net income, it is also clear that expenses directly attributable to the rental property (utilities, maintenance, repairs, real property taxes etc.) should be deducted from the gross rental. It is not clear whether a "depreciation reserve" should be created.

EXAMPLE: T is trustee of a trust which includes improved real property which is leased. During the year, T receives $12,000 income and pays $2,000 in utilities, leaving net cash receipts of $10,000. If T does not establish a reserve for depreciation, T should pay the full $10,000 to L, the life beneficiary. This would not compensate R, the remainderperson, for the drop in value (if any) of the property. On the other hand, if T establishes a reserve for depreciation, T would charge the income account with a reasonable amount, e.g., $1,000, computed in accordance with generally accepted accounting principles and pay the net income of $9,000 to L. The $1,000 retained as a depreciation reserve would be invested for the benefit of the principal account (and would, itself, produce income for L).

Unless the trust instrument provides otherwise, the trustee is under a duty to establish a depreciation reserve in order to preserve the value of the principal. Alternatively, the trustee may sell the

property and invest in a proper trust investment
which does not require a depreciation reserve.

7. WASTING ASSETS, DEPLETION

At common law, realty was generally considered
to be the singularly indestructible asset with all
other assets being "wasting" assets in the sense
that they are used up in the production of income.
Livestock were considered to be typical personalty
of the wasting type. Leasehold interests in land
and the mineral rights in the land were also capable
of being consumed. We have considered one type of
amortization: Depreciation is the method of amor-
tizing tangible property. If the property is intangible, "Depletion" serves the same purpose. Among
the wasting assets (i.e., assets which are subject to
depreciation or depletion) are copyrights, patents
and franchises.

Although it would seem that if depreciation and
depletion are required for rental property, they
should be required for any other asset, different
rules have been applied historically. Some states
recognize the "open mine" doctrine by which the
trustee may allocate to income all receipts from an
existing asset of a wasting nature (e.g., the settlor
put an "open mine" into the trust).

The Uniform Principal and Income Act (1931 Act)
§ 10 and Uniform Principal and Income Act (1962
Act) § 11 provide that income from wasting assets
shall be allocated to income up to 5% of the inventory value of the wasting asset each year, with the

balance being allocated to principal. Separate rules exist for timber and "natural resources in, on or under land," Uniform Principal and Income Act (1962 Act) §§ 9, 10.

8.   UNPRODUCTIVE AND UNDERPRODUCTIVE ASSETS

Amortization (Depreciation and Depletion) is required for assets which produce so much in the way of receipts that it is questionable whether all the receipts are income. On the other hand, there are some assets which produce little (or no) income; these assets tend to favor the remainderperson (who ultimately receives the wealth) over the life tenant (who would have received greater income from another investment).

Although most authorities are in agreement that the income beneficiary is entitled to a portion of the proceeds upon the ultimate sale by the trustee of an unproductive asset, there is substantial disagreement among the Restatement and the uniform acts (Uniform Principal and Income Act (1931 Act) § 11 and Uniform Principal and Income Act (1962 Act) § 12) as to whether there is a duty to sell, what constitutes "unproductive property", whether the rule applies to sales at a loss (Only the Uniform Principal and Income Act (1931 Act) would not apply the rule to a loss.) and the formula for computing the delayed income (including what percentage return should be allocated to income and when the period should commence).

The following approach may be helpful in dealing with unproductive asset problems:

a. Is there a potentially underproductive or unproductive asset? This question requires analysis of both the productivity and the type of asset involved. A low rate of return (i.e., relative underproductivity) is not enough; the property must be objectively underproductive, perhaps to the extent that the productivity is only token. While the uniform acts draw the line at a return of one percent or less, the Restatement, 3d, Trusts (Prudent Investor Rule) § 240 requires only "an income substantially less than an appropriate yield on the trust's investments." Unproductive land has typically been involved in this rule and most authorities extend the rule to mortgages which are foreclosed with some recovery. Case law has not been as quick as statutory law to extend the rules to unproductive personalty, especially when it is of relatively low value. The rule probably should apply to all personalty of considerable value which was acquired as an investment (e.g., gold coins) rather than as a chattel to be used (e.g., furniture).

b. Is there a duty on the trustee to sell the asset? The trust instrument is controlling. It may direct a sale, on the one hand, or authorize or direct retention of the asset on the other hand. If the trust instrument is silent, the Restatement and uniform acts generally impose a duty of sale. Note that apportionment of the proceeds upon the ultimate sale of unproductive assets turns upon the duty of the trustee, but determines rights between successive beneficiaries. The trustee may be subject to liability in situations where apportionment is not made (e.g., because the asset was sold at a loss in a jurisdiction which has enacted the Uniform Principal and Income Act). Normally, however, the focus is upon dividing the sales proceeds between the successive beneficiaries.

c. Which type of payment formula should be used and with what numbers? The theory of the Restatement and uniform acts is that the income beneficiary (or the estate of the deceased income beneficiary) is to be reimbursed for delayed income. The approach used is to give a return to the income first and allocate the balance of the sales proceeds to principal. This gives all windfall gains to principal, but also charges all losses to principal. In New York prior to the adoption of the Uniform Principal and Income Act (1962 Act), the apportionment to principal and income attempted to share the loss on foreclosed property between the two accounts. This was accomplished by figuring the total amount of interest owed and the total amount of principal owed and then apportioning the loss on the foreclosed mortgage between them. Thus, if $900 principal and $100 income were owed on a foreclosed mortgage or other debt and only $100 was recovered, New York would apportion $90 to principal and $10 to income while the restatement and uniform act approaches would satisfy the $100 debt to income first and allow principal to bear all the loss.

Under either system, it is necessary to determine the period and amount of the delayed income. Normally, the period and amount of the income would extend from the time that the duty to sell arose (i.e., when the property became unproductive or when it was received in the trust if then unproductive) until the date the beneficiary received the income. The Uniform Principal and Income Act (1931 Act) § 11 (but not the Uniform Principal and Income Act (1962 Act) § 12) stated that the duty to sell would be presumed, in the absence of evidence to the contrary, to arise one year after the property became unproductive in the trust. The amount of the delayed income is also subject to wide variance. In some cases, such as bad debts, the court uses the rate of return which the particular (unsuccessful) investment should have produced. Restatement, Second, Trusts § 241 requires the use of the "current rate of return on trust investments," thereby building in flexibility and its concomitant uncertainty. The uniform acts suggested a straight percentage, five percent being suggested by the Uniform Principal and Income Act (1931 Act) § 11 and four percent being suggested by the Uniform Principal and Income Act (1962 Act) § 12. All authorities use simple, as opposed to compounded, interest. Similarly, all both charge the income account with whatever small amounts of income it may have received during the period and divide up the net proceeds after allowing all applicable charges against the proceeds of the sale of the unproductive property.

9. LIABILITIES AMONG BENEFICIARIES

Normally trust duties are owed by the trustee to the beneficiaries and few duties are owed by the beneficiaries to the trustee or to each other. The interest of a beneficiary in the trust may be subject to an equitable lien or charge because of a debt to the trust, including a debt resulting from a breach of trust. The breach of trust may be by a beneficiary who is also trustee or because of profit from or participation in a breach of trust or because the beneficiary agreed to be liable for a loss. An agreement by a beneficiary to create a debt to the trust or a lien against the beneficiary's trust interest is valid if there was no improper advantage taken of the beneficiary, the beneficiary is not under a legal incapacity and the trust does not contain an effective spendthrift clause.

If a beneficiary owes money to the trust, the trustee is under a duty to withhold payment to the beneficiary until the debt is eliminated. The trustee, however, cannot withhold payment or assert a lien against the share of the beneficiary in order to satisfy a debt owed to the trustee personally.

B. BENEFICIARIES AGAINST TRUSTEES

1. REMEDIES OF BENEFICIARIES AGAINST TRUSTEES

Any beneficiary (contingent or vested) or group of beneficiaries can maintain an action against the trustee to enforce the trust. Although a guardian

ad litem can maintain an action on behalf of a trust
beneficiary who is under a legal disability, no person (including the settlor) other than a beneficiary
can seek the assistance of the court of equity to
enforce the trust. Although the beneficiary may
also use a court of law to obtain a fixed sum or
specific item which the trustee is under an immediate duty to pay or deliver, all other actions to
enforce the trust are instituted in a court with
equitable powers.

The trustee is liable to the beneficiaries for all
breaches of trust duties and for profits made by the
trustee in the administration of the trust even if
there is no breach. The beneficiaries generally can
choose from one or more of the following remedies:

• Specific enforcement of the trustee's duties;
i.e., requiring the trustee to go forward with his or
her duties.

• An injunction against the trustee violating his
or her duties.

• Redress of the breach of trust in the form of
money damages based upon the action which the
trustee should have taken, possibly with interest.

• Affirmation of action by the trustee even
though not permitted by trust terms or local law.
The beneficiaries are allowed to accept winning
gambles of the trustee.

• Removal of the trustee and appointment of a
new trustee. In some cases, a receiver is appointed
in lieu of a trustee.

● Denial of compensation. This remedy is used only in egregious cases.

Since a number of alternatives are available and any one or more of the beneficiaries can sue to enforce the trust, the court will accept the choice of all beneficiaries if they all have capacity and agree. If not, the court will generally impose the remedy which is most beneficial to the trust as a whole.

Beneficiaries generally have their choice of approach to the measure of damages by charging the breaching trustee with any one of the following:

a.   Any loss resulting from the breach; or

b.   Any profit made by the trustee in the breach; or

c.   Any profit which would have accrued had there been no breach by the trustee.

When the trustee's breach involves specific property, the beneficiaries are permitted to trace the specific property to restore it to the trust unless it has been acquired by a bona fide purchaser for value without notice of the breach of trust. The trustee may breach a duty to sell or not to sell, to buy or not to buy. In any of those breaches, the beneficiaries may affirm the action taken or may insist upon the profits (or item) which would have been in the trust if the trustee had performed his duties without a breach.

As a general rule, a trustee is not allowed to set off the losses incurred in one breach of trust by the gains made in another breach of trust, but the trustee is liable for only the net loss if the breaches are not separate and distinct. There is some uncertainty in this area as to what breaches are separate and which are the same breach. Among the factors which are considered in determining whether separate breaches have occurred are whether the same trust property is involved, whether successive dealings with the same property are involved, the time elapsed, timing of breach(es) and accountings by the trustee, the good or bad faith of the trustee (e.g., intention to misappropriate, intentional breach or inadvertent breach) and how consistently the trustee has dealt with the trust property.

EXAMPLE: In breach of trust, T invests the entire $50,000 of a trust in certain bonds which are not a proper trust investment. He sells these bonds for $30,000 and makes a proper investment in other bonds, which are sold for $35,000. The proceeds are invested in speculative stocks, an improper investment, but sold for $55,000, a gain of $20,000. Neither the $5,000 gain on the proper investment nor the $20,000 gain on the improper investment is offset against the $20,000 loss on the first improper investment. The transactions are separate because of the time interval, the intervening investment and the general policy of not wishing to encourage the trustee to take further risks with the trust property in an effort to "break even."

Generally a trustee is not liable for the acts of a cotrustee or predecessor trustee unless the trustee knew or should have known of the breach by the other trustee, participated in it, or failed to take steps to rectify it upon discovery. A trustee is also liable for the acts of a cotrustee or an agent if the trustee improperly delegates the power or fails to exercise reasonable care in the supervision or (in the case of agents) selection of the agent.

2. TRUSTEE FEES

Trustee fees may be fixed by agreement, trust provision, statutory schedule or by the court supervising the trust. Modern corporate trustees generally have fee schedules which are adhesion contracts for most trusts, but tend to be negotiable in the case of multi-million dollar trusts. The schedule may be set out in the trust instrument or not. Even when not set out in the trust agreement, the corporate fee schedule tends to be enforced despite problems of the Statute of Wills and parol evidence rule. If the trust agreement provides a fee schedule, that schedule will be followed unless it was the product of overreaching by the trustee or there are reasons for deviation, such as a change in circumstances which makes trust administration far more difficult. Almost all jurisdictions have statutes which permit trustees to be compensated; more than half of them merely state that the trustee shall be entitled to "reasonable compensation." About a fourth of the states set out fee schedules, usually based upon the principal value or the income of the trust. These fee schedules are sometimes phrased as maximums.

Charges for various functions of the trustee may be imposed. A "set-up" fee may be requested for initial services and a "distribution" fee for partial or complete terminal services. The main charge is usually an annual fee expressed as a percentage of principal (.5% to 1.00% is the common range) or income (5% is a common figure). The method of phrasing the base for the annual fee should not be confused with the allocation or apportionment of the expense to the principal or income account.

The trust or statute may simply provide that the trustee is entitled to "reasonable compensation." As a practical matter the size of the trust (or its income) is often very determinative, but writers traditionally state that the court in setting or approving the reasonable fees will consider, in addition to trust wealth, the skill and diligence of the trustee and the results of the trust administration. Most jurisdictions allow the trustee extra compensation for extra services such as complicated sales of major trust assets, tax work or legal work. The risk of self-dealing is present when the trustee employs himself, herself or itself to perform a service which an independent agent (e.g., a realtor, accountant or attorney) could also perform.

Except in New York, multiple trustees (whether cotrustees or trustee and successor trustee) traditionally share a fee fixed by trust agreement or statute. In the jurisdictions where "reasonable" compensation is allowed, the fees are generally required to be based upon the services performed by each trustee and therefore tend to be more, in total, than the reasonable fee of one trustee.

If a trustee has breached trust duties, the court may, in its discretion, deny some or all compensation or grant some or all compensation. In fixing "reasonable compensation," the court may take the fidelity of the trustee into account. The court does not deny compensation in all cases. Normally there must be a serious breach of trust such as misappropriation, repudiation of the trust, intentional commingling of trust and personal assets or intentional failure to keep records and render accounts. When the breach has been less serious, such as errors in judgment, failure to use skill and care or failure to diversify, the court is less likely to deny compensation. In theory, denial or reduction of compensation is not a penalty for the breach, but rather reflects the poor quality of the services rendered. At least one case has denied compensation to a trustee who performed acts which would have been a breach of trust but for an exculpatory provision in the trust provision; the trustee was not liable for the breach, but also was not entitled to be compensated for his services as trustee. If the trustee is both liable to the trust for a breach of trust and also entitled to compensation, a lien against the compensation is usually given to the trust.

A trustee can waive, expressly or impliedly, the right to compensation. An implied waiver has been found in instances where the trustee distributed the principal or income of the trust without reserving funds for trustee's fees and later sought such fees from the beneficiaries. A change in circumstances on the part of the beneficiaries (or the death of the life tenant) would strengthen the case against a retroactive allowance of trustee's compensation.

3. INDEMNITY OF TRUSTEE

Except for statutory provisions such as Uniform Probate Code § 7–306, the trustee is personally liable to third parties for torts, contract claims and claims arising out of property ownership. If the trustee is not at fault (and, if at fault, to the extent the trust is benefited by the action), the trustee is entitled to indemnity from the trust assets. The indemnity may be in any of the following forms:

• Paying the claim from trust assets. (Exoneration)

• Reimbursement from the trust assets to the trustee who pays the claim from the trustee's personal assets.

• Retaining trust assets (i.e., an equitable lien) until the trustee is repaid amounts owed.

• Obtaining a declaratory judgment in equity that a judgment obtained or about to be obtained at law against the trustee is against the trustee in that capacity and not individually.

• A small minority of states follow the English rule of permitting the trustee to obtain reimbursement from a trust beneficiary when the assets are inadequate. In most of those cases, special factors such as one or more of the following existed: The trust was created for a business purpose; there was an agreement by the beneficiary to reimburse; the beneficiary was also the settlor; or there had been a prior distribution to the beneficiary who had not subsequently changed his or her position.

The ability of the trustee to pay from trust assets or seek reimbursement, if not at fault or in breach of trust, is itself not a breach of the duty of loyalty even though the trustee is given a lien and a claim which is hostile to that of the beneficiaries. The trustee is not, however, entitled to interest on money used to pay trust expenses.

The trustee is not allowed indemnity if there is no benefit to the trust and the liability arose as a result of a breach of trust duty. If the trustee, in mistaken good faith, exceeded his powers in incurring an expense and some benefit accrues to the trust, the trustee is entitled to indemnification to the extent of the lower of the benefit to the trust or the amount expended.

EXAMPLE: Trustee properly employs a servant who negligently injures a third person. The trustee is liable to the third person upon the principle of respondeat superior, but is entitled to reimbursement from the trust estate. If the trustee had improperly employed the third person (or had committed an intentional tort), the trustee would remain liable, but would not be entitled to indemnity from the trust assets.

In a few states there has been a recognition of the trustee as a juristic person, but the vast majority

still require the two-step process by which the liability is first imposed upon the trustee as an individual and then his right to indemnification is separately determined on a basis of whether he was
acting properly or whether the trust derived any
benefit from his mistaken actions if he was acting
improperly.   See Uniform Probate Code § 7–306.

C. RIGHTS OF THIRD PARTIES
1.   TRUSTEE LIABILITY
TO THIRD PARTIES

A procedural morass, remnant of the historic
division of law and equity, faces the claimant
against a trust.   At common law the trust and the
trustee were not juristic entities.   An action could
be maintained only against a trustee individually.
If the trustee was not in breach of trust and if the
trust was solvent, the trustee could be indemnified
from the trust assets.

Many states maintain this archaic distinction.   A
creditor of the trustee cannot have legal (as opposed
to equitable) enforcement of a judgment against
trust assets; he must attach or levy execution upon
the personal assets of the trustee.   Naturally, a
number of exceptions have developed.   All of the
exceptions require that the third-party creditor seek
enforcement in the court of equity.   The following
are the clearest of the exceptions which are recognized:

• The trustee would be entitled to exoneration,
but does not have personal assets which the creditor

can reach: For example, the trustee is bankrupt, dead or out of the jurisdiction.

• Even though the trustee was not entitled to exoneration (usually because he acted in breach of trust), a (typically contract claim) creditor may be allowed to reach trust assets to the extent a benefit was conferred upon the trust, unless other factors prevent such equitable relief.

• The terms of the trust provide for liability of the trust estate directly (usually simultaneously providing that the trustee shall not be personally liable): This provision is usually found in Massachusetts business trusts, but is relatively rare otherwise.

• The trustee specifically contracts with the third person that the third person shall look to the trust and not to the trustee personally. Courts disregard the self-dealing aspect of such contracts in order to fashion another exit from the uncomfortable rule of trustee liability. Most of the questions in this area stem from attempts to interpret a contractual term to see if the liability has been shifted from the trustee, individually, to the trust. Signature "as trustee" alone is probably not enough to effect such a change in liability, while a clear statement that the third party agrees to look to the trust and not to the trustee personally for payment or a signature "as trustee and not personally" does permit and require the third party to look only to the trust assets. This can be disadvantageous to the creditor in situations where the trustee is more solvent than the trust. A provision of this type may be ignored by a court of equity if the trustee has, by an unrelated breach of trust, diminished the trust estate so that it cannot satisfy the obligation. If the trustee purports to execute a contract as trustee and not individually, but does not have the authority to execute such a contract, the trustee is liable individually to the creditor for breach of the implied warranty of authority (and not on the contract itself, although that contract provides the measure of damages).

There has been a tendency to seek other means of allowing a creditor to impose liability directly upon the trust assets without the intervening personal liability of the trustee, including such statutory forms as the Uniform Trusts Act which was enacted in six states. The analogies of principal and agent law and the lack of corporate limited liability for acts which are ultra vires suggest possible trends for the development of trust law.

Of course, if the creditor has a security interest in specific real or personal property contained in the trust, that security interest can be enforced.

Since the trustee's individual liability remains a shield to the trust in most jurisdictions, it follows that liability of the trust beneficiary to creditors of the trust is rarely found. The general rule is that a trust beneficiary is not liable for a contract, tort or other debts imposed purely because of the ownership of the property. The few exceptions to this

American rule of no personal liability for debts of the trust are as follows:

• Specific agreement by the beneficiary (with the creditor or the trustee) to be liable. Commercial lenders therefore seek the "co-signature" of the beneficiary.

• Receipt by the beneficiary of all or substantially all of the trust assets from the trustee. Tracing of the assets is permitted unless they are in the hands of a bona fide purchaser for value without notice or unless the beneficiary has so changed position that it would be inequitable to hold the beneficiary personally liable.

2. THIRD PARTY LIABILITY TO TRUST

Third party participation in a breach of trust could arise whenever the third party pays money to a trustee or acquires trust property.

Formerly there existed a duty on the part of any person paying money to a trustee to see that the funds were properly applied to trust purposes. This rule has been rejected or severely limited in almost all jurisdictions today.

A third person can purchase property from a trustee and acquire it free of trust if the sale is not in breach of trust. No duty exists to inquire as to the power of the trustee to transfer negotiable property, but the transferee of non-negotiable property from a trust is under a duty to inquire as to the power of the trustee to transfer the property.

Similarly, one who accepts trust property in payment of the trustee's personal debt is guilty of participation in a breach of trust. Beneficiaries may sue a transferee who is chargeable with notice of the trust, its terms or the breach of the terms jointly with the trustee.

The recipient of trust property sold in breach of trust receives it "subject to the trust" unless the recipient is (or claims through) a bona fide purchaser for value without notice. A transferee with notice can be compelled to restore the property to the trust or pay its value or its proceeds if the transferee has disposed of it. The transferee is entitled to credit to the extent the transferee paid for the property and the trust has received the benefit of the payment. A donee of the property also must restore it (or its proceeds) to the trust, but is not required to surrender any gain or make up any loss resulting from a sale of the property.

Defenses to liability of the third-party participant in a breach of trust (or recipient, without consideration or with knowledge of the breach, of trust property transferred in breach of trust) include the following:

• Informed consent (or release) by the adult competent beneficiaries who would otherwise be able to maintain an action. The consent may be given before or after the act which would otherwise be a breach of trust.

• Estoppel by reason of an active or passive misrepresentation of a fact (such as the existence of a

trust or the non-existence of the power to transfer)
made by the beneficiary upon which the third party
justifiably relied, will prevent the beneficiary from
asserting the breach of trust.

● The statute of limitations may apply or the
matter may have been reported to, and approved
by, the court in an accounting.

● Laches—an unreasonable delay on the part of
the beneficiary, which makes it more difficult or
impossible for the defendant to make an adequate
defense—will bar the remedy of the beneficiaries.

Third parties who deal with the trustee in a
situation in which there is no breach of trust should
ordinarily be sued by the trustee and not by the
beneficiaries. The trustee insulates the beneficiaries from the need to participate in legal actions.
Even under statutes requiring that legal actions be
maintained in the name of the real party in interest, a trustee of an express trust may sue without
the need to join the beneficiaries in the lawsuit. If
the trustee is unwilling or unable to bring suit, the
beneficiaries are required to bring a suit in equity
to compel the trustee to do the trustee's duty; to
avoid circuity, the third parties may be joined in the
equitable action by the beneficiaries.

D. TERMINATION OR MODIFICATION
OF A TRUST

A trust can be terminated or modified by any of
the following occurrences:

• Revocation by a settlor who possesses the power of revocation. Totten trusts are generally conceded to be valid and revocable. The power of revocation of other trusts is granted by statute in a few states, but generally must be expressly reserved by the settlor. If the settlor mistakenly failed to reserve the power to revoke, the trust may be reformed to include an express power of revocation.

• Rescission or reformation of the transfer of property into trust is available on the same bases as rescissions or reformations of transfers of property generally—fraud, duress, undue influence or mistake.

• Termination in accordance with the terms of the trust. Some trusts are designed to last for a specified period (such as eleven years) or until the happening of some event (such as the death of the life beneficiary). Additionally, the settlor may grant the trustee or a third person the power to terminate the trust.

• Subsequent impracticality, impossibility or illegality may lead to the termination of a trust which was initially practical and legal, but which encountered difficulties which were not provided for by the settlor.

• Consent of all beneficiaries (assuming they are sui juris) if no material trust purpose is defeated by the termination. A spendthrift provision in the trust usually prevents such a consensual termination. The additional consent of the settlor permits termination despite the defeat of a material trust purpose.

● Merger which occurs when the trustee and the beneficiary are the same person either because of the terms of the trust or conveyance of the entire beneficial interest to the sole trustee. The spendthrift trust sole beneficiary who becomes the sole trustee possesses the merged estates, but is said to have the power to reinstitute the spendthrift trust within a reasonable time or to take the property free of trust.

Upon termination of the trust, the title to the trust property may automatically vest in the beneficiary because of statutory rule (generally applicable only to realty), the terms of the trust, the Statute of Uses being applied to an active trust which became passive or because the estate given to the trustee was limited to the duration of the trust (such as a trust of the property for the life of the beneficiary-life-tenant with a legal remainder). In the usual case, the title remains in the trustee. The trustee has the duty to make an accounting and transfer possession (and title, if still in the trustee) to the beneficiaries entitled to it. The trustee may retain the property under a lien for the trustee's compensation or reimbursement for expenses, but distribution should be made within a reasonable time under the circumstances of each case.

*

INDEX

References are to Pages

341

REPUBLICATION—Cont'd
Codicil, satisfaction, 141
Exoneration, 110
Incorporation by reference, 110
Multiple documents, 109
Pretermission, 110

RES, TRUST
Generally, 195–204
Debt, 198, 202
Future property, 196–197, 199–200
Non-assignable property, 196–197, 199–200, 201–202
Undivided interest, 198–199, 202–204
Wasting asset, 197, 200–201

RESIDUE
Bequests and devises, 144, 148–149

RESIGNATION
Trustee, 210

RESULTING TRUSTS
Generally, 244, 245
Retained interest, 206

RETAINER
Generally, 142–143
Anti-lapse, renunciation, slayer, 142–143

REVIVAL
Generally, 91–93

REVOCABLE
Trusts, anti-lapse, 123–124
Will characteristic, 80

REVOCABLE TRUSTS
Generally, 172, 251

REVOCATION BY WILL
Gift causa mortis, by will, 108
Totten trusts, 258–259

REVOCATION OF WILLS
Generally, 80–101
Act, 87, 89
Divorce, 138
Express, 84–87

†

9